ACCOUNTING—
A SOCIAL INSTITUTION

Accounting—
A Social Institution

A UNIFIED THEORY FOR THE MEASUREMENT OF THE PROFIT AND NONPROFIT SECTORS

Julius Cherny
Arlene R. Gordon
Richard J. L. Herson

PREPARED UNDER THE AUSPICES OF THE
VINCENT C. ROSS INSTITUTE OF ACCOUNTING RESEARCH,
STERN SCHOOL OF BUSINESS, NEW YORK UNIVERSITY

Foreword by Joshua Ronen

Quorum Books
New York • Westport, Connecticut • London

Library of Congress Cataloging-in-Publication Data

Cherny, Julius.
    Accounting—a social institution : a unified theory for the
measurement of the profit and nonprofit sectors / Julius Cherny,
Arlene R. Gordon, and Richard J. L. Herson.
      p. cm.
    Includes index.
    "Prepared under the auspices of the Vincent C. Ross Institute of
Accounting Research, Stern School of Business, New York University."
    ISBN 0-89930-690-X (alk. paper)
    1. Human services—Evaluation. 2. Social accounting. I. Gordon,
Arlene R. II. Herson, Richard J. L. III. Title.
HV41.C4428 1992
657'.98—dc20   91-25524

British Library Cataloguing in Publication Data is available.

Library of Congress Catalog Card Number: 91-25524
ISBN: 0-89930-690-X

First published in 1992

Quorum Books, One Madison Avenue, New York, NY 10010
An imprint of Greenwood Publishing Group, Inc.

Printed in the United States of America

The paper used in this book complies with the
Permanent Paper Standard issued by the National
Information Standards Organization (Z39.48-1984).

10 9 8 7 6 5 4 3 2 1

Contents

SUMMARY

THE PROFIT SECTOR

Economic and Accounting Model

THE NONPROFIT SECTOR

Taxonomy

Accounting in the Nonprofit Sector

COMMON CHARACTERISTICS OF THE PS AND HSOs

Marketing

Management, Accounting, and Reporting

Organization of Product/Service Delivery

Success and Survival

APPLICATION OF MEASUREMENT CONCEPTS

Goal/Mission

Attribute

Metric

Periodic Reporting

Units of Accountability

Other Criteria

MEASURING THE PS AND HSOs BY THE SAME ACCOUNTING SYSTEM

SUMMARY

ACCOUNTING LITERATURE

Accounting in the NPS

Discussion of Accounting Literature

HUMAN SERVICE LITERATURE

Framework and Methodology

Efficiency

Other Organizational Elements

Cost/Benefit Analyses

Multiple Indicators

*General Accounting Office (GAO) and State
Evaluations*

Discussion of Human Service Literature

Exhibits

Foreword

Economic historians have been involved in studying the commercial and technological evolution of our civilization and how such development influenced, and has been influenced by, changes in the accounting and legal systems. As B. S. Yamey writes, "economic historians have emphasized . . . that systematic bookkeeping (i.e., double-entry bookkeeping) has been essential to the development and rise of modern capitalism." The rationalistic pursuit of unlimited profits, so the thesis runs, would not have been possible, or would not have been so effective, without scientific accounting as an instrument in the hands of the entrepreneur.

The objectives of accounting could be broadly defined to include the promotion of an optimal allocation of resources, or even equity or welfare considerations. The installation of accounting or information systems that would quantify what the price mechanism occasionally fails to capture can serve this monitoring function. In that case the definition of accounting principles and standards will facilitate the achievement of optimal resource allocation within the economy or the maximization of social welfare. One would have to consider, however, whether the cost of measurement may well fall below the benefits of realignment of resources toward greater effectiveness.

The pursuit of private profits under modern capitalism as measured by its accounting system is justified by the assumption that society as a whole is better off from the perspective of the optimal production of goods and services. The present work extends this notion of profit, where the private interest is directly benefited and society only indirectly, to a conception of profit where the private interest and society's well-being are direct objects of accounting.

Within for-profit organizations operating in the private sector, market prices are alleged to properly measure the social cost consumed and the social benefits conferred. The invisible hand of Adam Smith is credited with the ability to equate social benefits with private benefits, and social costs with private costs, often interpreted as through the working of an unfettered, unregulated free market mechanism that yields prices as signals for resource allocation. But to the extent that corporations inflict harm in ways that cannot be internalized through the price mechanism or, conversely, if they confer benefits that are not internalized by the corporation or over which they cannot gain property rights because of frictions in legal markets, then the social optimality of resource allocation is compromised. The question then is whether monitoring or measurement mechanisms could be put in place to mitigate this deviation from optimality. Moreover, the large transfers of resources, for instance social security, welfare, medicaid and medicare, that constitute a significant part of society's economic activity require some kind of accountability. Can accounting objectives be defined to include quantification of social effects?

But what the deviations from the norm in the profit sector are, constitute the norm in the case of nonprofit organizations. In the latter organizations, seeking profit is not the alleged objective of the organization. Hence, no activities seeking to maximize profit are undertaken. In seeking its goals, a nonprofit organization undertakes activities that by definition are directed generally to the attainment of a social objective (as well as survival of the organization) not measurable in terms of private profits generated through the price mechanism. Hence, nonprofit organizations are left without an objective, comparable and economic means of quantification of the degree to which they accomplish their goals. Accounting in such an organization should have as an objective the proper measurement of the degree to which goals are accomplished. This process becomes difficult in the absence of the regulating market prices (to quantify revenues, costs, and profits) or by any other means of measuring the revenue generated. It is this difficult problem that this book addresses with respect to a particular subset of nonprofit organizations, namely human service organizations.

Human service organizations obtain resources from society to promote the economic self-sufficiency of their members or to protect them in times of need. While techniques for evaluating particular programs and organizations of this sort have evolved, there is still yet no generally accepted means to assess the degree to which the organizations have accomplished their particular goals, to evaluate the effective and efficient organization, to reward its management, to communicate performance results to the organizations' stakeholders, and to make comparisons among such organizations. Currently, the accounting systems of such organizations make do with the recording of receipts and usage of funds, together with supplementary measures particular to the organization.

As the authors of this book argue, in order to measure the social revenues that such organizations generate, it is necessary to calibrate the degree to which their professed social goal is attained over time. They propose capitalization of the net changes in the societal resources used by consumers of these organizations. The extent that individuals move toward or maintain economic self-sufficiency is the measure of the social revenues they generate. A unified system of accounting is proposed, based on the common foundation of consumer satisfactions/benefits for both sectors. The suggested measurement methods are also amenable to audit and verification. The normative proposals in this book raise questions for further investigation and assessment.

If the system suggested can be shown to be useful and implementable in human service organizations, insights gained from it may also prove to be valuable in improving measurement and accounting schemes in for-profit organizations. To that extent, this book may confer positive externalities.

Joshua Ronen, Director and Research Professor,
Vincent C. Ross Institute of Accounting Research,
New York University, Stern School of Business

Preface

This work began in 1981 with a request to the Bruner Foundation, Inc., from the Lighthouse, Inc. (formerly known as the New York Association for the Blind) for a grant to support the development of a performance evaluation system. We were aware that "effective decision-making requires both qualitative and quantitative information. Program evaluation says little about the context or system in which the program operates and makes no economic statement. Decision-makers consider the value of a program. . . . Therefore evaluations which do not address value issues have a very limited usefulness to decision-makers" (Arlene R. Gordon, letter from the Lighthouse, Inc., to Bruner Foundation, Inc., April 10, 1981).

We were involved in the project from the beginning as the principals from the two organizations. The proposals contained in this book resulted from the integration of our theoretical and extensive practical experience as well as differing viewpoints emerging from our three diverse backgrounds—accounting, economics, and social services. We believe that this multidisciplinary approach played a significant part in the development of this work and is critical to future efforts for the resolution of societal problems.

The Lighthouse was in the process of completing the implementation of a computerized client information system and was seeking to develop the methodology for measuring the organization's effectiveness and efficiency in achieving its mission. The board of directors had specifically requested that management institute an ongoing system for evaluating the effectiveness of the Lighthouse's service programs. The problem was of special interest to the Bruner Foundation because of its focus on developing methods for evaluating the results of its grant giving. Therefore, the process of developing the methodology became a joint effort between the two organizations both during and after the life of the grant. Bruner and the Lighthouse were key players in the launching of this work and, in different ways, have continued their support and interest.

First, to the Bruner Foundation, our deepest appreciation for their commitment to the importance of evaluation as an integral part of human service programs, for their grant to the Lighthouse to initiate this study, their support of the first presentation of these concepts to the National Association of Social Workers Management Conference in New Orleans in 1987, and for their continued financial support during the preparation of this manuscript. Our thanks go especially to Simeon and Joshua Bruner, chairman and vice-chairman respectively of the board of directors, and to Janet Carter, executive director, for their personal commitment and support for the continuation of this work.

Second, our deep appreciation to the Lighthouse board of directors and management for policy decisions that affirm the significance of research and evaluation as an integral component of the organization's mission statement to ensure the effectiveness of its programs. It made the investment in developing information systems and guiding practice that would provide the means by which the organization could implement these policies. A special thanks to Barbara Silverstone, executive director. Her continuing interest and support of this work are a reflection of her professional values and commitment to quality services.

This book has been through many phases, and its publication now is due in no small measure to the support of colleagues, friends, family members, and organizations. This support has been expressed in both intangible and tangible ways—a belief in our goals, encouragement, constructive criticism of the many versions, and, last but hardly least, through financial assistance. To all, individually and collectively, we say "thank you" for all of the foregoing and for your patience with what must have seemed a never-ending project!

A very special thank you to Dr. Arthur Gillman, who, as director of research at the Lighthouse in 1982, began exploring the question of what an integrated, comprehensive evaluation system should look like and how to develop and institutionalize such a system. His primary work raised many questions, which led us on to our quest for a conceptual framework and a methodology. Thanks also to Ellen Perlman Simon, Risa Pollack, and Gilda Gold at the Lighthouse, all of whom provided invaluable counsel and assistance.

Joshua Ronen, director of the Vincent C. Ross Institute of Accounting Research, Stern School of Business, New York University, recognized the potential value of what we were attempting to do, and we owe a special thanks to him for his encouragement and help through the process of turning our original first paper into this book. Rebecca Todd was particularly helpful with her careful assessment of the first full-length manuscript. Most important to the future of this work was Josh Ronen's request that this book be published under the auspices of the Ross Institute. This hopefully ensures its usefulness as a basis for the research needed to validate many of the concepts and approaches introduced here.

Gratitude must also be expressed to colleagues in human services, accounting, and economics who were kind enough to read our work at different stages and offer their suggestions. We do wish to single out two: Harold Lewis, who at the time was dean of the School of Social Work at Hunter College, City University of New York, for his interest in the subject, for reading the very first version, and for his constructive criticism and encouragement; and Robert Snyder, president and chief executive officer of the Center for Educational Advancement, Hunterdon County, New Jersey, for his permission to use the outcomes of the center's innovative programs as the basis for illustrating the workings of the model.

Then there are those whose diligence, patience, and steadfast dedication made possible the final production of this work. First our thanks to Eve Memoli who spent tireless hours typing the manuscript with its many revisions. Thanks are due also to Sarah Mavranek for her assistance with the literature search and with the expansion of the original paper. For their special interest and help with the last editing hurdle, our thanks go to Susan Freyberg and Claudia Shacter who gave generously of their time. From Arlene Gordon, a very special thank you for the dedication of Sylvia Woolf, Roslyn Kaufman, Carol Fein, Doris Preisick, among countless others, for their hours of reading.

Our greatest appreciation goes, of course, to the members of our families, to our friends, colleagues, and all those strangers whom we buttonholed at conferences, parties, on trains, planes, and in elevators, who listened, opened their ears, eyes, and minds and said . . . "Go to it!"

We have saved until last the one person whom we truly consider our partner in this enterprise and the unlisted fourth author—Edythe Herson. Her patience, forbearance, and above all, thoughtful and insightful comments, questions, and encouragement, despite what were often trying times of listening to us and accommodating to our schedules, made a contribution beyond the scope of any measurement system! It is her own value system, both personal and professional, that underlaid her steadfast support throughout these years.

Abbreviations

AICPA	American Institute of Certified Public Accountants
CES	Comprehensive Evaluation System
CIS	Client Information System
CPA	Certified Public Accountant
DM	Discussion Memorandum
ED	Exposure Draft
FASB	Financial Accounting Standards Board
FIS	Financial Information System
GAAP	Generally Accepted Accounting Principles
GAAS	Generally Accepted Auditing Standards
GAO	General Accounting Office
GAS	Group Association Sector
GASB	Government Accounting Standards Board
GGS	Group Government Sector
GSI	Gross (Societal) Income
HSO	Human Service Organization
LDG	Logical Data Grouping
MIS	Management Information System
M/P	Maintenance and Protective Model
NPS	Nonprofit Sector
NRC	Net Resources Consumed
NSI	Net (Societal) Income
PPS	Private Profit Sector

PS	Profit Sector
SEC	Securities and Exchange Commission
SPS	Societal Profit Sector
SS/I	Self-Sufficiency/Independence Model
SSI	Supplemental Security Income

Introduction

This work evolved from our attempt to develop a performance evaluation system to measure the effectiveness and efficiency of a human service organization (HSO). Our initial goal was to develop an integrated system that could be institutionalized and report on a continuing basis to all stakeholders on the outcomes of its service programs. As we broadened our approach to formulate such a system within a conceptual framework, and as we explored the origins of human service programs and organizations and the history and culture from which they emerged, we realized that this undertaking was also about freedom of choice. The individual without economic resources or in whom there has been little or no societal investment to develop human capital is generally not in a position to make choices. A society that provides resources to make possible the movement of all its members toward self-sufficiency also provides options. Individuals who can make choices relative to their pursuit of happiness contribute to creating a more dynamic society. Historically, through the transfer of resources to HSOs (both public and private), society has attempted to help its members achieve economic self-sufficiency. A system is needed that will enable society to have proof of the effectiveness of these transfers to accomplish this goal.

We identified the need for a measuring system to extend the visibility of nonprofit operations that would sufficiently disclose the effectiveness and efficiency of each HSO as it strives to fulfill its mission. However, there is a spirit and purpose within an HSO that must also be captured in measures of performance. At the focus of each HSO is an individual consumer-client whose needs are unique and whose identity must not be lost in the aggregation of service statistics. In answering calls for external performance reporting based on rational criteria for funding, the concerns must also be addressed of those who fear subjugation of client service to an inappropriate criterion. Therefore, any system created should not only record results of client functioning but also encourage client participation and recognize the contributions and interrelationships of staff and management and community to client progress. It is not enough to know what is counted or how it is counted. There should be an awareness of the impact of the system on client and staff behavior, their perception and motivation, how the system will integrate and interact with other community systems, and what the impact of results will be on the organization's policies and future.

Accounting is a social institution whose chief function is measurement. Given a statement of goals, accounting should measure the achievement of these goals. Thus accounting becomes a feedback system to report upon the differences between goals and their achievement. In a democratic society, the economic goal for its members should be continuing gains in their independence in terms of self-sufficiency, and satisfaction of their needs and wants from a consumption viewpoint. These are common goals in both the profit and nonprofit sectors. With this recognition, the putative differences between the two sectors are eliminated, and one accounting system for the measurement of societal goal achievement becomes feasible.

What became clear in the nonprofit sector, from both the literature and our own experiences, is that systems are generally available to assist organizations to measure and report on efficiency. Although recent research reports an increased focus on outcomes, efficiency is often confused with effectiveness; outputs are often viewed as outcomes. In a market economy, efficiency in the production of outputs is secondary to and subsumed under the effectiveness of outcomes. Accordingly, in this book, we use the term *effective* as the combined measure of efficiency and effectiveness.

The realization that the profit sector's activities and results reflect the achievement of a generally accepted societal goal (consumer benefits/satisfaction) led us to look more closely at the significance of the centrality of the consumer to the profit metric. However, since there was no measure of the economic value of services performed by human service organizations, there was no basis for the preparation of a statement of income for HSOs. A different approach was necessary.

We identified society as the ultimate consumer-beneficiary of human service programs. The goal of optimizing the economic allocation of societal resources required us to develop three propositions: Society is better off when all its members participate as fully as possible in the social system; society is better off by making its individual members less risk averse by providing support during times of need; and society is better off when there is an ethical and moral environment in which the individual can make choices.

With these propositions as the base, it then became possible to derive an organizational model of human service organizations based on outcome performance. The model incorporates a definition of the consumer and an attribute for measuring consumer benefits/satisfaction. By using an economic attribute to measure quality of life, the model recognizes the significant relationship between self-sufficiency and an individual's freedom of choice. This normative model for human service organizations and our analysis of the model of the profit sector led us to a unified field theory for the measurement of both sectors.

The proposed accounting system, derived from the organizational model, provides an economic measure of the effectiveness of human service organizations. The economic measure, like that of the bottom line in the profit sector, is a primary indicator of the success of the organization in achieving its mission. As with all measurement systems, it plays a major role in shaping the behavior of the organization—its board, staff, and most important, its clients. It contains an integrated management information system, which gives recognition to client outcomes, staff, and management performance. In addition, there are internal reports for use by all levels of staff, as well as for the board and external stakeholders such as funders and the public. The most significant result of the proposed organizational model for the HSO is that it causes the organization to focus on outcome.

The accounting system derived from the organizational model can be implemented immediately by any HSO. The broader social policies emerging from the societal model will require political decisions by society. We believe that the model can serve as a basis for reexamining the current accounting model of the profit sector and can offer as well a method of addressing broad social problems.

We have organized the presentation of our work into three parts. Part one presents in two chapters an overview of the purpose, problem, proposed solution, short-term consequences and long-range implications. Chapter 1 is an executive summary of the book; in chapter 2, an organizational model for HSOs is developed. Principal implications and consequences of the organizational model are highlighted.

Part two provides an expanded discussion of the theoretical and empirical foundations for this work. Chapter 3 briefly details the history and culture from which the societal model emerged. Chapter 4 then develops the three propositions that form the conceptual framework of the system. Chapter 5 details the methodology of how a measuring scheme is developed and what elements comprise such a scheme, and how the methodology is applied in the fields of economics, human services, and accounting. The current profit and nonprofit accounting systems are then analyzed in chapter 6 from the perspective of their comparability and how they merge into a unified system for measuring the performance of both profit and human service organizations.

Chapters 7 and 8 offer a literature review and empirical evidence and applications. A review of the literature in chapter 7 describes practitioners' attempts to apply/develop systems for accountability and reporting. This literature is reviewed from the perspective of the preceding three chapters. The professional literature discusses their attempts to deal with the issues of measuring the goals and results for achieving improved economic and quality-of-life outcomes of programs for children, the aged, the handicapped, and other disadvantaged groups. Some empirical applications of the proposed unified accounting system to an HSO are then presented in chapter 8 along with case illustrations.

Part three, in chapter 9, explores in greater depth the implications and consequences of the societal and organizational models and future research needs.

PART ONE

CHAPTER 1

Executive Summary

The purpose of this book is to present a performance evaluation system for measuring the effectiveness and efficiency of human service organizations (HSOs). These organizations receive either directly or indirectly transfers of resources from society in order to promote the economic self-sufficiency of its members or to maintain and/or protect them in times of need. This may be due to dependency incurred by reason of age, illness, disability, or socioeconomic circumstances.

HSOs, as well as most other organizations currently classified in the nonprofit sector (NPS), have been unable to quantify goals and measurement of achievement by commonly accepted criteria. While specialized techniques for the evaluation of particular programs and organizations have evolved, there is no generally accepted means for evaluating and rewarding effectiveness and efficiency, and for communicating performance results to stakeholders. This is unlike the profit sector (PS), which subsumes its performance measures within the profit metric.

For most organizations in the NPS, the current nonprofit accounting system is based on providing information about the receipt and use of funds, which offers little in the way of economic and management information. What is needed is a system that can measure, report, and analyze on an integrated basis, client, service, staff, and management cost and financial data. Such a system would provide a continuous and comprehensive understanding of the impact of services on individual clients and on the HSO, thereby permitting comparisons among organizations. "Service effectiveness should be the primary object of social welfare administration" and "the principal criterion of agency performance."[1]

A fundamental problem facing any society is the establishment of its goals on a prioritized basis that is consistent with its values, institutions, and history. Different societal goals may give rise to different allocations of society's resources.

Society's task, given a particular set of goals and institutions, is to develop the mechanisms for the optimal allocation of resources and the reporting systems by which it can measure its effectiveness and efficiency in achieving these goals.

In one respect this underlying problem involves the use of societal resources as opposed to private resources in the promotion of benefits for individuals. The organization that provides such services can be private or public, religious or secular, voluntary or governmental, profit or nonprofit, or combinations of these types. What is of importance is that all organizations that use resources provided by society be held to the same standard of outcome.

As will be analyzed in greater detail, private resources can be used for private benefits, group resources can be used for government and group benefits, and group resources can be coupled with private ones for individual benefits. This book applies to the last group, where the individual is either a recipient of services directly paid for by government or indirectly from organizations that are funded through tax benefits. This is distinguished from the benefits and services received by individuals as members of society at large, such as access to museums and parks, police protection, transportation facilities, defense, and other societal services needed to maintain the system. It should be noted that as we attempted to establish a system for a segment of the NPS as presently constituted, it became clear that significant reclassifications within the PS and NPS were required.[2]

An organizational model is needed for HSOs that will optimize society's use of resources for the benefit of both society as a whole and the individual members. Derived from this model, we present a general performance evaluation (accounting) system for HSOs, which can perform the function presumed by the standard financial accounting system in the PS. The PS accounting system derived from its model assumes that the optimization of economic benefits is based on the postulates of satisfaction of consumers ranked by preferences, product production according to consumer demand, profits/survival of the individual firm, and allocation of the firm's and societal resources—all within the framework of functioning market systems.

In summary, our intent is to develop a system that measures the effectiveness and efficiency of these HSOs in achieving their organizational and societal goals—a broad concept of stewardship. The system is based on defining an attribute that represents these societal goals and individual behavioral characteristics. The adoption of this model permits comparability of results, measuring the impact on the individual consumer-client, the organization, and on society and its resource allocation. It purports to respond to the current demands for accountability and to the numerous attempts by multidisciplines to define such a measure.[3] In essence, a profit metric is developed for HSOs as a part of a redefined NPS. This system has the potential to be applied to the PS. The PS's current model, however, cannot be applied to the measurement of the performance of HSOs.

THE CURRENT SOCIAL SCENE

Questions have surfaced regarding the direction of our society,
cost of government and its agencies, the usefulness of HSOs, s
sibilities/obligations to vulnerable groups, and the role of the indiv
ing social ethic. These social policy questions relate to the ethics and value system
of our society including such intangibles as the *good life, family, justice, equity,*
and *self-interest*. The issues revolve around the welfare state, its status, and the
extent of societal support for current social programs.[4] These include the protection of children and other groups such as the elderly, the poor, and the disabled,
and the social benefits and costs of education, training, health care, and the allocation of their costs to various sectors of society. These in turn raise questions about
the role and interrelationship of social problems and the sectors—private and
public, profit and nonprofit. Also to be considered are the societal costs of the
public sector—the maintenance of a system of government in an advanced
technological, energy-based economy with accompanying ecological and environmental effects and spreading problems of drugs, disease, and crime.

How to resolve these questions makes up a cacophony of concerns within the
pressures of the federal budget and trade deficits and the U.S. role in a world
experiencing revolutionary political changes and economic problems. Associated
with these concerns is a call for accountability and the question whether there
is an appropriate payoff for social expenditures. Rumblings have produced intellectual, emotional, and often frustrated searching for action, for answers, for
change. Calls for evaluation of outcomes are coming from all sectors of society.
The answers to these calls for the evaluation of efficiency and effectiveness can
be developed by criteria that bind together quantitative variables as to the amount
of goods and services, priority variables as to their group allocation, and quality-
of-life variables of ethics and human relationships.

To address these issues, an approach must be developed that considers the needs
and rights of the various groups within our present society and within the
framework of the assumptions underlying societal goals. The solution of these
problems may require an answer to more basic questions: What is society's purpose with respect to its individual members and the group? How does society
establish and prioritize its goals? How does it establish costs and benefits in order
to allocate its resources? How does it measure the effectiveness and efficiency
of such allocation?

When social scientists analyze society's current problems and each discipline
concludes that society is not functioning in an adequate fashion, then prevailing
social arrangements are in need of rethinking. In many respects the present trend
in the social sciences invokes the Kuhnian phrase "laden with anomalies."[5]

In addition to the chorus of dissonance coming from segments of society and
governments, the fields of human services, accounting, economics, political
science, and philosophy are attempting to deal with the current malaise. Problems
have been examined based on the methodological perspectives of each of these

disciplines, each recognizing aspects of the current scene from its special view-point. Problems are described and answers are prescribed for a particular part. None sees the total picture .

The review of the literature reveals three major issues. First, the current social scene demonstrates an ever-widening quest for an economic answer to ensure that current social programs are both effective and efficient. There appears to be an acceptance that these programs are intended to have an economic benefit and that an economic answer is required. Second, from the economic, accounting, and human service literature, increased attention is being paid to the same problem of measuring effectiveness and efficiency and the need to develop methods for evaluating these outcomes. Pragmatic issues arise related to the allocation of resources in the NPS and among their constituent groups, and the development of a method for carrying out this allocation. Third, an agreed-upon, unified framework is lacking in the fields of accounting and human services while the framework of economics often appears to have little relevance to reality. The approach proposed in this book provides an economically based framework for the delivery of human services and its accounting that responds to the limitations of conventional wisdom.

STATEMENT OF THE PROBLEM

How is a general performance accounting evaluation system developed for HSOs within our society? This problem is multifaceted and raises multiple questions; their resolution requires definitions. Recognizing that the questions are interrelated, for purposes of analysis they are presented from the perspectives of society and government, sectors, the firm or organization, the individual member, and other common factors to be taken into account.

Society and Government

How does society justify transfers of resources to the aged, handicapped, unemployed, homeless, sick, and other disadvantaged persons? Can government support to individuals by various types of social insurance at critical periods in their lives be justified economically? What types? Can concepts of self-interest, group interest, and societal interests be reconciled by government or in the political arena? Is it more costly for government to render direct services or to use private organizations for such services? Is there a trade-off between maintaining standards and local control? Is it more costly to make direct support payments to the vulnerable and disadvantaged populations than to train and reorient such populations? Can a measuring system be devised to answer these questions?

Can a system be developed that is congruent with the history and traditional culture of the society? How can concepts of competition and cooperation coexist within a society? Can a moral framework be prescribed or derived? Can the *ought* be economically measured? Can social program legislation be justified in economic terms, that is, in terms of costs and benefits? Can theoretical solutions be proposed that can be applied empirically? Should short-run, discrete answers to specific problems on an ad hoc basis be reevaluated in terms of more generalized approaches?

Sector

For HSOs in the traditional NPS, how does our society establish goals, prioritize and allocate resources in an economic manner and then establish a system to measure and to report on the effectiveness and efficiency of its decisions? From a sector point of view, can economic criteria for good and bad transfers be determined? From a measuring viewpoint, are there basic differences between the PS and HSOs, and can the same or similar system of measurements be used? Can a system for HSOs be based on economic foundations to optimize resources in the same sense that the PS optimizes the allocation of its resources based on the actions of the firms and consumer preferences? In this context, can profit be considered an appropriate measure of both efficiency and effectiveness? Can the firms within the present profit and nonprofit sectors be redefined in terms of their goals and contribution to society as opposed to their present classification in terms of taxability? What is the role of tax policy relative to tax exemption and/or the deductibility of payment to eleemosynary institutions.

Firm (Agency/Organization)

How are efficiency and effectiveness determined in the absence of a statement of income for HSOs? Can incentives be established to reward successful management in HSOs? Can the measurements of efficiency be separated from effectiveness? For the organization that provides the services, the HSOs, how can income be defined? Can a statement of income as used in the PS be developed to measure appropriately the outcomes in HSOs? Can criteria for quality of life be defined in terms of economic measurement? Have issues of funding for HSOs masked the larger question of their goals and measurement of outcomes? Should for-profit companies operate in the human service field; and the complementary question, should HSOs function in the traditional profit areas? Is there "unfair" competition when this occurs?

Individual

Who is the consumer and what is consumer satisfaction in the field of human services? Can a market be defined when the client is not the payer? How will needs be determined and prioritized in such a market? What attributes can be developed within accepted measurement methodology?

Common Factors

How do the above questions relate to some of the "broader domestic woes": the lack of quality of the work force, the disorganization of family life, increasing cost of the health system, crime and drug abuse, the budget deficits, declining investment in the infrastructure, and the cost of environmental cleanups?[6]

To address specific questions, a broader perspective is required. A step up to a higher level of analysis facilitates the development of a conceptual framework, within which specific questions can be subsumed and solutions proposed.

MODELS

Models define sets of logical relationships. Accordingly, model building can apply to questions of society, to sectors within the society, to industries within the sector, to firms and organizations within the industry, and to individuals in various roles such as consumers or producers. These are hierarchical relationships. An accounting model is a set of logical relationships to which measurements have been applied; accounting systems incorporate the techniques and working rules for the operationalizing of a model. An accounting system is needed that is responsive to the nature of the questions dealt with. Accordingly, a hierarchical model with three levels is presented—propositions for a societal model, for the organizations or firms (HSOs) in the NPS, and for the behavior of individual members of society. When the term *model* is used in this book, it refers specifically to the model of a performance evaluation system for the individual firm or organization. References to the other models will be specifically identified as the societal model or the individual/consumer model.

This hierarchy of models is essential from a logical point of view. The development of the model required both moving up to the societal level and down to the level of the individual societal members. For such a model to measure what it purports to measure, the societal goals within which HSOs function must be explicitly presented. The measuring system induces the implementation of these goals by the actions of stakeholders within the society who respond to the measuring system. Thus, such a system becomes meaningful when placed within the framework of these goals and the institutions of the society in which the organization functions. Likewise, the societal and organizational models must be in harmony with the behavioral characteristics of the individual members of that society. This also allows the measurement of how well off are the ultimate beneficiaries of the model—the societal members.[7]

Therefore, while the focus of the book is on the organizational (firm) model, its development needs to be placed within the context of a conceptual framework that sets forth both societal and individual goals. This approach is not unlike the current normative model that has been adapted by the PS. Even under continual criticism, this model serves for the PS as an explicit statement of the operations of the firm, within the framework of implicit societal goals and individual behavioral characteristics. The model developed here for HSOs with its more rigorous development of societal and individual goals rests on a stronger theoretical foundation than that used by the PS.

At all times, the underlying question must be kept in mind—should the emphasis of an economic system be to make the individual better off in the expectation that society is better off; or the reverse, to make society better off so that the individual on average is economically better off? Our position, as presented in this book, is that when society is economically better off, on average its individual members are better off.

HISTORY

Society from biblical times has allocated resources, both public and private, to care for the sick, the lame, and the poor. In the twentieth century, with the industrialization of Western society in particular, attention began to focus on attempts to bring or restore persons outside the mainstream to economic self-sufficiency. The capitalistic society embraced more and more of the concepts of a welfare state, particularly as they centered on either training individuals for productive work and/or providing supports during illness or re-training/education for coping with new technologies. The public sector (government) assumed leadership in the 1930s during the depression by massive public works and then in 1935 with the passage of the Social Security Act. The number and scope of such programs exploded in the 1960s with the "war on poverty" and with the passage of civil rights and affirmative action legislation. These, in turn, served as a basis for an activist disability rights movement, and for legislation to provide services for disabled persons. During this same period there was expansion of legislation for rehabilitation, special education, and other programs for women, children, and older Americans.

Currently, these programs are carried out with the use of societal resources, either directly by government or by voluntary HSOs with combined funding from the government, and by individual and corporate donors. These HSOs are included in the potpourri called the NPS, which has been the subject of several studies. These analyses point up the problem of estimating the functioning, size, and significance of the sector and its components within their present classification, and revisions have been called for.[8] The logic of the societal and organizational models would appear to support a proposal for a changed taxonomy (see Exhibit 4.1).

SOCIETAL MODEL AND ITS PROPOSITIONS

In order to achieve societal goals and to optimize societal resources, a societal model embracing three basic propositions is developed. In summary, these are: All member of society should have the opportunity to pursue independence and self-sufficiency; society should provide support during critical and vulnerable periods so that its members are unafraid to take risks; and incentives should be established for ethical behavior, which would incorporate considerations of both community and competition. These three propositions express the societal goals that are the basis of the societal model.

Within a society, and basic to the notion of a social system, is the concept that its population is made up of people who at one and the same time collectively comprise the social system and function individually within it. Yet at any point in time, there are always members of society who, for various reasons, are wholly or partially outside the social system in some significant respect. The first proposition states that the social system is better off with more participants than with fewer.

The second proposition is that the social system is better off when it encourages risk taking or discourages its participants from being risk averse.[9] For its own best interest, to ensure the freedom of pursuit in a society of increasing complexity, the role of government should be to "undertake actions that lessen uncertainty" for its members, "actions that cannot be taken by individuals acting alone."[10] Moreover, government policies create a state of confidence; this, in turn, affects investment decisions (influencing savings, investments, gross national product, and technological developments).[11] There should also be included incentives for the individual members to invest in human capital—education, training, and health care.[12]

Government policies such as the creation of social security, unemployment insurance, and medical coverage likewise encourage societal members to be risk takers. To incorporate the above goals, it is in society's own best interest to provide the necessary foundations for pursuit to all of its members. Such provision serves as an insurance policy for societal members, both for financial immediacy and for long-term stability.

In considering the ethical behavior of societal members as it relates to the economic-political sphere, it now becomes clear that the either/or assumptions given by the proponents of a completely competitive economy versus government-intervention society require restatement. The third proposition argues that society needs both the economic benefits of competition and a strong ethical/moral system to encourage cooperation. The use of either system by itself could ultimately destroy the functioning of the society. A completely competitive society eventually eliminates most of the competitors and also results in increasing societal static as in costs of litigation and conflicts. An egalitarian society tends to eliminate the creative economic forces for production of goods and the good life.

Thus, the three propositions state that the combined competitive-ethical society should reduce friction, include more functioning people, and encourage risk taking and dynamism. The concomitants of the first and second propositions should likewise induce the desired social behavior of society's members. These propositions follow from axioms relative to economics and from the recognition of the individual as part of the group. When the ethical goal can be given the attribute of an economic good, the quality of life becomes measurable.

Society, in setting goals and in allocating resources, requires a system for measuring the effectiveness and efficiency by which they are achieved—a system that incorporates individual, organizational, and societal effects of resource allocation. A measuring system that focuses on results—on outcomes—can have a profound effect on the behavior of all stakeholders in working toward the fulfillment of these goals.

THE ORGANIZATIONAL MODEL

Types

As previously defined, there are two types of HSOs. Those whose mission is to increase the self-sufficiency of their clients to effect a decrease in their clients' use of societal resources will be referred to as the Self-Sufficiency/Independence (SS/I) organizations. The second type, serving the more frail and vulnerable persons in our society, with its goal to hold constant their current functioning and to retard their inevitable decline, has as its mission preventing a decrease in the self-sustaining ability of its clients. This will be referred to as the Maintenance and Protective (M/P) organization. The organizational model is described in detail for both types of organizations in chapter 2.

Definition of Effectiveness and Efficiency

Effectiveness is the satisfaction of the needs and wants of the greatest number of people. Efficiency is the delivery of the greatest amount of goods/services using the least amount of resources within a certain time frame. These definitions are not consonant with popular usage and with the second definition of *Webster's* (third edition): *effective* is "producing a definite or desired result; efficient"; and *efficient* is "producing the desired effect or result with a minimum of effort, expense, or waste." The confusion between these terms is abetted not only by popular usage but also by *Webster's* in listing *efficient* as part of the second definition of *effective* and also showing *effective* as a synonym for *efficient*.

Elements of the Model

The propositions establish the framework of societal economic goals in harmony with our society's history and culture. These propositions underlie the development of an economic measuring system for the HSOs in the NPS in response to the questions raised in the Statement of the Problem. An examination of the nature of the problem is required to devise a measuring system that can give answers. The key elements on which the organizational model is based are: consumer satisfaction and benefits together with the role of markets in the PS and for HSOs; quality of life—the development of a quantifiable attribute; the firm in the NPS—the role and functions of HSOs; and accounting systems—addressing the questions of measurement.

Consumer Satisfaction and Benefits. In the PS, in accordance with the assumptions of neoclassical economic theory, profit is intended to measure consumer satisfaction at the realized level of efficiency serving as a measure of society's and its organizations' contributions to well-offness. Given this description, it would appear that there should not be any distinction between the sectors—they both should seek to optimize consumer satisfaction. The apparent conceptual distinction between these sectors is a consequence of the historic separation of the consumer from the payer in the case of the HSO. The problem of whether there is a need for the creation of a different accounting system for the HSO is resolved if we can understand and demonstrate that the payer, whether society or the consumer of the service, is better off by reason of the payment.

The basic problem that initiated the development of the model was the lack of a bottom line for the HSO as in the PS. In the PS, there is the assumption of an optimal allocation of resources based upon consumer satisfaction and the acts of self-interest produced through the interlocking market actions of consumers and producers. Individual preferences arising from the satisfaction of wants and needs are called utility functions by economists. In the simplified utility model, the consumers presumably prioritize their demands based on their hierarchy of choices. Producers respond by bidding for resources and labor, the factors of production. According to this theory, the optimal allocation of societal resources is thus based on the choices in the markets by consumers and the reactions of producers. As part of this allocation process, entrepreneurial profit—the bottom line—represents the difference between revenues generated and costs incurred.

The same set of assumptions applies to the HSOs relative to consumers who prioritize their requests for services based on their needs. HSOs should also respond in their allocation of resources based on their prospective profits, measured under the model by societal income. The difference between the consumers' actions in the PS and the HSO is that for HSOs, society is the payer, and the measurement of gross revenue is in terms of societal income generated.

In looking at the problem, the goal of a performance evaluation system for HSOs is to develop a single monetary measure to function in a manner similar to the PS, accepting the limitations of a single measurement. It recognizes that such measurement has a profound effect upon the behavior of stakeholders; therefore the proposed model also incorporates desirable societal goals as stated by the propositions. This model contains a system for the direct measure of societal benefits. Society pays for the individual consumers, and their gains can be aggregated at all levels—individual, firm, and sector. Accordingly, the underlying axiom for the development of the model is in terms of consumer benefits regardless of payer.

Quality of Life. Within our society, the requirements of work and self-sufficiency and a sense of independence, dignity, and self-esteem are related, often equated. In essence, there is one calculus for the individual member within society based on the goal of the achievement of economic self-sufficiency and independence. The societal model in effect recognizes that there is one scale applicable to all its members. There is a break at the point where economic self-sufficiency has not been realized, and accordingly the use of societal resources may be required.

If consumer satisfaction could be equated for both sectors, the artificial differences between them would vanish. As described in chapter 2, the value of services or revenue is developed based on the measurement of the overall mission of HSOs, the improvement of the quality of life for their clients. The economic attribute selected to define quality of life is the client's movement toward, or maintenance of, self-sufficiency, which is also the goal of the participants in the PS.

The Firm (Organization). Profit or net income is determined in the PS by deducting the costs and expenses from revenue earned and presented in the statement of income. HSOs currently present no statement of income, only a statement of receipts and expenses. What they lack is the dollar denomination of outcomes, a concept of earned revenue (or gross income or sales) for the preparation of a statement of income. Except for two missing links, HSOs could measure their results and account for their use of resources in a manner comparable to the PS. The two missing links are: a definition of earned revenue for inclusion in the statement of income and a method of ensuring that the earned revenue reported in such statement of income can be part of the funding cycle for the individual HSO. The proposed organizational model develops a system for computing earned revenue derived from the concepts of the societal model.

The universal attribute selected by the PS is monetary profit. Relative to the first link, a universal attribute has been similarly selected for HSOs, which measures in monetary terms the movement or maintenance of their clients toward self-sufficiency. The HSO's gross revenue is defined as the aggregate monetary value of such movement and termed its gross societal income (GSI). After deduction of its program and administrative expenses, the balance is its profit and termed net (societal) income (NSI). To develop the second link, it is necessary that society provide a means and source of funding to complete the cycle by rewarding the effective organization. It is proposed that eligibility for public contracts together with tax deductions by individual donors be limited to the extent that GSI has been created by the HSOs.

It is clear that successful entrepreneurial behavior in the PS, measured by profit, depends upon optimizing revenues in response to market analyses of consumer demands in comparison to expenses of operations. Similarly, in the NPS, HSOs should analyze their missions based on the needs and wants of the consumers and their abilities to move clients toward self-sufficiency. The attribute for defining revenue in order to measure outcome effectiveness is measured by the change or maintenance in the individual client's use of societal resources consumed in comparison to the individual's subsequent productivity or functional capacity. This is termed Net Resources Consumed (NRC). The revenue earned by the HSO, the SS/I firm, is computed by aggregating the present value of the change in NRC for each client over that individual's prospective working life. For the M/P firm, the value of the results is based on standard measures of functioning. Thus the model bridges the gap between the PS and the HSO by recognizing the centrality of the consumer in both sectors, establishing the congruence of mission and outcome to market and profit. The equivalence relationship that mission (Ms) implies outcomes (O) is similar to market (Mk) implying profits (P). [Ms →O ≈ Mk → P] also clarifies the role of efficiency in both sectors. In order to measure efficiency, based on standard units of time, the accounting and management techniques for both sectors also become interchangeable, conceptually and in application. As in the PS, standards of efficiency for HSOs become operable only within the framework of a particular set of market alternatives or market actions. An organization in a market economy allocates its resources in an efficient manner after it has optimized its market or outcome strategy. At best, efficiency factors may play a limiting or peripheral role in affecting the strategy of market or outcome efforts. Efficiency, based on outputs, should not be confused with outcomes (effectiveness), any more than production is confused with sales in the PS. For HSOs, a standard unit of service as a management control measure can be related to standard costs. This permits the essential aggregatability of multiple service units, however unique each service, which permits client, service, and financial information to be summarized and analyzed. Thus, once the relationship of efficiency to effectiveness, or outputs to outcomes, is understood, then all the varied and sophisticated techniques that have been developed in management and cost accounting, such as job and process cost systems, standard costs, applications of overheads to direct costs, variance analysis, and others can be applied to both sectors.

Accounting Systems. Accounting systems are economic measurement schemes that address two questions: what should be measured and how it should be measured. In the case of financial accounting, Ijiri defines accounting measurement as "the measurement of the economic performance of an entity." He emphasizes that "among the economic performance measurements encountered in accounting, the most typical one is, needless to say, income measurement."[13] Therefore, for the purpose of this proposed system we must make clear the concept of income measurement. Profit is another way of referring to income measurement. Profit (positive or negative) is the difference between revenues and the costs related to the production of those revenues. In the standard financial accounting system, profit is that which should be measured. Whereas the activities of the organization are denominated in money terms, this is not the purpose of organizational activity. Too often the measurement has become the message. An analysis of the profit metric points up that profit is the central factor of financial accounting, that our economic system is based on consumer satisfaction as the major element as reflected in sales revenues, and that the minor element is the sales-related costs. Our economic system, by implication our financial accounting system, is driven by the political-economic principle that "Goods, to be goods, must satisfy wants of one or more persons—wants for security, comfort, discovery, expression, achievement, and so on. Goods are the vehicles that carry satisfaction of human wants."[14] Because of a scarcity of resources, however, not all wants can be satisfied. In the long run, in accordance with economic theory, only those wants that can be satisfied at a profit will be satisfied—only those wants where costs are less than revenues.

From a review of the current accounting system for HSOs as to what is being measured and how it is being measured, one could presume that its goal is to report on an organization's ability to raise and spend money. By comparison, organizations in the PS are economically evaluated presumably by what they do for society through the satisfaction of individual wants, without assigning value judgments to such consumer decisions.

Operational Components

Through a client information system (CIS) and a financial information system (FIS), the accounting system builds on information theory and appropriate good practice in order to provide for the accumulation of data concerning the client, family, and community. Other pertinent data include treatment (i.e., service goals and specific objectives), initial prescription, changes, standard and actual service units given, costs, outputs and outcomes that can be aggregated on the individual, program, and organizational level. The internally generated common data bases provide feedback for the decision making at all levels within the organization, for reporting as required to stakeholders, and for analyses of multiple causal factors. This constitutes and is referred to as the comprehensive evaluation system (CES).

The CIS contains all data regarding the client, vital statistics, educational, medical, and work service history, treatment goals, program implementation, case notes, and so on. From a measuring point of view, it is in effect a job order accounting plan with a projection of time period, time costs, program completions (outputs), and outcomes. It becomes the basis of the feedback loop focused on the needs and accomplishments of the client.

The FIS has the principal function of recording the financial data and the time-related costs involving the client and the organization in terms of service units—standard and actual. By an appropriate chart of accounts, it maintains the regular financial accounts as well as cost accounts relating to client, program, and cost center. The FIS also incorporates the preparation of budgets and standard costs. The establishing of an appropriate management information system (MIS) requires the use of the same basic data for the measurement of efficiency and effectiveness of an HSO's resources for the client, program, and cost center's regular operations. The CES integrates and reports on program outputs, client outcomes, the HSO's profits, and combines the basic data for planning, research, and efficiency, reporting to the appropriate stakeholders.

As will be described in chapter 5, the model is in conformity with measurement methodology—the specifying of goal, defining an attribute, providing a metric convertible into dollars, as well as developing an accounting system that responds to the requirements of periodicity, relevancy, comprehensibility, and auditability.

IMMEDIATE CONSEQUENCES AND LONG-RANGE IMPLICATIONS

Within the framework of the societal and organizational models, the proposed accounting system for HSOs will focus all stakeholders on a common value system. The measure of effectiveness and efficiency based on client outcomes stated in economic terms, that is, societal profit, should induce behavioral changes among the stakeholders toward this goal. The adoption of the organizational model for an HSO should have significant consequences and implications. These are described from the perspective of the firms (HSOs), sectors, professions, government, society, and future research.

The Firm

The accounting for all firms becomes comparable based on society members' behavior as consumers to optimize their satisfaction and benefits. Profit as a measurement of effectiveness of outcomes becomes reportable; moreover all firms can use the same techniques of measuring efficiency (outputs) of their operations.

The system derived from the organizational model, based on societal profit, measures the effectiveness and efficiency of HSOs in achieving their individual and societal goals. The adoption of this system permits comparability of results among organizations in terms of outcomes, dollar bottom lines, in other words, profits. As developed in the organizational model, the profit measures the impact on the individual consumer-client, on the organization, and on society and its resource allocation.

The immediate behavioral consequences on stakeholders include greater emphasis upon the assessment of client changes. These changes focus on outcomes rather than program outputs. This requires a longitudinal period of follow-up after termination of client-consumer services. Likewise, using a common data base, there can be continual internal monitoring of effectiveness and efficiency as a feedback loop resulting in a direct validation of programs, staff, and management performance. The integrated data base also establishes the foundation for reporting to other stakeholders such as directors, the public, and funding sources, and it supplies a method to evaluate the achievement of the organizational mission. The system not only provides the framework for internal and external reporting and controls, but it also can be used as the basis for planning, ad hoc studies, and research, and for developing incentive compensation for staff and management.

There is an equivalence relationship of market (and its products) and profits (outcomes of market) to mission (and its programs) and outcomes (outcomes of mission): therefore the statement that market implies profit is similar to mission implies outcome. In the PS, efficiency does not stand alone; it is a concomitant of the determination of market needs for its products. Likewise for the HSO, efficiency can only be monitored after, or together with, the determination of mission and programs to answer needs for the optimization of outcomes.[15] Conceptually, there is no more of a problem in determining efficiency for firms using transfer resources than for private resources. Procedures are equally applicable that relate to internal control, an integrated management information system, job order costs, standards, budgets, hierarchical reporting, and so on.

In order to fund the societal income generated by HSOs, it will be necessary to have significant changes in the tax law. Deductions by donors should be limited to the societal income generated by the donee. This process completes the funding cycle for the HSO and improves the efficiency and effectiveness in the allocation of societal resources. The proposed change in tax policy rationalizes the societal goal of allocating resources. The reliance of HSOs on the outcomes of their performance for sources of funding (i.e., the generating of gross societal income) should have a significant effect upon their functioning. The individual HSO can concentrate more on operations and less on the generating of funds.

The model can be installed without delay for any organization that has a state-of-the-art client and financial information system. For full societal effects, changes in tax policy and implementation of the propositions would be necessary. However, even without such changes, the information contained in the statement of income should be of significance to all stakeholders relative to the outcome of the mission. These results should be of particular interest to funding sources and should present HSOs in a different light—permitting an appropriate ranking of their performance and presenting objective evidence of their societal contribution.

Sectors

Historically, boundaries between the two sectors lessened as nonprofits borrowed management and cost accounting techniques from profit-oriented firms, for example, management by objective, zero-based budgeting, and other procedures. More recently, the PS is learning from work done by some firms in the NPS about the significance of defining mission, engaging in strategic planning, and motivating staff.

Based on the proposed organizational model, the movement to a unified system of accounting for all firms in a redefined profit sector (which includes private profit and HSO organizations) now becomes feasible. It further points the way for the application of the measuring system to other segments of the NPS, which like the HSOs directly serve individuals, that is, health and education. Given the applicability of the societal propositions in chapter 4, measuring concepts in chapter 5, and the elements of consumer satisfaction and benefits and quality-of-life goals for societal members, it may be possible to create measurement of income based on these criteria for these segments.

Moreover, the model may provide a method for dealing with the cost of externalities, heretofore discussed but not considered in the statement of income of the individual firm in the PS. These financial statements are flawed to the extent that their measurement criteria do not consider societal costs in the economic values created. Sales and service revenues and costs of the individual firm do not reflect the broader societal and environmental effects of their products.

Previous discussions have led us to the recognition that the common goal for the profit-oriented firm is to optimize consumers' economic benefits and satisfaction. The proposed conceptual framework for measuring the effectiveness and efficiency of HSOs is based on the same element, consumer benefits and satisfaction. An analysis of the operating characteristics of firms in both sectors likewise demonstrates that they function in a similar manner, face similar problems, and resolve them in a similar fashion. Moreover, measurement concepts are equally applicable to the PS and to HSOs in terms of the defined criteria of specificity of goal (profits), definition of attribute (satisfaction/benefit), metric (unit measure convertibility into dollars), and other factors (the potential of periodicity, relevancy, comprehensibility, cost, and auditability). The equating of mission with market and outcome with profit permits a unified field theory of measurement applicable to both sectors. Thus, the model dissolves the measurement and reporting differences between them. The profit to society earned by HSOs can be directly measured by clients and aggregated for the organization as well as for a redefined sector.

With the dissolving of differences, many of the prior problems of the relations between the sectors also dissolve. With the same method of accounting and measurement, all markets become open to all firms; all pay taxes (income, real estate, sales, etc.); firms offering similar services paid for by societal resources must be held to the same standard of accountability; all can compete for customers and personnel based on rules established for the same playing field. Where there is a private payer who uses services and pays for such services from private resources, presumably the individual's actions are covered by the model of the market and the PS. It follows that when private payers use the services of an HSO, they likewise should be paying market prices. The same services and skills are required for an HSO regardless of who pays. The payment for such services affects fund raising, staff attitudes, and staff compensation. These changes should have societal ramifications, simplifying regulations and reducing costs of frictions between the sectors. These ramifications of the model can be considered as a specific illustration of the resolution of particular problems by a step-up in the level of analysis.

The elimination of differences between the PS and NPS (as previously discussed) has extensive implications in providing new ways of approaching problems and as an impetus for change. HSOs will be viewed in a different light as society recognizes their significant contributions to its well-offness.

The Professions

There should be significant effects of the models on the fields of economics and accounting as well as in the political science arena.

The defining of revenue and the consequent potential for an HSO to prepare a statement of income accomplishes "mission impossible" for the accounting profession. Up to this point, HSOs have had no means to measure the value of their services rendered to clients, that is, their revenues generated, and accordingly, a statement of income could not be prepared. The concept of societal income overcomes this gap by measuring differences in the clients' NRC, the economic value of the movement, or maintenance of clients relative to self-sufficiency. A statement of income can be integrated with the existing statement of support, revenues, and disbursements based on the mandated application of generally accepted accounting principles (GAAP). The model provides a conceptual framework that could minimize some inappropriate applications of current accounting pronouncements, such as its emphasis on cash flow. It is believed that this misapplied emphasis has contributed to the recent savings and loan debacle and the merger/leveraged buy-out mania of the 1980s. Accounting systems should encourage the production of goods; the financial system, the message, should not be substituted for the medium.

The present PS model disregards social costs and requires an indirect measurement of societal well-offness based upon the questionable concept of the aggregation of the individual consumer's preferences. The movement of HSOs' clients toward self-sufficiency may be a sounder measure of revenue than are market prices in the PS. This movement is a direct measure of societal benefits with the potential of incorporating costs of externalities and the summing of incomes, which eliminates the problem of the summing of individual utilities raised by Arrow.[16]

We propose a changed taxonomy based on the source of resources, whether private or the group and the application of resources, whether for the benefit of particular individuals or for a group (see Exhibit 4.1). Resources used for the direct benefit of an individual, whether private in the private profit sector (PPS), or societal in the societal profit sector (SPS), such as HSOs, can be accounted for on a profit calculus. These become the micro segments. Resources used for the benefit of a group can be provided from private or societal sources. Group segments can then be accounted for on a nonprofit basis. One group includes private organizations such as foundations and associations called the group association sector (GAS)—commonly referred to as the independent sector—and the other, the group government sector (GGS). The latter's function is to maintain and/or better the society and its infrastructure. These become the macro sectors.

For the professions and various disciplines within the social sciences, new ways of approach are shown and the interdependence of the disciplines is emphasized.

Government

The general performance evaluation (accounting) system gives various governmental bodies on a national or local level information to assist them in making political decisions. The societal model contains the societal value goals and the accounting system, the feedback to measure the achievement of these goals established by the political body.

Tax policy should be reexamined in light of the logic of the organizational model and the changed taxonomy. It is clear that all firms in the micro profit sector, the PPS (Box 1) and the SPS (Box 3), should pay income taxes and that organizations in the macro nonprofit sector, the GAS (Box 2) and the GGS (Box 4) should not (see Figure 5.1). What about tax deductibility by donors?

The model responds with a specific guideline: Deductibility is given to donors that purchase the societal revenue earned by HSOs. However, policy decisions are required relative to contributions to organizations in the macro sector that are devoted to society's betterment: the arts, religion, research, the civic sector, and so on. These decisions should depend on the development of models and measuring systems for this sector and its segments (see chapter 9, Future Research).

The same measurement system derived from the organizational model can be applied to any governmental unit providing direct services. The function of government should emphasize the need of local control and local organizational inputs to reflect local needs and conditions. However, government should provide the standards that in turn require the collection of data for the evaluation of outcome with measurable objectives. As the federal government transfers block grants to states, and states to cities and to local communities and to local entities, the reporting of outcomes should be comparable, based on national standards. However, it must be determined whether government contracting to HSOs, which provide measurable incentives, whether in the PPS or SPS, may provide a more effective and efficient allocation of societal resources.

Society

The implementation of the organizational model redirects board, management, and staff behavior to focus on achievement of societal goals that support the fundamental societal missions. This should result in a more effective and efficient allocation of societal resources by: (1) increasing the number of people in or moving toward the economic mainstream, (2) providing a measurement of profit and risk, and (3) promoting ethical behavior. The concomitant effect of these propositions is to improve the moral environment of the society and to reduce its frictions by: (1) inducing client-consumers to join the system; (2) creating an appropriate environment to help the needy, the victims of genetic lottery and other chance events; (3) recognizing the benefits of both cooperation and competition; and (4) encouraging investment in human capital. A society that emphasizes investment in human resources—education, training, and health—as well as encouragement of risk taking and the other goals contained in the propositions, should be more dynamic, creating economic benefits for its members. As a concomitant, more societal members should recognize the benefits derived from cooperation as well as competition.

In effect, the measurement of revenues of the HSO (societal income), while computed on an economic basis, has a positive influence on ethical behavior within the society. The system induces the particular organization and society to look at how to better the position of individuals, thereby improving the lot of the community as a whole. The model responds to societal problems prevalent in the current scene. In a world of limited resources, the system of accounting is in harmony with a Western humanistic viewpoint.

The propositions that have been developed and the related organizational model to implement such propositions cover the individual as a direct recipient of services rendered or paid for directly by governments or indirectly by organizations that receive tax exemptions. Accordingly, costs related to the consumer that are paid for or anticipated to be paid from societal resources should be accounted for on a current basis by the firm. Financial statements of organizations should reflect liabilities for such societal costs, an example being the cigarette industry. Such cost inclusion could also focus the accounting on the depletion of natural resources and the cost of environmental concomitants of industrial production. It could also increase the awareness of consumers as to their social responsibilities and liabilities from their use of tobacco, alcohol, and drugs.

The model may also assist in the resolution of other societal problems by providing an approach for the development of a measuring system for other segments of the SPS (health and education) as well as for the group sectors. It suggests that a basic societal consideration should be on balance to improve the economic position of its individual members—a principal goal for any society.

Future Research

Accounting systems derived from the societal and organizational normative models require support in the form of empirical studies and research by practitioners and academicians:

- Practical experience will help formalize methods for the computation of NRC as well as for the further development of specific attributes in the non–work related segments of human services

- Additional research is required relative to the application of the model to the PPS to incorporate societal costs and to provide a direct aggregatable measure of societal well-offness

- A major area involves the application of the organizational model to the two other principal segments of the SPS, health and education, where the individual is the direct recipient of services

- The changed taxonomy, where the group is the beneficiary of resources used (defined as the nonprofit or macro sector) suggests that the attributes and their corresponding money metric, which have been applied to the micro sectors, may not be appropriate to measure group-related outcomes. It suggests further that group well-offness may require attributes that can measure such factors as levels of health, education, leisure, arts, conflict resolution, and the environment

NOTES

1. Rino Patti poses the questions as to how to select, value, and prioritize appropriate services in order to achieve congruence among services, resources, and outcomes. The accounting system developed in this book incorporates his criteria and responds to the proposed dimensions for a management approach. Patti, Rino J. (1987, September–October). Managing for service effectiveness in social welfare organizations. *Social Work, 32*(5), 377–381.

2. Our focus is on the individual recipient and the nonprofit organization that provides human services. In effect, we initially followed a classification similar to Gronbjerg in a study of the poor in Chicago. "I exclude hospitals, arts, cultural, educational, and research organizations," which provide "highly specialized activities that serve the general interest." Excluded also are membership associations and social clubs as well as churches and religious congregations. Gronbjerg, Kirsten A. (1990, June). Poverty and nonprofit organizational behavior. *Social Service Review, 64*(2), 239.

There have been several studies that examine the nonprofit sector from the critical perspectives of its composition, growth, trends, and contribution to the economy including: Weisbrod, Burton A. (1988). *The nonprofit economy*. Cambridge, MA: Harvard University Press; and O'Neill, Michael. (1989). *The third America: The emergence of the nonprofit sector in the United States*. San Francisco, CA: Jossey-Bass. See Exhibit 3.1, which presents some data from these sources. However, see also the changed taxonomy proposed in chapter 4 and Exhibit 4.1, which represents a significant implication of this work. Relative to the nonprofit sector, various terms are used such as non-profit, not-for-profit, nonbusiness, and non-business. We use the term *nonprofits* unless for a direct quotation or within the context of a prior quotation,

3. Our literature review failed to disclose an integrated model that addresses internal performance and public accountability in the nonprofit sector. One related effort is a conceptual scheme that integrates control and evaluation criteria within a "benefit cost perspective." For a discussion of the model and its limitations, see chapter 7. Ramanathan, Kavasseri V. (1985, Summer). A proposed framework for designing management control systems in not-for profit organizations. *Financial Accountability and Management, 1*(1), 75–95.

4. Linn, Lawrence E., Jr. (1986, December). The new economics of social welfare: An essay review. *Social Service Review, 60*(4), 590–602.

5. "Discovery commences with the awareness of anomaly, i.e., with the recognition that nature has somehow violated the paradigm—induced expectations that govern normal science." Kuhn, Thomas S. (1970). *The structure of scientific revolutions* (2nd ed., pp. 52–53). Chicago: University of Chicago Press.

6. Kutner, Robert. (1990, January 8). Economic viewpoint. *Business Week*, 21.

7. We use the term well-off in accordance with the first definition in *Webster's* (third edition): "being in good condition or favorable circumstances." We will use the term well-offness as the state of being well-off. This is a more generalized statement than the way in which the term well-offness is used by Hicks. "Income is not the maximum amount the individual can spend while expecting to be as well off as before at the end of the week; it is the maximum amount he can consume." Hicks, J. R. (1978). *An inquiry into some fundamental principles of economic theory* (2nd ed., p. 176). Oxford: Oxford University Press.

8. Weisbrod, *The nonprofit economy*, and O'Neill, *The third America*.

9. Included among Keynes's explanations of unemployment are that "pervasive uncertainty is an inherent feature of a capitalist economy . . . [and] when the state of confidence is low, individuals will make decisions in a risk-averse fashion" McKenna, Edward, Wade, Maurice & Zannoni, Diane (1988, October). Keynes, Rawls, Uncertainty, and the liberal theory of the state. *Economics and Philosophy, 4*(2), 228.

10. McKenna, Wade & Zannoni, Keynes, Rawls, Uncertainty, 222.

11. The following quotation from Keynes underscores this viewpoint:

I expect to see the state, which is in a position to calculate the marginal efficiency of capital-goods on long views and on the basis of the general social advantage, taking an even greater responsibility for directly organizing investment; since it seems likely that the fluctuations in the market estimation of the marginal efficiency of different types of capital, calculated on the principles I have described above, will be too great to be offset by any particular changes in the rate of interest.

Keynes, John Maynard. (1964). *The general theory of employment, interest, and money* (p. 164). New York: Harcourt, Brace and World (Original work published 1935).

12. Schultz, Theodore W. (1981). *Investing in people—The Economics of population quality*. Berkeley: University of California Press.

13. Ijiri, Y. (1975). Theory of accounting measurement—In Studies in accounting research no. 10 (p. 51). Sarasota, FL: American Accounting Association.

14. Phelps, Edmund S. (1985). *Political economy: An introductory text* (p. 4). New York: W. W. Norton & Company.

15. "At some point, increments of service effectiveness can be achieved only at unacceptably low levels of output and efficiency." Patti, Managing for service effectiveness, p. 38. It should be noted that marginal revenue and marginal cost are calculable under the proffered model.

16. "If we exclude the possibility of interpersonal comparisons of utility, then the only method of passing from individual tastes to social preferences which will be satisfactory and which will be defined for a wide range of sets of individual orderings are either imposed or dictatorial." Arrow, Kenneth J. (1963). *Social choice and individual values* (p. 59). New Haven, CT: Cowles Foundation for Research in Economics at Yale University.

17. Repetto, Robert, & Magrath, William B. (1989, June). *Wasting Assets: Natural Resources in the National Income Accounts* (p. 68). Washington, DC: World Resources Institute. Reviewed in *Future Survey, 11*(11), (1989, November).

CHAPTER 2

The Organizational Model

The overarching societal goals of encouraging citizens to pursue economic self-sufficiency, to take risks, and to behave in an ethical manner provide the framework for a measuring system that induces goal-congruent behavior. From an analytic point of view, the fundamental goal common to HSOs is to improve the quality of life of their clients. Persons who are not economically independent within our society generally cannot equate their quality-of-life satisfactions with those of other members of society. The HSOs response to the needs and wants of their consumer-clients must be satisfied in an effective manner. What is required is to define in economic terms this response and to devise a method to measure changes brought about by the HSOs' intervention. Currently there is no attribute that measures the value of services rendered by HSOs, which the market performs for the PS; accordingly, the NPS cannot develop a statement of income as in the PS. There is no common denominator to measure quantity, quality, or value of services; only an accounting for funds that does not reflect service performance. Since stakeholders' behavior is influenced by the measuring system and its rewards, a change is necessary so that societal goals can be implemented. The model combines the perspectives of the client, the firm, and society.

The key components upon which the organizational model are based are: measurement of quality of life, definition of consumer satisfaction, questions addressed by accounting systems, and functions of HSOs. The model's major operational components are a client information system (CIS) and a financial information system (FIS), which generate the data and context for the development of evaluative processes referred to herein as a comprehensive evaluation system (CES). The system's external reporting medium, a statement of societal income for the individual HSO, utilizes the same data bases as the internal reports for the hierarchical levels of stakeholders. The effects of the system on the external reports and on the internal design for decision making and control, the management information system (MIS), are then discussed.

The model combines an awareness of the goals and operating requirements of HSOs with measurement concepts. The system's basic elements—its unifying goal, its attribute, and its unit of measure are discussed in chapter 4. We then demonstrate how the model responds to the remaining criteria for a measuring system—matching of periodic flow of inputs and outputs, integrating external and internal reporting to stakeholders, and other criteria such as relevance, costs, and auditability.

An analysis of the dynamics of the system is presented. The chapter concludes with a summary statement of consequences and implications of this organizational model.

ELEMENTS OF THE PROPOSED SOLUTION

The key elements supporting the model are as follows:

1. Purposes addressed in their broadest sense by accounting systems
2. Underlying definitions of consumer satisfaction and markets in the PS and NPS
3. Factors and assumptions in the measurement of quality of life
4. The role and functions of the human service organizations

It is from these elements, within the perspective of the propositions, that the organizational model is developed.

Accounting Principles

Accounting principles are discussed to address the question of their use in measuring performance. They must also be examined relative to the potential of their being adopted, or adapted to the measurement of the performance of HSOs. In the absence of an explicit authorized conceptual framework, how do accounting principles work? Generally accepted accounting principles (GAAP) include concepts for accounting practitioners to follow, such as the use and continuity of historical costs, the financial statements to be prepared, the definitions for assets and liabilities, and criteria for income recognition, materiality and relevance. The organizational model requires the development of a missing component for a statement of income and a theoretical framework in which to place such statements. There appears to be little awareness by the accounting profession that such income statements must be placed either in a framework similar to the underlying propositions of the PS relative to optimization of consumer satisfaction and consequent allocation of resources, or that a new set of propositions must be developed for the HSOs. This book responds to both of these either/or statements.

By promulgating a set of guiding societal propositions and by developing a reliable attribute for the measurement of earned revenue, an appropriate set of measurements is developed for HSOs. Significantly, the application of the proposed model to the PS may portray more precisely the operations of that sector if and when societal criteria take precedence.

Accounting can be thought of as a method of measuring resources used and income generated within a specified time period as well as the status of the assets and liabilities. Accounting questions arise since compilation of the revenue generation and resource consumption cycles do not generally correspond to the reporting period. Thus, financial accounting systems reflect in their accounting cycle the longer of the reporting time requirements or the actual operational process cycle time. Accounting problems diminish with the increase of the time period: Given an accounting cycle of a decade in comparison to a year, they become minimal (without getting into the question of price changes); presumably, in heaven, with unlimited time and boundless resources, accounting questions disappear. In those cases where the operating cycle time is greater than the reporting time, appropriate intracycle estimates facilitate the periodic reporting of financial results. These estimates, or evaluations, are made through the use of GAAP.

The application of accounting principles in the PS is discussed in chapter 6. Such discussion emphasizes that profit reporting contains myriad estimates based upon applications of GAAP. It can be asserted that nearly every amount that appears in financial statements in the PS can be considered an estimate. This has not deterred the preparation of financial statements in the PS based on its model; nor should it.

Accounting principles differ from economic theory, which separates interest on capital from profit as well as including the interest component in other computations. Coming closer to economics, accountants have also attempted to deal with price changes as affecting the valuation of fixed assets and the evaluation of investments at market value in lieu of cost.

Accounting rules are based, in a broad sense, on the twofold principle of recognizing income only in the case where there is an arm's length transaction for the exchange of goods or services with a party outside the organization (customers); or recognizing loss only when there is objective evidence external to the enterprise to support the valuation. It should be noted that if the enterprise does not make any bona fide sales, it does not have any earned income. The original cost basis remains pervasive to accounting, particularly for fixed and intangible assets. Their allocation to the income statement is through appropriate (sometimes arbitrary, however generally consistent) methods of allocation to future periods by depreciation and amortization of such costs.

The other place where intracycle valuation principles usually play their most significant role is in the area of inventories. It is obvious in the case of manufactured goods that are in the state of being produced (work in process) or are in a finished state. In these circumstances, the rule is not to recognize added value; only the accumulation of related cost is permitted. This accounting convention is further modified by the criterion that if the goods that are being or have been produced will not be sold at a price that is in excess of the accumulated cost, the inventory has to be valued at less than accumulated cost, giving rise to a loss—the rule of the lower of cost or market.

Revenue Defined. Profit is generally defined as revenues less expenses; revenues are defined as measures arising from delivery of goods or the rendering of services during a period. This definition is modified by the realization convention—that is, the converting of noncash resources into money and money equivalents. It is assumed that if someone pays or agrees to pay for some item or service, that person is receiving the desired outcome from the purchase, namely, the satisfaction of some need; and that which is given, such as money, is marginally less valuable than the satisfaction received.

The critical difference in the financial accounting systems of the PS and HSOs lies in the seeming difficulty in arriving at a suitable and workable definition of revenue for HSOs. Clearly, every nonprofit organization is supposed to produce an output in order to achieve an outcome in accordance with its mission. The problem is that in most cases, output is substituted for the outcome qua mission. Therefore, if a definition of revenue having the properties as discussed above could be developed for the HSOs, then the major difference between the two sectors would be dissolved. Moreover, all the methods and techniques of accounting systems already developed would be available whether for the PS and HSOs, and potentially for other segments of the NPS. More important, from society's point of view, the more effective and efficient organizations could be identified.

This presentation of a measurement system is limited to HSOs whose mission is either to improve the self-sufficiency of their consumer-clients or to maintain their level of functioning, thereby minimizing the clients' use of societal resources. The first step in the construction of such a specific accounting system is the development of an attribute to measure improvement or maintenance. Given the broad range of meanings that can be attached to the word *welfare*, an attribute is defined by an equivalent concept, or a surrogate, that measures change in "self-sufficiency" and that can be transformed into monetary terms.

As stated, the two properties that are necessary for a definition of revenues are a measure of enterprise outputs and of measurable outcomes (the attributes) during a period, and the realization principle, for example, a sale being made. Another way of describing this process is defining a *market* with a *willing buyer* and a *willing seller*. An analysis of these two properties in the context of what is referred to as HSOs in the current NPS with its defined attribute can provide a suitable and workable definition of revenues for the HSO.

The terms used to describe a market are supply, demand, price and quantity. The word *market* in economics is generally taken to mean a social mechanism through which individuals interact with each other. In the PS markets, the recipient of the output, the economic beneficiary of the outcome, and the payer for the outcome are presumed to be the same person. In the proposed HSO accounting system the benefits go to the consumer-client paid for by society and measured by the increase in the societal income generated, the change in the client's self-sufficiency. Both benefit—the direct consumer of services and society.

In addition, markets can be classified by their structures, the degree of competition. One type of market structure applies in particular for finding a substitute for net realizable value. A monopsonistic market is a market where there is a single buyer. In the case of the use of societal resources, then society is the buyer. Economic theory states that for the monopsonist in this market structure the optimal condition is when marginal benefit equals marginal cost. The point where this equality holds can be viewed as being net realizable value.

Having developed an abstract measure of net realizable value, we approach operationalization from the point of view of the marginal benefit to society. As noted, the outcome that society usually seeks is either the improvement in or maintenance of a citizen's welfare. What is being suggested is that the marginal benefit to society is the present value of the money (resources) saved given its commitment to its citizens in their movement toward self-sufficiency. The resources saved in this analysis are estimates, as is most of the information contained in accounting reports.

The Consumer

In the PS, the attribute of profit measures consumer satisfaction at the achieved level. In theory, it serves as a measure of the organization's contribution to society's well-offness. Entrepreneurial effectiveness reflects response to consumer demand, together with efficiency in the use of resources; this results in the entrepreneurial rewards called profits. If a similar attribute (profit) to measure consumer satisfaction for HSOs could be developed, then society would have a consistent measure for both the PS and the NPS.

Quality of Life

Quality of life has a functional relationship to the autonomy of the individual. As the Dole Foundation eloquently but simply states, "We identify ourselves increasingly with our occupation, our life-style, status, hobbies and avocations. . . . There is substantial dignity in being able to support oneself and make basic choices in life-style."[1] It is assumed that there is a goal generally followed by individuals in our society to increase their economic independence and self-sufficiency. This becomes a measurable calculus on a continuous scale, applicable to those who are successfully participating in the social system and those unable to do so—a break at the point of those who are independent and are producing society's income and those to whom society has allocated resources. For individuals who are not full participants in the social system, continual assessments can evaluate their movement toward specified goals that include increased levels of functioning, autonomy, self-sufficiency and/or independence, which can be translated into an economic calculus. As developed in chapter 4, such measures are based upon the assumption that such changes lead to an economic improvement in the quality of life. Thus, in the proposed model, participation in the social system is measured by the surrogate of achieving improved levels of functioning translated into the change in economic independence of the individual. This applies also to individuals who are frail and more vulnerable and where the goal is to maintain the level of functional independence and thus avoid increased dependence on societal resources. Maintenance or improvement in independent living skills may not only contribute to their autonomy, but also may reduce the cost of operating the institution or providing in-home services.

It should be pointed out that a measuring system that contains the surrogate measure of independence should tend to induce management and staff behavior toward this mission. It should also furnish a dominant common goal for clients and other stakeholders.

HSOs

What has been learned from the PS is the pivotal role of the firm. Its effective response to its market and the efficient organization of the factors of production, distribution, and administration results in profits—its market revenues less their costs. These actions by the individual firm correspond to the economic theory of the PS, which optimizes consumer satisfaction and, according to its system, society well-offness. As will also be expanded upon in chapter 6, the firm in the PS and the HSO play key roles in determining their mission, exploiting markets, and marshaling the factors of production. The major difference is the payer—the consumer in the PS based on perceived satisfactions and benefits is similar to the consumer-client, the direct recipient and beneficiary of the services rendered by the HSO; however, society is the payer and the beneficiary (together with the consumer-client). Is society getting its money's worth? Is the HSO effective in the use of these transferred resources? A financial statement of income of the HSO could provide the answer in terms of its profits. This, of course, requires a measure of the value of its rendered services paid for by the use of societal resources.

Based on actions of the PS, it is essential to recognize that criteria of efficiency do not stand by themselves—they must be related to market criteria in order to optimize profits. It is apparent that the mission of an HSO is equivalent to its market, and therefore its success in performing its mission should be measured by the outcomes of its programs; this is similar conceptually to market product success and profits in the PS. Thus it can be stated that mission is to market as outcome is to profit. And, as in the PS, relative to market and profitability, it is only after determining mission and its outcomes for the HSO that the most efficient use of resources can be planned for and calculated.

The above discussion may in part provide the justification for the complex phenomenon that has been referred to as human service organizations. These organizations are hybrid entities, having characteristics of both public and private organization types that fulfill their special role. They are like private organizations in that their decision making is private and they compete with profit and other nonprofit organizations for the factors of production (labor, material, etc.)

as they attempt to satisfy human needs. They are like public enterprises in that they cannot withhold their products from the market and their accountability is public, based on varying accepted societal values. In a competitive economy, PS enterprises, by their very nature, have to be primarily economically self-serving, and in a democracy, public enterprises are politically self-serving, and thus are dependent on achieving a consensus and are often slow to respond. In contrast, HSOs should only be self-serving by serving others. The problem then evolves into one of making sure, by incentives and accountability, that HSOs are in fact serving others in an optimal fashion. In a society of increasing anonymity, HSOs would have to be invented if they had not already evolved to their present position.

Net Resources Consumed. There is a common denominator of an HSO's performance that is consonant with the societal goals embodied in the propositions: the improvement of the quality of life of its consumer-clients specifically defined as their movement toward economic self-sufficiency and relative independence. If the value of this intervention by an HSO could be quantified, then an HSO's income could be determined.

Individual participation and society's well-offness is being proposed in an economic sense, and its degree is determined in relation to the attribute measure termed net resources consumed (NRC). NRC is defined as the difference between an individual's income and use of societal resources, defined in monetary terms. The minimum consumption baseline is equal to that allowed at the poverty level (or at a prescribed percentage above). The use of some standard consumption level is essential to ensure that the measure of change in clients' NRC is not achieved by reduction of their consumption level. A fully participating individual can be identified as one whose NRC is zero or positive, that is, his/her production as measured by earned income equals or exceeds his/her consumption. A partially participating individual is one whose consumption exceeds production; a nonparticipating individual consumes, but does not produce. For example, if a client who enters an HSO program has an NRC of $10,000 (there were direct or indirect $10,000 transfer payments to the individual by government), and exits the HSO with an NRC of zero, it is assumed that the HSO has brought the client to a state of full participation in the social system. If the client earns $8,000 per year, then the change in the client's NRC in the amount of $18,000 is the basis of the value of the intervention by the HSO. Such savings of societal resources, the individual client's change in NRC, can be calculated as the present value of an annuity for a specified period, for example, the estimated working life of the consumer-client, discounted at an appropriate interest rate. The gross revenue generated by the HSO is the total of their individual clients' changes in NRC.

Credit is being given to the HSO for the client's progress. Approaching the result in this way not only makes the system tractable and in keeping with concepts of measuring systems, but also establishes what can be defined as the system's goal. When using this concept of NRC, the goal of the HSO is to reflect a positive change in the clients' level of NRC. The cost to HSOs of programs, the value of the resources devoted to the clients' services, together with administrative expenses, must be deducted in measuring the net gain to society, termed net societal income (NSI). The above illustration of NRC applies to HSOs whose goal is the increase in clients' self-sufficiency, the SS/I. A similar approach can be applied to the maintenance and protective model (M/P) as discussed later in this chapter.

Discussion of Elements

The individual pursuit of economic self-interest in the PS has been presented in terms of the consumers' satisfaction of their needs and wants arising from the use of their resources based upon their preferences. Both sectors seek to satisfy the consumer. Consumer satisfaction is a basic postulate in the PS, and the results are then imputed as to society's well-offness. For HSOs, consumer satisfaction is defined in terms of the movement toward economic self-sufficiency of its members who use societal resources. The firm in each case presumably responds appropriately in terms of the effective and efficient use of resources, which results in profits. In the PS, the measurement of society well-offness is indirect and imputed; for the HSOs, society well-offness becomes a direct measurement.

THE MODEL'S OPERATIONAL COMPONENTS

Client Information System (CIS)

A client information system provides data for feedback reporting of actual services to those predetermined at the time of intake, actual costs in comparison to predetermined costs by client, cost center, and program, and an assessment of outcomes. Thus the CIS offers a profile of the individual client, his/her present status, past history, and present problems. It includes a statement of his/her self-assessment of present functioning and goals for the future. While portraying the individual client, the information should be recorded in such a way that it may be aggregated and provide a record of clients seeking and receiving services for hierarchical levels of staff and for other stakeholders.

The second major task of the CIS is to record the projected service plan and the actual services received. It includes staff assessment of the plan, projected service units for the plan as agreed upon by client and staff, and a record of periodic reassessment, changes in original estimates of required service units, and information at termination of service including final assessment (output) and actual service units utilized. Additionally, as a third component, this service history includes information on reimbursement for services such as client payment and/or third party reimbursement. A fourth component records outcome data including timing of follow-up and data necessary to measure a client's movement toward self-sufficiency. Chapter 8 offers more specific details about a CIS.

The Financial Information System (FIS)

While the CIS is the recording instrument for client information, the FIS is the calculating instrument, necessary for converting the disparate, individualized service unit to a common, comparable base. It also performs the traditional recording and summarizing of information for control of operations so that all costs are accumulated both in service units and dollars based on programmatic functions. In addition, it maintains the usual detailed functional expense accounts such as salaries, fringes, overhead, general administrative and fund-raising costs. The FIS also integrates the billing of services to clients and third-party payers, the maintenance of inventories, departmental transfers, and other related functions. It also serves as the "bookkeeper" for the MIS in terms of record keeping for budgets, standard and actual operations, and variance computations.

The FIS must reflect the operational structure of the HSO in terms of its functioning and the need of hierarchical reporting, appropriately classifying programs, cost centers, departments, and expense functions consistent and congruent with the agency's operations and the goals established as defined by its mission. Further along in this chapter, included under the heading Accounting Factors—Internal Reporting, there is a discussion of budgets, standard costs, and variances. Chapter 8 also gives a more detailed discussion of an FIS together with examples of a worked-out budget.

The Comprehensive Evaluation System (CES)

The CIS and FIS constitute the foundation for client tracking and cost and service control procedures; taken together they form the CES. The system provides the "hard" and "soft" data on a continual basis; the reference to hard data incorporates statistical information arising from accumulation of service units and dollar costs; soft data refers to subjective evaluations by clients, staff, or outside consultants. It should again be emphasized that while efficiency is a laudable objective, it must be subordinate to outcome analysis. As has been stated heretofore: mission implies market as outcome implies profit. Therefore, as in the PS, without considering the framework of the market and sales revenues, efficiency by itself is of little significance. Efficiency factors together with variances can be analyzed only when alternative outcomes are considered. Moreover, with integrated data bases, such reports are available for analysis by various staff and management personnel and, when summarized, for the board of directors and other appropriate stakeholders.[2]

THE FINANCIAL STATEMENTS

The Self-Sufficiency/Independence Model (SS/I)

Outputs are used for efficiency calculations and represent the program effects of client changes as measured on some functional scale. Outcomes reflect the effect of program outputs relative to the longer-term goals of the client. The proposed model is capable of generating measures of outcomes and effectiveness by individual, by type of clients, by programs, and by staff members. The summing of these outcomes generates a measure of revenues for the entire agency, the gross (societal) income (GSI); this can be presented in a manner comparable to that of the PS in terms of its statement of income. This financial statement reflects an HSO's contribution to society's well-offness. It measures how the organization fulfills its mission in producing a positive outcome for the client and consequently a reduction in cost for society. After all costs of service provision and administration are considered, the aggregate measure of contribution, or net societal income, is computed (the comparable term in the PS is net income). With appropriate allocations NSI can be computed for individual clients, client mixes, programs, staff, and the particular HSO, and/or for groupings of HSOs.

An example of a hypothetical HSO statement of (societal) income is illustrated in Exhibit 2.1. No dollar amounts have been included for presentation purposes; see chapter 8 for details of an actual case study in which numbers are presented. Each of the components of this financial statement in Exhibit 2.1 is discussed.

Revenues. For an HSO, revenues include the total of GSI generated by consumer-clients and fees and other income from other sources. The first step in calculating NSI is to compute GSI. This is the summation of each individual

Exhibit 2.1
Statement of an Agency's Net (Societal) Income

For the Period Beginning xxxx and Ending xxxx

Revenues		
Gross societal income	$xxx	
Fees and other income	xxx	
Total revenue		$xxx
Less: Related program expenses @ standard cost		xxx
Gross profit @ standard		xx
Standard program expenses (as above)	xxx	
Actual program expenses	xxx	
Efficiency adjustment		x
Gross profit @ actual		xx
Less: General and administrative and research expenses		xx
Net (Societal) Income*		$ x

* Before taxes measured by income.

client's GSI. GSI for an HSO client is in turn defined as the present value of the change in his/her NRC. The procedures used in this calculation start with client intake. At that time, the HSO calculates the money value of all the services and stipends that the client is receiving from society. At some point after the client disengages from the HSO, for example, a year, there is client follow-up. Assume, for example, that at the point of intake, a client's NRC measures $-\$4,000$ represented by supplemental security income and Medicaid support. A year after client closure, his/her NRC is $+\$7,000$, a job at minimum pay including medical coverage. In this case, society can be considered better off by an amount equal to the present value of the change in payments to the client, that is, by $11,000 a year for the actuarially computed balance of the client's work life. To reflect the time value of money, the $11,000 societal *annuity* must be discounted at an interest rate. Based on criteria in chapter 5, an objective auditable interest rate can be associated with a U.S. government bond whose maturity date is closest to the terminal date of the client's actuarially determined work life. In effect, this is the cost that society pays on its long-term borrowings in the treasury bond market. Actuarially, an annuity of $11,000 per year for 20 years discounted at an annual rate of 10%, an assumed treasury rate for a 20-year bond, amounts to $93,650. The societal income is the revenue generated by the HSO for a particular consumer-client. Gross revenue generated is the total of all clients' societal income.

Related Program Costs. The program costs while the client is actively engaged with the HSO are accumulated at their costs as inventory. These costs are only offset against the client's societal income at the appropriate period after client closure as stated above. Until that time, the accumulated costs are carried on the balance sheet as inventory. The accumulated costs incurred for clients who leave prior to program completion should be removed from inventory and charged to current operations. When the amount of the inventory at the beginning and end of a period is not material relative to the number of client closures within the period under review, that is, to its GSI, all program expenses may be directly deducted.

The Efficiency Adjustment. The difference between the program costs at standard and the actual program costs is the measure of efficiency; it is included in the statement of (societal) income as expense (or income) for the period while the client is engaged with the HSO. When the efficiency adjustment is not reflected on the statement of (societal) income, then related program costs will be presented and deducted at actual. Financial statements in the PS for "outside" stakeholders ordinarily report upon operations without this disclosure. Obviously, there is no effect on the bottom line, the agency's net (societal) income, since the efficiency adjustment cancels the difference between the program costs at standard and program costs at actual.

General and Administrative and Research Expenses. As in the PS, the last set of deductions represents costs associated with general and administrative, research, and other period services. The larger HSO might separate these costs as well as other functions such as public education and marketing.

The application of the model significantly affects current fund-raising expenses as is evident from the discussion later in the chapter on the funding cycle and tax policy. Cost of fund-raising should be incurred only for HSOs that do not generate societal income. Under the proposed model, such efforts at fund-raising would suffer from the inability of the donors to receive tax deductibility for their contributions.

The Maintenance and Protective Model (M/P)

We now turn to a discussion of the second type of HSO—the Maintenance and Protective (M/P) model. These organizations serve certain persons in our society in order to maintain their existing functional level. They have as their mission preventing a negative change in the self-sustaining ability of their clients. The political decision for the establishing of these organizations also has economic considerations. As will be more fully developed in the subsequent chapter, in assuming certain responsibilities relative to these persons, society also benefits. However, society needs to be able to measure how effectively and efficiently its resources are being used for these groups and how this resource allocation affects the economy.

HSOs that manage these programs are perceived from a modeling point of view as the same as those HSOs whose mission is to increase their clients' ability to be self-sustaining. They are essentially on a continuum with the SS/I model. The other criteria of a measuring system and operational components remain similar for both types of HSOs—and with the usual caveat—the need to supplement any single measurement with other quantitative and qualitative indicators.

The statement of (societal) income for the M/P agency mirrors that of the SS/I (see Exhibit 2.1).

The elements for measuring and funding the system for the M/P model are largely in place, namely:

- Government contracting systems with specified criteria for bidding, reporting, and financing reflecting various client population mixes; these in turn are based upon individual clients' continuing functional assessments

- Various functional assessment scales that consider the individual's ability of maintaining self and functional scales that measure client's capacities to carry out activities of daily living. These scales can provide objective measures or ratings that on an individual basis can be related to a service plan. Even in the absence of formal scales, the act of program prescription, with clinical or specific output criteria, performs the same function. These become the basis of output measurement—the completion of programs at predefined levels

- National health surveys that consider the relationship between an individual's ability to carry out the activities of daily living, age, and disability

- Mortality schedules in the life insurance industry

- Schedules of morbidity (life insurance industry) based upon functioning, physiology, disease, age, and demographic location

- Blue Cross/Blue Shield—Diagnostic related group (DRG) data
- Performance and environmental quality standards established by various government agencies relative to staffing, food, space, and other environmental quality factors

In preventing functional decline, there should be a reward to organizations for the relative maintenance of the individual on a functional scale. The reward must be measured by whether individuals are relatively better off at the end of a period than a standard measuring system would indicate for their peers. A rate guide must be developed, not unlike the DRGs under which hospitals are paid, drawn from the available elements listed above. As an incentive, the HSOs should receive the amount saved. This could be calculated from the specific savings attributable to the year based on the functioning of the client at the conclusion of the year. As an alternative, the HSO could receive as income, on an annual basis, the present value of the savings with an interest rate for a comparable U.S. government bond. The latter is conceptually closer to the rewarding of the SS/I agency with the discounted present value of the savings resulting from their outcomes.

The SS/I and M/P models are, in essence, a continuum and are so presented in terms of their measurement. For the M/P, the question is answered as to how well an individual continues to function. Within the maintenance of established quality standards, this is determined by the degree of effectiveness of clients' maintaining their existing level of functioning against the standards in the relevant morbidity and mortality tables. Even if all of the savings were given to the HSO, society would benefit. Such rewards reinforce societal goals by supporting society's members during times of crisis (making them unafraid to take risks) thereby encouraging ethical behavior.

It should be emphasized, however, that for political decision making, economic comparisons among different types of HSOs should not depend only on the models developed herein; the choices for the allocation of resources among competing groups are political decisions. The goal of the organizational model is to make possible valid comparisons among HSOs with similar missions, for example, among specific groupings of SS/Is and M/Ps, and to provide society with economic information to assist in the allocation of its resources among the competing groups.

OTHER FACTORS

Funding Cycle and Tax Policy

The answer to the question as to how society can reward HSOs that attain their goals has been proposed. However, the creation of societal income does not provide cash flow for the individual HSO. If the creation of societal income could be converted into cash for the individual HSO, then: first, the meritorious or successful HSO would be rewarded for its effectiveness; and second, the cycle of outputs and outcomes into sales and cash or its equivalent would be completed as in the PS. Then the above two objectives could be accomplished by the reporting system proposed with this model.

Both individual donors and governments must be in a position to reward the individual HSO based upon its performance. To ensure, or at least to give a higher probability for the successful accomplishment of the above-stated goals, a basic change is required by Congress and the Treasury Department. Tax deductions for charitable donations to HSOs should be limited to the extent of the HSO's gross societal income. In that event, the contributors would be in the position of judging by objective criteria the more effective organizations, or would risk the loss of the income tax deduction, the societal tax subsidy. If a market could thus be created for sale of such societal income credits and corresponding limits imposed for tax deductibility of contributions, then society indirectly would support those organizations that create societal income through the present medium of income tax deductions. Governments would be required to allocate any direct funding on the basis of the HSO's statement of (societal) income. Accordingly, restrictions would have to be placed on direct government funding or contracting of services to implement the model.

The result of either solution would mean that fund-raising efforts by the individual HSO and community drives for funds would likewise be limited by this measurement. From a societal perspective, tax subsidies would automatically represent the societal costs of tax incentives for the creation of gross societal income. Assuming an effective federal and state marginal tax rate of 40%, society would be paid off in $2.50 of value for each $1 invested in tax deductions. In the event there is an insufficient demand for tax deductions in terms of the supply of HSOs' gross societal income generated, it could be in society's interest to increase the effective rate of benefit to purchasers. There could be other societal savings in administration and monitoring costs as well as increases in income from the multiplier effect of increased consumer spending.

As an alternative, the treasury could reimburse the individual HSO for its gross societal income net of income tax due on its NSI, based on the filing of an audited annual report. This alternative approach fails to establish a market for tax deductions that prioritizes the activities of HSOs by market actions. Such a market allows society to make choices among various endeavors as well as among particular HSOs. The market would, in effect, evaluate preferences based on the prices of the available tax deductions.[3]

With both the PS and HSO calculating and reporting revenues, it follows that HSOs should also be liable for federal and state income taxes on their net income. The convergence of the two sectors means that all companies become profit oriented in terms of the measurement of the effectiveness and efficiency of their operations. The liability for taxes by all companies eliminates the discussion and dissension that presently exist relative to "fairness" as well as the complexities involved in tax reporting for HSOs that function with "hybrid" operations.

Criteria for Measurement Systems

The proposed accounting system meets the defined criteria as presented more fully in chapter 5. The model responds to the organizations' mission, specifies an attribute for goal measurement, contains a metric, establishes the mechanism for external and internal reporting on an integrated and continual basis to stakeholders, and considers such other criteria as relevance, communicability, auditability, and cost of the system.

The accounting systems for the two sectors converge once the key problem of quantifying the attribute of goal measurement is resolved. As is expanded upon in chapter 6, the overall goal and mission of the sectors become the same—consumer satisfaction. Only the direct payers differ. Accordingly, the measuring criteria, the matching cycle for income and expenses for the preparation of internal and external reports, and other criteria can be applied in common with the principles, techniques, and applications also used in the PS.

Accounting Factors—External Reporting

Balance Sheet and Statement of Cash Flow. The balance sheet and statement of funds will continue to be prepared as under current requirements. However, as a result of the creation of the statement of (societal) income, certain balance sheet adjustments will be required to reflect inventories in the preparation of financial statements. The cost of the clients in programs, equivalent to work in process in the PS, and the cost of clients classified as case closures before outcome assessment, equivalent to finished goods in the PS, would be included at cost as an inventory of clients. It should be noted that client closure takes place only after the relevant follow-up period for placement. GAAP has grappled with questions relating to inventory valuation at actual, standard, or replacement (market) costs as well as the inclusion of direct or indirect overheads at actual or standard costs. Even the handling of positive efficiency variances (i.e., profit anticipation) relative to inventory evaluation has been dealt with. Accordingly, as it relates to inventories, the preparation of financial statements does not require the construction of a new set of accounting principles; rather, it necessitates the application of existing concepts to an *industry* and to a set of circumstances for a particular organization.

As has been described above, the balance sheet must also reflect a receivable for the estimated market value from the generation of gross societal income for the period, that is, the amount of such gross societal income less an appropriate adjustment for a market discount factor. The cash flow statement will also incorporate this factor. Likewise, to reflect the content of the previous argument relative to income taxes, the required federal and state tax expense and its liability would be reflected in these statements in accordance with GAAP.

The preparation of financial statements for the HSO such as the one outlined above is feasible. Dealing with inventory valuations has been conceptually well defined. Actuaries have developed techniques that are suitable for longitudinal follow-ups and that include estimates for the possibilities of retirement and employment dropout, for changes in family labor force participation, and for group-specific mortality and morbidity rates. The system can also incorporate adjustments to initial estimates and for subsequent changes in client societal participation. It should be pointed out that actuarially based computations and the present value technique are pervasive in GAAP and extensively employed in PS practice as well as in human services.[4]

Because the foundation for this model has a conceptual framework similar to the PS, in other words, consumer satisfaction, the model's implementation should also find direct support in current accounting practice and concepts. GAAP as employed by the PS includes appropriate accounting theory, and generally accepted auditing standards (GAAS) have developed auditing practices that become equally applicable to the HSOs, including: (1) clearly stated principles distinguishing between period and deferred costs; (2) reflections of extraordinary items and corrections of a previous year's financial statements; (3) footnotes to financials including statements of principles, restrictions on assets, and other relevant disclosures; (4) actuarially based computations and present value concepts; (5) sampling techniques for handling large volumes of data; (6) principles of cost accounting involving allocation of overhead costs, joint costs, and so on; and (7) accounting industry guides and standards for industry reporting. Thus, the practices and standards already developed by the PS can be applied to the normative model for HSOs. Definitions and conventions of practice that are familiar to firms and practitioners need not be redeveloped.

Like any other industry, there are accounting problems that are peculiar to HSOs. These would include questions relative to the equity section of the balance sheet and to donations of time and money (restricted and unrestricted) that are not incorporated in the calculation of an HSO's gross societal income. Valuation and reporting of volunteer hours, donations unrelated to gross societal income and their related fund-raising costs, segregation of overhead expenses by types of consumers for special reporting: these are illustrations of industry-specific questions.

Accounting Factors—Internal Reporting

Efficiency relates to output and is a result of how the agency has made use of available inputs to create outputs. As emphasized in chapter 1, efficiency should be related to and calculated in terms of the effectiveness of its outcomes. Efficiency analysis commences with the juxtaposition of projected and actual output and projected and actual cost based on the data and information provided in the total MIS, which includes the CIS, the FIS, and all budgetary and standard cost data—and the CES, their integrated reports.

Internal control and reporting for HSOs is based on actual and standardized time units of performance that can be added and valued in money terms. An integrating system is needed for communication among the hierarchical levels of management and to stakeholders. It utilizes a common data base for the reporting of effectiveness and efficiency of operations, is central to internal control, and can provide data for staff evaluation and for incentive compensation. Conceptually and practically the same system can be applied to the SS/Is and the M/Ps for the measure of efficiency since it is based upon the same standardized time unit, which can be valued in money benefits. The concomitants of standardized time units are budgetary control, standard costs, and variance accounting.

Budget. Once the account classification system has been established, the requisite client service and projected cost budgets can be built. Because these budgets will serve as a foundation for later efficiency analyses, they should be constructed to reflect projected client mix and service output levels. Without this, comparisons of projections to actual may not be accurate, if not downright misleading. When prepared properly, the budget should contain projections for a specific client mix, a specific program mix consistent with capacity levels, and the absorption of direct and indirect program and overhead costs. More sophisticated budgeting can reflect the client and program mix variables. There should be a separation between direct identifiable departmental or cost center expenses, prorated allocable expenses that relate to a group of departments or cost centers, and proratable expenses applicable to the agency as a whole. Obviously, the greater the identifiable and specific allocable expenses, the less the general overhead ratio. When capacity and anticipated usage are projected in terms of time units, then the standard cost per unit is readily determinable. Management consultants and cost accountants have presented arguments relative to the advantages and disadvantages of cost absorption being based upon capacity or anticipated usage.

An example of a typical HSO budget is provided in chapter 8. In the illustration, total costs for each center are determined by first summing direct salaries (account and program) and direct identifiable overhead. To these, indirect allocations of other overhead salaries and overhead expenses are then added. Their preparation involves continual feedback and feed-forward, with the balancing of client needs with facilities and resources. The time that must be devoted to budget preparation is rewarded by the creation of planning and decision-making tools. Service units within a cost center have a common time base and therefore a cost equivalence. However, the balancing of client mixes and their program needs with staff availability and physical facilities points out in advance problem areas, necessary trade-offs, and the feasibility of achieving the operating goals.

Standards and Service Units. Much of the information contained within the CIS has so far been expressed in terms of standard service or time units, such as conference time, therapy time, client-related administrative service, and so on. To operationalize the system, these units must be transformed into standard cost units. Use of the standard time units allows aggregation and comparison. The projections about client mix, program services, agency capacity and costs can be converted from planned service units to standard costs. Projected plans can then be compared against actual results—for individual clients, client groups, programs, cost centers or departments, and the entire agency. In general, their use engenders a certain flexibility that makes possible the manipulation of data for the purpose of analyzing effectiveness of outcomes and efficiency factors for hierarchical reporting.

Variances. The model offers the opportunity for the preparation of variance reports that focus staff at the service provider level or management at any level on the variances of actual from standard. Standard cost analyses will revolve around variances computed between the actual dollar costs of service provision and such standard costs (see chapter 8).

Variance accounting is derived from specific data, whether in monetary or service unit terms; variances also are a more effective tool for action than summaries or averages. Since variance accounting is based on specific standards and oriented to performance within an organization, only exceptions to such standards may need to be reported to various management layers for action. It is possible to program computers to prevent management overload of information so that only significant (as defined) variances will be printed on reports. It is the hierarchical management levels' function to investigate the causes of variances as well as to review the standards and procedures when variances recur.

Variance accounting can also be used in nonmonetary areas when management formalizes agreed-upon goals, such as open service requests and the number of new clients who have not started programs.

The System's Dynamics

The actions of the organizational model, together with the propositions, require a review from the perspective of the dynamics of management and staff behavior. Although the basic features of the model have been presented, questions must be addressed about possibilities for manipulation of results within the framework of the system before any claims of performance are made: (1) will the model encourage manipulation in the selection of clients; (2) can management or staff manipulate standard costs (which measure efficiency) to advance their own position to the detriment of the agency; (3) are the measurements related to externally established standards and are they auditable; (4) is the proposed system too complex, too costly to install and operate; (5) what happens to the dropouts and the "nonsuccessess" and their costs. Each of these questions will be discussed. The replies apply to both the SS/I and M/P models unless otherwise indicated.

In response to the possibility of manipulation, it is unlikely that the system could be biased in the selection of clients. Organizations have a given amount of fixed costs. If management were to select clients where change was difficult to effect, there might not be a sufficiently broad base of income to absorb this fixed cost. The period expenses would overwhelm the HSOs gross societal income and in turn create a net societal loss, something management would presumably wish to avoid. If, however, the HSO tended to select clients where change was easy, it would probably not earn a sufficient societal income. The change in the NRC of such clients would probably be lower than the change for an average client. In fact, an argument could be made that management would choose clients most in need of its services because their marginal change in NRC would be greater. To optimize measurement results, management would tend to balance client mix, facilities, needs, and the potential of client change.

The answer to the second question as to whether staff and/or management could "play" with efficiency reporting is generally no. This cannot be done where there is any type of integrated budget and standard cost accounting system in place. For example, assume that management attempted to demonstrate efficiency in its operations by the initial overstatement of the amount of standard hours required for a particular client service. A standard cost system would reveal the fact that the total number of projected hours would exceed agency capacity. In any event, net (societal) income reflects the combined measures of effectiveness and efficiency. While the overstatement of standard hours might lead to a positive efficiency adjustment, it would also increase standard program costs, thus offsetting any advantage. There could be no effect on the bottom line.

The answer to the third question is yes on both scores: the measurements are related to externally established standards and are auditable. The critical calculations for the evaluation process are externally generated. For the SS/I, the change in NRC is an independent measure, based on initial and final net societal resources used or generated by the client. The interest rates on U.S. treasury bonds, which are matched to the period of the estimated working life of the client-consumers, are externally available. The interest (discount) rate, therefore, is market determined. Of course, there would be the tendency for management to evaluate client intake data at the most pessimistic level. Scoring influences behavior of participants, creating problems which auditors in the PS must also deal with.[5] Representatives of government agencies responsible for the maintenance of quality standards and contract outcomes would make site visits and/or review reports. Likewise, the financial statements prepared under the proposed model could be examined by outside auditors to the same extent as those of profit-seeking enterprises.

The question whether the proposed system is too complex or too costly to install and operate should be framed within a given set of assumptions relative to appropriately functioning agencies. Whatever the size or complexity of the agency, the model makes use of the existing data required for quality service in today's environment. It must be assumed that essential client, service, and financial information is being collected and reported upon in a systematic fashion. The model proposes an integration of these data. The preparation of the statement of (societal) income is derived from the existing records, in particular from the CIS at the time of intake and records of client progress and costs through case closure. Then, only one additional calculation is required, the computation and aggregating of the change in each client's NRC.

When there is no measurable outcome, the costs applicable to dropouts and to clients where there are no successful results in terms of the original goals, that is, no measurable changes, then all costs are expensed in the period's statement of income. In a market economy, there are limits to the marginal productivity of labor in comparison to wages paid. Accordingly, some members of the population will remain in supported employment or with other kinds of direct societal supports. Society should continue to fund such programs from an economic standpoint since marginal productivity below wage scales is better than no production; it can often be demonstrated that the cost of such work programs is offset in part by family opportunity costs. Moreover, such support is in keeping with the insurance concepts developed in the second proposition to protect societal members against risks, and with the ethical concomitants of the third proposition.

SUMMARY

The optimal satisfaction of needs and wants underlies consumer decisions in the rendering of human services with society as the consumer-payer in the use of its resources. The satisfaction of needs and wants for the quality of life has been defined in terms of the consumer client's goal of becoming self-sufficient. This represents the HSOs' market, and their success is measured in terms of their ability to improve or to maintain people's ability to be self-sufficient. The measurement of this movement becomes the revenue of the HSOs in the same manner as the sale of products and services satisfies consumers in the PS.

For the SS/I model, it is measured by the surrogate attribute of the economic benefit of such a change in each client's net societal resources consumed, specifically defined as the present value of the change in the client's dependency on societal resources. For the M/P model, it is measured by the societal resources saved by the consumer-clients being maintained at their optimal functional level, in the face of clear and measurable evidence that unaided, the individuals would have increased their dependence on society. Such a definition of revenue provides the framework for the preparation of the missing statement of (societal) income. Within a unified accounting framework, accounting questions are responsive to GAAP. The statement of (societal) income permits reporting to stakeholders on a comparable basis for HSOs. In order to complete the funding cycle, the amount of such net societal income must become part of the HSO's cycle conversion into funds. This could occur based on a proposal to extend and integrate tax deductibility of donations to HSOs and the use of tax credits to the extent of their GSI. The other foundations of the model are functionally similar to the PS in accounting for efficiency. They include techniques for intake control and assessment of clients, standard cost accounting, and hierarchical reporting, among others discussed in chapter 6. The proposed measuring system provides attributes and applications required for external reporting and internal management of operations. The system has two operational components, a CIS and an FIS. Their union, using common data bases, generates the essential data for evaluation reports about the HSO's operations referred to herein as the CES.

The normative model has been presented. In chapter 8 some empirical applications illustrate the particular workings of the model in terms of the CIS, the FIS, and the CES; there is also presented a sample budget together with standards and variances for internal analysis and a statement of (societal) income for an HSO based on an actual case study.

CONSEQUENCES AND IMPLICATIONS

Consequences and implications of the organizational model have been presented in chapter 1 and are expanded upon in the discussion in chapter 9; five are briefly highlighted here: the accounting system for the preparation of a statement of income for HSOs, the feasibility for a unified system of accounting for the profit private sector and the HSOs, the potential for application to other segments of the societal profit sector, changes in the field of economics, and, the most significant, the effects on the client and the agency.

The development of the organizational model makes possible the preparation of a statement of income by the individual HSO. HSOs' revenues are defined in units of attribute that reflect their goals. A method is proposed to establish a circular closed system so that the revenues generated in accordance with such statement of income are included as a component of their funding cycle. For measuring efficiency, HSOs can continue their own approaches to management based on standard time, budgets, controls, and other techniques that are conceptually and in practice the same as used in the PS.

In chapter 6, the consequence of this model's applicability to the PS is explored. The potential of moving to a unified system of accounting for all firms becomes feasible, where private or societal resources are used for the satisfaction of or benefits to the individual.

The model induces a changed taxonomy. The new system of classification points the way for the potential applications of the measuring system to other societal segments (see Exhibit 4.1). Given the applicability of the societal propositions, measuring concepts, the elements of consumer satisfaction, and benefits and quality-of-life goals for societal members suggest that similar measurements of income can be created for such other human service segments as health and education.

The current system of accounts in the PS reflects the ability of the individual firm to play the game based on the prescribed rules. With an accounting model that underscores the acquisition of cash, the current system may also measure acquisitiveness and greed. Profit in the PS is a combined measure of effectiveness and efficiency based on economic assumptions of optimizing societal well-offness, as previously stated. However, for a more rigorous accounting theory, the profit measurement developed in the model may be superior to the method of computing profits in the PS based on its current model. Present financial statements are flawed in that their measurement criteria do not consider societal costs in the net economic values created. Sales and service revenues of the individual firm do not reflect the broader societal and environmental effects of their products. The model may provide a method for dealing with the cost of externalities, not considered in the statement of income of the individual firm in the PS. The present PS model also requires an indirect measurement of individual consumer's satisfactions. When the individual is better off, it is assumed that private welfare is equal to or greater than social welfare—a derived computation for estimating societal well-offness. The compilations under the normative model measure social welfare directly, in other words, where social welfare is equal to or greater than private welfare in order to determine society well-offness.

For the human service organization, the conceptualization of societal income has the greatest potential impact. It directly affects the organization, practitioner, and consumer-client. It has the potential for permitting the establishment of national, state, and local standards for funding of HSOs to carry out politically agreed-upon societal goals. With the current push for privatization and contracting for services, the model provides a method of public accountability based on common measurements. It also provides the basis for recognizing and rewarding enterprising and innovative management and practitioners. It permits comparability of results among organizations. The ultimate goal of promoting economic self-sufficiency, the essence of the organization model, contributes to the realization of potential for the consumer-clients not only by committing societal resources for effective assistance to those in need but also by involving them in a meaningful way in establishing and striving for the achievement of such goals.

NOTES

1. *Case Statement (1985).* The Dole Foundation (220 Eye Street, NE, Washington, DC 20002), 2. One way of measuring the dignity and quality of life is on an economic basis. Dignity is the goal or the by-product of work, and as such it is not only relevant to economic outcomes but also to the quality of the society. Society should provide the means and motivating factors for an individual to express his or her independence, capability, and identity. This combination of independence and motivation is basic to quality-of-life concepts. While there does not seem to be any direct measure, it would appear that quality of life relates to the autonomy of individuals, their ability to make choices, their dignity.

2. See chapter 8 for a listing of reports that an integrated MIS should generate.

3. It has been determined that income taxes are not economically neutral. The tax system has been used for what has been perceived as socially desirable incentives and/or penalties: home ownership, charitable deductions, oil exploration, forestation, urban rehabilitation, investments in building and equipment, excess profits, gasoline-alcohol-cigarette consumption, small business incentives, historic restoration, and others. A recent entry to this list includes the partnership of private corporations and nonprofit community organizations to stimulate housing for low-income families. Apparently, the sole returns for this investment consist of tax credits.

4. Financial Accounting Standards Board (FASB) Discussion Memorandum (DM). (1990, December). Present value based measurements in accounting. Listed in Exposure drafts outstanding. (1991, March). *Journal of Accounting,* 138.

5. For example, in allocating purchase price in mergers and acquisitions in the PS, it is generally advantageous for management to reduce inventory and receivables and correspondingly increase the remainder of the allocation to fixed assets and excess (goodwill). This procedure favors the calculation of immediate earnings for the subsequent period since fixed assets and excess are subject to longer amortization periods.

PART TWO

CHAPTER 3

Societal History:
Background of the Problem

This chapter reviews the history and culture from which the propositions for the societal model emerged and the principles from which the elements of the proposed solution are derived. We then go forward in subsequent chapters to present, first, the propositions underlying the societal model, and then to examine methodological issues for a measuring (accounting) system for the allocation of societal resources, the convergence of the profit and nonprofit accounting systems, a review of previous attempts at solutions to the problems of measuring effectiveness and efficiency in the use of societal resources, and some empirical applications of the organizational model. The last chapter projects the immediate consequences and long-run implications of the proposed models and unified accounting system.

We assume that the modern capitalistic state considers the promotion of full employment and economic security as the mainstays of its missions to promote the general welfare. The history and analysis of the modern welfare state, as reviewed below, offer considerable support for the social programs of the welfare state provided they are work-oriented and protect middle-class entitlements. Social programs that are work related or designed to promote self-sufficiency and independence appear to be more politically acceptable. This is also evident from an examination of press and television reports, government releases, and academic writings.

Within the context of the modern welfare state, there is also an intellectual ferment regarding the economics of our society and the need for a changing ethic. Concomitantly there has been a long search for a system for evaluating the effectiveness of societal transfers to ensure an appropriate allocation of resources.

HISTORY AND PHILOSOPHY OF GOVERNMENT

Two opposing viewpoints lead to substantially different conclusions about the nature of human capacity and its potential for directing the affairs of society.[1] In the unconstrained outlook, individuals are endowed with the abilities to master the complexities of their environment, to make "collective decisions" for "deserved outcomes," and to develop policies for the common good, for example, economic planning versus laissez-faire, judicial actions versus judicial constraint. The constrained viewpoint sees the regulation of society as beyond the capability of the individual to devise specified programs to achieve stated goals. Rather, it reflects a confidence in pointing society in the direction based on traditional values and depends upon unfettered systems to create social processes such as markets and constitutional government with judicial restraint, for example, the establishing of appropriate rules applicable to all its members. In effect, this difference in viewpoints emphasizes the contrast between the common good and the public interest. The common good has its roots in Western humanistic thought with the emphasis on the community. This concept of community includes individuals whose own "good is . . . bound up with the good of the whole." The concept of public interest, on the other hand, is from the seventeenth and eighteenth centuries, in which social good arises from "the aggregation of the private interest of individuals."[2]

Historically, in the United States, these differing philosophies on the role of government date back to the Declaration of Independence and are embodied in the creation of our Constitution. The Declaration of Independence states that among our inalienable rights are life, liberty, and the pursuit of happiness (pursuit). The Preamble to the Constitution presents the goals for the new society among which are to establish justice, insure domestic tranquility, and promote the general welfare.

Hamilton, Madison, and Adams on one side, influenced by Smith, Hobbes, and Locke, were the protagonists of a stronger federal center that would provide protection for the person and his property by the development of commerce, a stable currency, and by voting control by men of property. On the other side were Jefferson and Paine, influenced by Condorcet and Godwin, the protectors of the personal liberties of the individual against the power of a strong central government. Both systems are contained in the Constitution's rules of the game— stability ensured by a system of checks and balances, and protection of the individual by the first ten amendments, the Bill of Rights. During the ensuing 200 years, government's function as a guarantor of liberty often resulted in conflicts and trade-offs between personal and property rights. However, the central role of government as the guarantor of the individual's right of pursuit has remained above challenge, embedded in our culture, in myth as well as in fact. Perhaps this right of pursuit is "what America [has] always preached and found so hard to practice."[3]

Slavery cast it shadows over the nineteenth century. The country also struggled with issues around property rights, domestic and foreign trade, the westward movement, inventions and technology, tariff and currency questions. Along with the development of the robber barons were the know-nothings and the muckrakers. William Jennings Bryan was crucified on his cross of silver while hard currency prevailed. There were periods of exploitation of resources mixed with attempts at preservation of the environment, some protections at the workplace, and the emergence of a limited craft union labor movement. These developments continued into the twentieth century. Schlesinger refers to approximate 30-year periods of restricted government with rugged individualism, followed by more active government and concerns for the individual that he calls "the cycle of private interest and public purpose."[4]

Based on an expanding economy and an apparently mobile society, mainstream republican virtues dominated American thinking into the early part of the twentieth century. The folklore of the rugged individual persisted until the Great Depression, which shook but did not affect the conceptual centrality of the market. The decade of the 1930s accomplished a nonviolent revolution in the role of government in providing old-age and unemployment supports, public assistance, work-supported programs, control of the excesses of the private sector by regulations of the securities and banking industries, and other social reforms. While interrupted by World War II and its aftermath, these are the conceptual foundations of the welfare state—society's increased acceptance of responsibility for the poor, the aged, the unemployed, and other disadvantaged groups. Government's responsibility to full employment, enacted during the Truman administration, became a key pillar for subsequent social legislation. The climax to this revolution was the war on poverty commenced during the Kennedy and Johnson administrations that extended and increasingly formalized society's obligations to the disadvantaged.

Thus, it is only in the last thirty years that social engineering for the redistribution of income based on changing definitions of rights has significantly affected the social order, referred to as the welfare state. In the debate between John Rawls and Robert Nozick on government's function in society, Rawls's approach to government is that it should ensure that principles of justice are embedded in society's function; Nozick would limit government's role to providing protection, as the referee in maintaining the rules of fair play. Even though both would disagree sharply as to government's specific agenda in the resolution of current social problems, both recognize the right of pursuit.[5]

Among human service theorists and practitioners, there has been considerable discussion regarding the modern welfare state—its origins, viability, and future direction. Some emphasize the blurring of boundaries between the traditional voluntary and private sectors, in particular the increasing privatization of public functions. Others emphasize the significance of full employment and the supplementary provisions for those family supports needed in the event of injury, illness, unemployment, and old age. They comment that the welfare state is essentially healthy, is approaching a centrist position, and is focused on allocations of societal resources, whether public or private, for the promotion of self-sufficiency.

In looking at the history of the past three decades, Blau documents how the predominantly liberal ideological consensus of the 1960s fragmented into theories of the right, center, and left. He stresses the empiricism of postwar practice and the "positive attitude for the welfare state as a vehicle for gradual reform." The conservative reaction, according to Blau, is based on "minimal government" as developed by Frederick Hayek, Milton Friedman, and Charles Murray. Further, he states that other conservatives stress the centrality of the marketplace and are proponents of workfare and stricter controls. The centrist view, as presented by Blau, recognizes the limits of the welfare state and the need to balance social problems with economic factors—which also include "social spending and an investment in human capital." The radical view attributes to the responsibilities of the welfare state the "(1) regulation of the poor, (2) accumulation and legitimation and (3) ensuring the existence of a future work force/maintenance of the non-working population." Blau then concludes that theories of the welfare state are in many ways a debate about rights, rights of entitlement to a social wage, property rights, personal rights, and community rights such as medical care and affordable housing. Theorists in the future should "set forth their assumptions about the question of rights."[6]

Stoesz outlines "a theory of social welfare in the United States . . . to explain how political and economic forces shape the structural institutions of social welfare."[7] He "emphasizes the role of interest groups in defining social welfare. . . . The interest groups of the social welfare industry are classified, and the viability of each group is evaluated according to the dynamics of bureaucratization and privatization." These include traditional providers of the voluntary sector, welfare bureaucrats of the welfare state, clinical entrepreneurs in private practice, and human service executives in corporate welfare. The emerging "professional monopoly . . . reconciles . . . professionals for autonomy with the imperatives of a market economy." He points out that "human service corporations [private] have established prominent—if not dominant—positions in several human service markets."[8] Stoesz concludes that the traditional providers, that is, the voluntary health organizations, are becoming the representatives of populations that have been neglected or excluded from the societal mainstream. Presumably the voluntary health organizations would attempt to function consonant with traditional goals of self-sufficiency and other cultural norms. Their influence has been decreasing because of the dynamics of structural interests— bureaucratization and privatization, the latter identified with the market economy. A possible threat to private practitioners is the emerging development of human services supplied in industry by in-house services.

The evolution of the modern welfare state is traced by Atherton. In discussing the position of the right and the left he emphasizes the "work-connectedness of the bulk of social welfare programs and the positive effect of the social insurances on retirees, survivors, injured workers, the unemployed, and their families." Most programs were designed to provide income after retirement, during or following disability or other critical events. He also quotes Ramesh Mishra, who "identifies several factors that gave the welfare state its legitimacy. First, Keynesian economics provided an economic rationale for state intervention designed to 'ensure a high level of economic activity and full employment.' '' Atherton goes on to state that there has been ''public approval for the curtailment of expensive programs that are not perceived to be effective'' and ''rejection of the notion of substantive equality by the voters.'' He believes that the mass of people will accept and pay for programs that appear to have value and are effective and fair. Atherton further states the ''the masses also favor a balanced, mixed economy and will react when they perceive the balance to be shifting too far in either direction.'' Further, they vote ''on a pragmatic basis rather than on strict ideological lines.'' Therefore he believes the programmatic welfare state will continue including its social insurance programs and public assistance with an emphasis on work and cost-effective programs.[9]

The movement toward what is characterized as the middle ground of self-sufficiency is also emphasized by Kohlert:

A rare consensus is resolving family policy dichotomies. People of divergent philosophies and loyalties are beginning to agree on a policy of giving support to achieve self-sufficiency. . . . In the late 1980s, pragmatism is more in evidence; efforts more often are centrist—to help individuals and families become self-supporting and self-sufficient with a realistic understanding of the limits of resources.[10]

Questions have also been raised as to whether the current welfare state is focusing on the underlying issues causing chronic poverty. According to Atherton, poverty has been addressed primarily when it is work related. Unlike some countries in Western Europe, in his opinion, there are many underlying causes in the United States that account for the failure to eliminate poverty—racism, language problems, sexism, ethnic diversity, and the lack of integration of the chronically poor into the work force. Even the common assumptions as to the role and commitment of HSOs in caring for the poor may be misguided. In a study of poverty and the behavior of HSOs, Gronbjerg also points out that the commitment of non-profits to the poor is not independent of the incentive provided by government funding for the poor—funding takes precedence over commitment.[11]

The issues that have surfaced and crystallized in the decade of the 1980s about the welfare state are summed up in an essay by Linn. He reviews the studies that emerged in the Reagan years, reexamining the role of government and the private sector, presenting both conservative and liberal viewpoints about whether benefits of transfers outweigh the costs. More important, from Linn's perspective as a basis for determining future policy is a careful presentation of economic transfers. He sets forth a dilemma: ''The main policy choice is typically posed as between a larger or smaller welfare state. . . . [However,] analysts of social policy tend to ignore the significance to the low income population of non-governmental transfers of income and services and of the social networks that they represent.'' He emphasizes the distinction between primary and secondary consumer income and, after delineating the significant size and sources of the latter among the poor, concludes that these "express belief in family, mutual support, self help and community. . . . By attempting to understand public significance of these transfers, we may discover an avenue toward constructing a new generation of social policies founded on enduring American values and the realization of human needs in the American economy."[12] His conclusion appears to reinforce the significance of local control—an extra dimension, a multiplier effect arising from family and neighborhood support. The accounting system proposed in this book resolves aspects of the problem of local control of programs and their funding from federal block grants to states, and from states to local contractors or governments. A common system of reporting and accountability within national policy can incorporate objective standards and definitions for data collection relative to evaluation of outcomes.

CURRENT SCENE

Having traced, albeit sketchily, the evolution of the welfare state and some of the issues currently being raised, we turn next to examples of specific questions being asked about the effectiveness of particular social programs. All of these questions require an economic answer to justify their initiation, continuation, or expansion. To highlight some of these questions within a chorus of dissonance, the discussion is grouped around four themes: reactions of governments relative to their policies and programs for the disadvantaged populations; the potential for work and mainstreaming of the handicapped and older worker; the support needed for the aged; and strategies relative to consumer awareness. The need for a new social ethic and other relevant items, all bearing on the issue of allocation of societal resources and social costs, are then viewed from the broader perspectives of the nonprofit sector and the need for a changing social ethic.

Government

Calls for measurement have reached Congress, and the national bureaucracy has responded. There have been many actions by the federal government and the General Accounting Office (GAO), a response in part to requests by Congress for answers on the effectiveness of social programs relative to their costs in pending legislation. Other federal government agencies have likewise reacted to this overall question. The calls for comments on priorities, promulgation of new regulations, and requests for proposals demonstrate the increasing focus on performance criteria, the search for outcome measures, and concern about the efficiency and effectiveness of programs designed to increase the self-sufficiency of the individual and family.[13] These references from the Federal Register and other governmental reports all contain a common goal, the ability to measure the achievement of (or improvement in) economic self-sufficiency following program completion.

Congress is seeking to understand the outcomes of public expenditures for programs designed to increase the economic status of women, children, minority groups, and other disadvantaged persons. There is not only the problem of the measurement of different programs within each group,[14] but also there is an apparent conflict between the generations about claims for increased allocation of resources. While the elderly push for their share, there is growing concern about the increased poverty level of children, especially in the minority groups. Many state and city agencies have also attempted to evaluate the efficiency and effectiveness of their various programs. They are still seeking an appropriate cost-benefit methodology for outcomes (see chapter 7).

Employment of the Handicapped and the Older Worker

Attention has been focused on untapped potential sources of labor, the handicapped and the older person, who will contribute to counteracting a shrinking labor force. There is a growing body of gerontological literature relative to the issue of continued employment for older persons. Appropriate economic measurements to demonstrate the value of proposed changes relative to their employment are needed. Such changes would require a shift toward a longer-term and preventive system of care for older workers.

In the case of individuals with developmental disabilities, there is a need to demonstrate on an economic basis that society should not miss the opportunity of making productive use of this potentially large supply of labor. An economic measure that informs society on the change in self-sufficiency of these disabled persons and their ensuing contribution to the economy would assist the decision-making process. Many leaders call for tapping into this unused reservoir of labor.

The Dole Foundation was founded

to encourage opportunity for disabled persons in competitive employment . . . millions of disabled Americans are unemployed who are willing and able to work; they want the dignity of greater economic independence and a chance to contribute to their communities. An estimated 8% of the U.S. Gross National Product (G.N.P.) goes out in government and private payments to these same disabled persons. Clearly, providing the means to "mainstream" handicapped individuals into the job market is sound economic and social policy. Various sources estimate the number of persons with disabilities in the U.S. able to work but unemployed, at about 5 million. . . . We know that government and private programs and cash benefits for unemployed disabled persons **now cost over $200 billion a year**.[15]

A measuring system is needed to determine the answer to the economic questions posed by the Dole Foundation.

Moreover, there is a need for vocational rehabilitation program reform in order to help people placed in employment to make it on their own, including additional ongoing maintenance and support. Griss cites Bowe, a leader in the field of disability, stating that in this regard, "America is spending ten dollars on dependence among disabled people for every dollar it expends upon programs helping them become independent"; and that the challenge of disability policy is to recognize that "it is far more expensive to continue handicapping America than it would be to begin rehabilitating America."[16] Again, a measuring system that can confirm Griss's assumption relative to the economics of the costs of training and economic outcomes in comparison to the costs of supports to this particular population would be meaningful.[17]

Basic changes must also be instituted in medical priorities and government rules:

Chronic conditions and disabilities have emerged as the major health problem of the later 20th century. But our cure-oriented, medically based health care system is ill equipped to meet the needs of persons with disabilities who often require other kinds of services to maintain themselves at home or at work.[18]

The political decision has been made in part by society in terms of its political preferences. The passage of the Americans with Disabilities Act, which addresses job discrimination and requires accessible transit systems as well as accessibility of public accommodations, increases opportunities for the integration of the handicapped into the work force.[19] More accessible workplaces are provided without the necessary commitment to training to fill the workbenches.

The Aged

The question of the aged can be approached in three ways: providing social and health supports that make continued employment possible; ensuring that society rewards those who work, and their families, by providing basic retirement income and by taking care of them when they are frail and vulnerable; and reflecting the societal application of ethical principles.

Increased emphasis on chronicity and disability has surfaced as a result of focus on the present and projected dramatic increase in the numbers of older persons, particularly the "old-old"—those most at risk. The pressure for increased allocation of resources for health and long-term care systems has caused many to identify critical issues that need to be resolved. A central issue is "what should the quality of life be in old age, and how much of society's resources should be used in its achievement?"[20]

A review of the issues related to the rehabilitation of elderly persons points out that the primary health care system follows the cycle of illness, treatment, and recovery, and that rehabilitation treatment is often not included in the current system of health care. There is built-in tension that exists between standardized costs that apply to a total population and the need for individualized treatment.[21]

The significance of treating the chronic medical problems of older people as well as the need to establish patient outcomes from medical care services are also subjects suggesting the need for change.[22]

In the model proposed in chapter 2, it should be recognized that self-sufficiency is being measured directly as an economic measure; the maintenance of an optimal state by older persons is on a similar value scale to a positive change in self-sufficiency by others. Such a measure reflects the best interest of society, the implications of the propositions underlying the societal model proposed in the subsequent chapter.

Consumer Activism

As in the PS's attempts to develop consumer awareness relative to its products and services, HSOs have applied concepts of consumer satisfaction following much the same path developed by Ralph Nader. There are attempts to affect consumer behavior by education and to effect significant change in their patterns of stress, diet, exercise, and so on.

The lack of a coherent government policy in the area of vocational rehabilitation and the disenchantment with the medical model of care have encouraged the independent living movement. There is a change within the health care sector from disease treatment to prevention. There is also an emphasis upon self-help, a shift from centralized to local control, to improved service systems for people with disabilities, to coordination between public and private sector initiatives, and to the development of community strategies for health and human services.[23]

For several decades debate has raged around the question of "universal health care—coverage as to population, type of illness, health service, providers, pricing, service of funding and regulation."[24] Faced with growing concern over rising costs and inadequate insurance, most lawmakers agree it is time for a national policy that generates quality medical care at a reasonable cost for all Americans. While business and labor express concern, "there is no agreement over what a national health policy should look like."[25]

Disease prevention and early detection and treatment through primary care will both improve the quality of life and reduce the cost of health care according to Robbins. Even the large current expenditures do no ensure appropriate distribution of health care and results. Robbins emphasizes that a national effort is required to focus on appropriate control of environmental hazards (air, water, workplace), and on discouraging the use of alcohol and cigarettes. There must be a national policy to encourage the development of primary care, particularly for the poor, the young, and the elderly.[26]

There is a growing awareness that structural and demographic changes within the society call for new strategies. The "help the handicapped" goal may need modification or replacement within the framework of self-sufficiency and self-help. Foundations are commencing to fund programs that return the handicapped to active participation in society. They, and the public, must consider not only work but also the collateral issues of equal access to facilities in order for them to achieve independent living. As consumers, it is argued that the mentally and physically impaired should participate in decisions affecting their own lives. This perspective needs to be incorporated into a service delivery system that changes the patient's position to one of independence. Disabled persons take the position not only that boards of the service agencies should represent the populations they serve but also that individuals with disabilities should control program services.[27]

The empowerment of individuals to direct goals and treatment also affects the delivery of services. It brings the concepts of consumer benefits and satisfaction into alignment with the PS. There is also a developing consumer satisfaction evaluation movement to incorporate consumer perspectives relative to program progress and service delivery. However, "so far the results are infrequently used."[28] Consumer satisfaction studies are of questionable use by themselves; but, if correlated with outcome measures, they could heighten awareness about consumers' reactions and preferences and contribute to improved service performance.

The Nonprofit Sector (NPS)

Within the current scene, the chorus of dissonance may echo static emanating from the currently defined taxonomy of the NPS. The present role, functioning, size and inconsistencies in the classifications of the NPS have been examined by writers such as Weisbrod who studied the role, activities, financing, and regulations pertaining to nonprofit organizations, a mixture of elements of government, group, and private enterprises. He points out how little is known about this segment of the economy and its overall contribution to society and its functioning. Nonprofits must be considered within other elements of societal economic policy as they affect both the profit and governmental sectors.

This sector lumps together about one million organizations, two-thirds of which do not qualify for tax deductibility of contributions. It includes many tax-exempt service industries, including health, educational, and social services, associations such as museums and foundations, religious and civic organizations, health promotion, education and research, as well as non–tax deductible memberships and clubs. Weisbrod raises the question of the comparative advantage of different institutional forms in a mixed economy. The nonprofit sector includes hybrids, private organizations that are nevertheless unable to reward management and are limited in their ability to provide incentives for efficiency. His analysis includes the sources of funding in terms of charitable donations, sales of goods and services, donation of voluntary labor, and presents a statistical profile of this sector.[29]

After a scholarly and patient analysis, he presents some public policy recommendations: (1) nonprofits should be encouraged to provide collective goods and be restricted in their business activities, related or unrelated to their tax-exempt purpose, that compete with private profit firms; (2) interlocking control of firms should be abolished from both sectors; (3) the Internal Revenue Service should be replaced as the principal regulator by an agency more sympathetic to its needs; (4) a comprehensive statistical program about the size, composition, outputs, funding sources, compensated and volunteer labor, and interactions with the market economy should be developed.[30]

Based on Weisbrod and other studies, O'Neill concurs about the diversity among organizations in the NPS. His goal, like Weisbrod's, was to present an analysis of what he terms The Third America, the historical development of its major subsectors, their funding sources, size, significance to the economy, policy questions, and trends.[31]

"We have more accurate information on soybean production in the United States than on America's third sector."[32] This lack of complete and consistent data is evident in Exhibit 3.1, which presents some statistical data about the nonprofit sector taken from Weisbrod and O'Neill. These data are presented in an attempt to evaluate the relative significance of this sector and its segments under its current classification system. As explained in chapter 4, based on our proposal for a changed taxonomy, it is our opinion that the significance of the third sector to the economy is grossly understated.

Changing Ethic

A civilized society shows compassion and caring for all members of the community, and provides opportunity for all to earn a livelihood. The art of civilized government is to combine self-interest and civic values (the two major types of human motivation) so that society reaps the benefits of each. But most economists use a neoclassical model that ignores civic values . . . and reveals an incomplete view of the role of self-interest.[33]

Is there a connection between overall society welfare and the welfare of social programs? What are the correlations among physical and mental health, the quality of life, personal satisfactions, and the quantity of economic goods? How can we apply economic measures to ecological and environmental issues? How do we reconcile private property, current living standards, and the concern over acid rain and the greenhouse effect? In a civilized society, what allocation of resources should be made to the groups that do not contribute to the functioning of that society? Can a civilized society mesh the advantages of competitive and free-market economies with a system of ethics? Can quality-of-life characteristics, diversity, and user preferences be incorporated within an economic measuring system?[34]

From such diverse publications as *Social Work* and *Business Week* come editorials and commentary pointing out the conflict between the human fallout caused by free-market enterprises and ethical questions raised by an economic system that causes large groups of the population to be outside the social system. *Social Work* discusses "the values of caring and independence," including caring for children, declining status of children ("thirteen million live in poverty—three times the number of a decade ago"), the health of children and older youths, cost of health care, employment opportunities, and the distribution of income and wealth, including the growth of a permanent underclass.[35] A *Business Week*

Exhibit 3.1
Compilation of Data on the Nonprofit Sector

Description	Year	Comment	Amount	Reference
Number of firms in NPS	1985 1985		886,658[a] 873,000	Table A.9, p. 176[1] P. 6[2]
Tax exempt firms	1985	501(c)(3)	366,071 370,000	Table A.9, p. 176[1] P. 6[2]
Total revenues	1985 1986	501(c)(3) firms "annual funds"	$314 billion $300 billion	p. 63[1] p. 7[2]
Nation's assets (NPS proportion)	1975 1987	Includes foundations	1.8% $500 billion (approx. 10%)	p. 64[1] p. 8[2]
Number of employees	1977 1977 1986	501(c)(3) Est. full-time equivalent 7% of workforce	4.95 million[b] 9 million 7.7 million	Table A.11, p. 179[1] p. 65[1] p. 6[2]
Volunteer labor	1985 1987	Full-time equivalent 15 billion hours	6 million $150 billion	p. 66[1] p. 7[2]
Gross national product (NPS proportion)	1975 1982 1975 1986	501(c)(3) & 501(c)(4)	15.1%* 9.5%** 3.2% 6-7%	Table A.4, p. 171[1] Table A.10, p. 178[1] p. 8[2] p. 7[2]
National income originating in NPS	1985 1986	Includes volunteer labor	4.4% 7%	Table A.5, p. 172[1] p. 9[2]

* The non-profit sector "accounts for about 6 percent of the gross national product and 18 percent of the national service economy....This figure does not include the revenue of the 370,000 nonphilanthropic nonprofits; other studies have indicated that the latter constitute about 10 percent of all nonprofit financial activity....Yale economist Gabriel Rudney has calculated that American nonprofits in 1980 had expenditures exceeding the budgets of all but seven nations in the world (Rudney, 1981, p. 3)." (page 7)[2] See, however, Weisbrod, Table A.10, Gross receipts of nonprofit social welfare organizations which shows that 501(c)(4) organizations account for approximately 20 percent of the combined 501(c)(3) and 502(c)(4) gross receipts; this total represents 9.5 % of GNP. (p. 178)[1]. The 15.1% is reported by Weisbrod is from the study of Raymond W. Goldsmith, The National Balance Sheet of the United States, 1953-1980 (Chicago: University of Chicago Press, 1981), Table 62, p. 147.

[1] Weisbrod, Burton A. (1988). The nonprofit economy. Cambridge, MA: Harvard University Press.

[2] O'Neill, Michael (1989). The third america - The emergence of the nonprofit sector in the United States. San Francisco, CA: Jossey-Bass.

(a) Data from Table A.9, pp. 176 & 177[(1)], 1985.

Active Exempt Organizations	IRS Classification	886,658
Religious, charitable	501(c)(3)	366,071**
Social welfare	501(c)(4)	131,250
Labor, agriculture	501(c)(5)	75,632
Business Leagues	501(c)(6)	54,217
Social, recreation clubs	501(c)(7)	57,343
Fraternal beneficiary societies	501(c)(8)	94,435
Other	501(c)(9) etc.	107,710

(b) Data from Table A.11, p. 179[(1)], 1977.

Tax Exempt Service Industries

Industry	Establishments (# of)	Expenses (billions)	Payroll (billions)	Paid Employees (thousands)
Total	165,614	$ 85.37	$ 41.69	4,950
Health services	12,307	43.96	22.85	2,431
Educational	9,160	14.03	7.22	932
Social services	40,983	8.29	4.12	676
Subtotal	62,450	66.28	34.19	4,039
Other				
Membership	82,666	12.07	4.41	600
Amuse. & Rec.	7,138	2.13	.94	122
Museums, etc.	2,252	.61	.27	32
Sundry	11,108	4.28	1.88	157

** Religious institutions do not have to file yearly reports to the IRS and are not included in this total. There are an estimated 350,000 churches, synagogues, mosques (p. 20)[(2)] "In 1987 $44 billion, nearly half of all private funds contributed to charity, was donated to religion" (p. 21)[(2)]. "In 1986, local religious congregations...employed over a million people and had revenues and expenditures of $40 billion" (p. 21)[(2)]. They gave to charity $7.5 billion in 1983 in comparison to foundations and corporations combined donations of $6.6 billion. (p. 23)[(2)]

article emphasizes the triumph of the system of free markets both in the United States and the world economy; however, it points out that there is still the need for the computation of costs and benefits for economic actions not directly measured within the system of free markets. The question of the trade-off of efficiency and equality is raised particularly as it applies to the destruction of family life and the significant differences in income distribution among age groups, between whites and blacks, among educated groups and "the underclass," the chronically poor. The article also points out the need for "shoring up the educational system," and "nonmarket incentives" such as "altruism" and "human will and cooperation to achieve a more equitable society," and the need for "programs that encourage self-sufficiency."[36] The search for partial solutions has also been reported in publications of the Council on Foundations.[37]

The issues raised relative to the need to reconcile public and private interests and to generate the concept of greater community are discussed in an interview with Daniel Yankelovich. He stresses that "society is struggling to find the middle ground between the old ethic of sacrifice for others and the new ethic of looking to one's own inner needs and potential and self-expressive desires." He comments that "self-seeking social Darwinism" should be replaced by the American "innate generosity and . . . sense of fairness." There should be "an emphasis on equality of opportunity . . . a belief in education as a way in which acceptable inequality is achieved . . . and an emphasis on hard work and effort," to which should be added the social ethic of commitment. Taking advantage of "the desire for participation and the right to participate" makes it possible to "take such an incredibly diverse society as ours and give it some stability and cohesiveness."[38]

Many articles have also appeared that call for economic evaluation of ecological, medical, and other scientific and environmental problems. These also raise ethical issues and stimulate the political will to reconcile individual rights with group interests.[39]

SUMMARY

Our history and culture, leading to the present welfare state, demonstrate the continuing dichotomy between the rights of the individual and the collective. The current social scene demonstrates the need for a way to allocate resources for programs perceived to be for the betterment of society. At the same time, solutions are being sought, consistent with our societal values and history—all in the face of what appear to be declining available resources, increasing needs, and changing attitudes. There is general confusion and distrust of solutions to these problems and the institutions available for their solution—government and/or the NPS.

The solution to the questions raised in this chapter require a system's change, rather than a system's revision. In a mixed economy of government, for profit and nonprofit institutions, the choice of particular institutions to meet the demands of society can focus the analyses of the optimal use of resources. A changed societal model leads to a changed taxonomy.

Society has developed from a conceptualized model of a mechanical clock to that of an organic system. Any organic system, in order to survive, must adapt and continually repair itself during its process of change. The adaptation has been through the growth of competition; a repair process is also required. The following chapter provides a framework of societal propositions that embody both group considerations and individual concerns, recognizing that elements of both need to be incorporated into our social system while maintaining an appropriate tension between both philosophies.

NOTES

1. Sewell, Thomas. (1987). *A Conflict of visions*. New York: William Morrow.

2. Jennings, Bruce, Callahan, Daniel & Wolf, Susan M. *The public duties of the professions*. (1987, February). (Supplement) Briarcliff Manor, NY: The Hastings Center.

3. Lewis, Flora. (1990, November 7). Foreign affairs: America sleeps. *New York Times*, p. A31.

4. Schlesinger, Arthur M., Jr. (1986). *The cycles of American history* (pp. 23–48). Boston, MA: Houghton Mifflin Company.

5. McKenna, Edward, Wade, Maurice & Zannoni, Diane. (1988, October). Keynes, Rawls, uncertainty and the liberal theory of the state. *Economics and Philosophy 4*(2), 221.

6. Blau, Joel. (1989, March). Theories of the welfare state. *Social Service Review*, *63*(1), 26–38.

7. Stoesz, David. (1989, March). A theory of social welfare. *Social Work, 34*(2), 101–107.

8. "In 1985, two human service corporations reported annual revenues that exceeded the total contributions to the United Way of America, $2.6 billion. Moreover, each of these corporations employed more than 80,000 workers, by far more than the number of state and local public welfare employees in any state in the United States ['Statistical Abstract,' 1988]." Stoesz, A theory of social welfare, 104.

9. Atherton, Charles R. (1989, June). The welfare state: Still on solid ground. *Social Service Review, 63*(2), 167–178.

10. Kohlert, Nance. (1989, July). Welfare reform: A historic consensus. *Social Work, 34*(4), 306.

11. Gronbjerg, Kirsten A. (1990, June). Poverty and nonprofit organizational behavior. *Social Service Review, 64*(2), 239.

12. Linn, Lawrence E., Jr., (1986, December). The new economics of social welfare: An essay review. *Social Service Review, 60*(4), 590.

13. An example of federal government concern is seen in the Administration on Developmental Disabilities' (ADD) invitation for public comment on its policy position "to reduce dependency and increase self-sufficiency among our most vulnerable citizens," in order for them to "live productive and independent lives, integrated into communities." Their goals were specified: "to increase family and individual self-sufficiency and independence through social and economic development strategies; to target Federal assistance to the most severely disabled; and to improve the effectiveness and efficiency of State

and locally administered human service programs.'' It further stated that: ''We have left an era when the trend was to assign to the Federal government an ever increasing responsibility for identifying the needs for social services and for designing programs to meet these needs. Public policy now articulates that public decisions are best made at the level of government closest to the target populations served.'' Department of Health and Human Services (1989, September 18). Developmental disabilities: Request for public comment on proposed developmental disabilities priorities for projects of national significance of fiscal year 1990 (Program Announcement No. 13631-89-4. *Federal Register, 54*(179), 38447-38449.

Another agency of the federal government, the Social Security Administration (SSA), sought proposals in order to induce more job placements and control and to monitor costs including (1) incentive payment systems, (2) cost effectiveness measures of employment services which includes ''computer management information systems designed to monitor the relationship of VR/employment services and outcomes based on specified performance criteria''; ''management reports permitting ongoing measurement of cost effectiveness'' of programs, and the effect of different types of services and persons, which should ''include employment outcome measures . . . related to service costs.'' Social Security Administration (1989, April 6) *Federal Register 54*(65), 13989-13992.

A *Federal Register* release relates to the Job Training Partnership Act (JTPA). In the ''two year study in progress, the JTPA system does not appear to have targeted services, particularly more intensive training, to those eligibles least ready to independently obtain jobs,'' and ''on-the-job training contracts were identified which subsidize inappropriately long periods of training for jobs requiring less skilled workers.'' The question is also raised as to how to judge the effectiveness of the JTPA system ''under varied local structures, and to innovate in planning and operating programs.'' Office of Special Education and Rehabilitative Services, Department of Education (1989, March 13). *Federal Register 54*(97), 10459-10467.

Funding priorities have been issued by the Department of Education for service activities that include demonstration projects for the provision of vocational rehabilitation services to individuals with severe handicaps in order to improve the outcomes of their employability and independent living. ''The purpose of this proposed priority is to solicit applications [regarding rehabilitation technology services] . . . to enhance . . . employability,'' and ''innovative strategies to promote vocational and independent living outcomes.'' Department of Education, Rehabilitation Services Administration (RSA) (1989, February 16). *Federal Register, 54*(31), 7156.

Another release provides notice of proposed rule making. It includes the ''Development of Evaluation Standards and Proposed Compliance Indicators.'' The latter would incorporate performance measures, the most important of which is ''the placement of individuals in competitive jobs at a reasonable cost to the Federal Government. . . . The actual placement rate and the actual cost per placement . . . are more important than a project meeting the placement and cost projections stated in its grant application'' (6808-6809). Specific program compliance indicators are included relative to the weights and minimum performance levels for each compliance indicator. Office of Special Education and Rehabilitative Services, Department of Education (1989, February 14). Proposed rules. *Federal Register, 54*(29), 6808-6811.

14. The GAO has developed ''a framework of general criteria for evaluating children's programs to be used by the Congress to help structure its evaluations of Federal programs.

The framework was designed to ensure that those evaluations are comprehensive and to permit comparisons to be made fairly between programs.'' Some GAO reviews and the Congressional Committee reports are listed in this article. Shipman, Stephanie (1989). *General criteria for evaluating social programs* (p. 20). Washington, DC: U.S. General Accounting Office.

15. *Case Statement (1985)*. The Dole Foundation. (220 Eye Street NE, Washington, DC 20002), 1–2.

16. While Congress has taken action to ''reduce this work disincentive for disabled SSI recipients, [it] has not been extended to SSDI beneficiaries . . . the Social Security System spent $16 million in 1987 reimbursing the VR [Vocational Rehabilitation] System for placing SSDI recipients in competitive employment, and $20.5 billion in cash benefits to disabled workers because they could not work.'' Griss, Bob. (1988, December–1989, March). *Access to Health Care 1*(3&4), 88. Washington, DC: World Institute on Disability.

17. Griss, *Access to Health Care*, 89.

18. Jeremiah Milbank, President of the J. M. Foundation, as quoted in *NY Ragtimes*, (1989, Summer) 7. New York: New York Regional Association of Grantmakers, Inc.

19. ''In July, the United States Congress enacted the Americans with Disabilities Act of 1990 (ADA) which seeks . . . to provide substantial protections to disabled Americans who are in, or seek to join, the work force. Among a number of provisions relating to the disabled is a requirement that employers, in certain instances, make accommodations for an employee's or job applicant's disabilities. . . . There are four other titles dealing with public transportation, public accommodations, public communications and architectural and transportation barriers.'' Staff. (1990, Fall). New federal protections for the disabled pose questions for employers. *Law Notes From Herold and Haines, 3*(2), 1.

20. Accordingly, it is important

to identify sources of problems in the optimal rehabilitation of elderly persons and to explore the implications of rehabilitation for increased well-being of older persons. The role played by culture, functional status, psychosocial factors, and the health care system was addressed. Concluded was that rehabilitation is undoubtedly beneficial for older persons and new directions for research are suggested.

Becker, Gayline, & Kaufman, Sharon. (1988, November 4). Old age, rehabilitation, and research: A review of the issues. *The Gerontologist, 28*(4), 459. The importance of an interdisciplinary approach to the field of gerontology has also been noted, as well as the current challenges of the increase in the minority older population, life and death ethical issues, and the need for a ''disease/functional model of health care with specificity.'' Silverstone, Barbara (1989). Aging in tomorrow's world: The challenge to gerontology. Keynote address at the 16th New York State Association of Gerontological Educators (SAGE). Cited in their newsletter (1989, Winter), 3.

21. ''To be effective, rehabilitation must be viewed as an individual rather than a collective process, with each patient optimally having a treatment program specifically tailored to his or her limitations.'' An individualized approach ''may undermine the sense of maintaining control over the policymaking process.'' The authors suggest that a flexible policy is needed to replace the all-or-none approach and should be ''focused on small incremental gains,'' which may ''be more cost effective, as it might be possible to return greater numbers of persons to higher levels of independent functioning.'' This strategy raises many questions and ''more research is needed in which the cost effectiveness of innovative programs and techniques and the length of rehabilitation for older persons is rigorously

analyzed.'' Such research could help establish policy guidelines wherein individual functioning can be maximized relative to costs and where the results are aggregatable for policy guidelines. Becker & Kaufman, (1988, August 20), Old age, rehabilitation, and research.

22. "In fact they need services which empower them to manage their chronic needs so that they live as independently as possible in their own homes, and function on their jobs, and participate as active members of their community. . . . This policy bulletin has examined five choices for improving access to health care for persons with chronic conditions." It provides a list of services in addition to primary care for which costs and benefits could be readily accounted for. The list provides external standards to serve as measurement surrogates. Griss, *Access to health care*, 89.

23. "The Rehabilitation Act Amendments of 1986 mandated the development of program standards and performance indicators to assess the performance of the federally funded Independent Living programs." The Rehabilitation Research Training Center established "an absolute priority [to] study and test strategies . . . regarding the effectiveness of individuals with disabilities . . . in achieving personal independent living objectives." This included "the quality of community services available" and their effect on independent living. (Rehabilitation Research Training Center, Department of Education, Office of Special Education and Rehabilitative Services. (1989, April 25). Notices. *Federal Register, 54*(78), 17899.

24. "AMRRC is a central resource on available and developing quality evaluation methodologies and programs which may have practical applications. The center convenes its members, donors, and interested parties in a variety of formats, forums, and around current projects. Partnerships have the greatest potential to have an impact on the science of measuring quality medical care services and patient outcomes. The ultimate goal is effective operational quality and cost evaluation programs." (1989, Summer). *Quality Review, An AMRRC Publication, 4*(1), 21.

25. Garland, Susan B. (1990, January 22). Washington Outlook. *Business Week*, p. 39.

26. Robins, Anthony. (1989, December 7). Prevention now. *Scientific American*. [Advertisement]. *New York Times*.

27. Curtis, Jody. (1989, November, December). The largest minority. *Foundation News, 30*(6), 18–23.

28. Budde, James, Petty, C. Ray, & Nelson, Christopher. (1989, October, November, December). Problems and benefits associated with consumer satisfaction evaluation at independent living centers. *Journal of Rehabilitation 55*(4) 62–68.

29. Weisbrod, Burton A. (1988). *The nonprofit economy* pp 1–159 Cambridge, MA: Harvard University Press.

30. Weisbrod, *The nonprofit economy*, 160–165.

31. O'Neill, Michael. (1989). *The third America: The emergence of the nonprofit sector in the United States*. San Francisco, CA: Jossey-Bass.

32. O'Neill, *The third America*, 5.

33. Davidson, Greg, & Davidson, Paul. (1988). *Economics for a civilized society*. New York: W. W. Norton. Reviewed in *Future Survey, 11*(9), 7. (1989, September).

34. "We have no consensus on what should be measured. Are we interested only in self-care, or in mobility, or in communication skills, or in a much more global measure, such as quality of life? . . . If a person can walk around the block physically, but does not do so because it's not safe, that's a quality-of-life issue. It may be necessary to include outside variables like that in order to get a complete picture." Friedman, Emily. (1989, August 8). Outcomes Analysis in Rehabilitation. *Utilization Review*.

35. Hopps, June Gary. Securing the future—What will we risk? (Editorial). (1989, July). *Social Work, 34*(4), 291.

36. Pennar, Karen. (1989, September 25). The new America—The free market has triumphed, but what about the losers? *Business Week*, p. 178.

37. "President Bush launched a 'points of light initiative' to encourage a national volunteer effort to help the homeless, the poor, illiterate, drug abusers, people with AIDS and other Americans facing severe problems. . . . Television producer Norman Lear has endowed a new foundation, the Business Enterprise Trust, with $1 million for the purpose of giving national awards to corporations and individuals who demonstrate courage, creativity and social vision in the business word . . . 'to . . . stimulate a discussion in business schools, among business people and in the country at large about the responsibility of business.' " Staff. (1989, September 15). In the news. *Council Columns, 8*(10), 4. Washington, DC: Council on Foundations.

A pamphlet about social investment by private foundations relates current efforts at program-related investments that include social investments such as program-related loans, guarantees, and equity investments as well as recoverable grants and investments in local programs to change a region's economy for social returns. Marble, Melinda. (1989). *Social investment and private foundations*. Washington, DC: Council on Foundations.

38. Nelson, Robert C. Changing public values: An interview with Daniel Yankelovich. *Kettering Review*. (1988, Fall). Dayton, OH: Charles F. Kettering Foundation. 40–48.

39. The "NSF will support high-quality research proposals . . . that could lead to significant public benefit if the research is successful," including "economic and social benefits to the nation." Staff. (1987, June 22). *Program Solicitations*. Washington, DC: National Science Foundation. The use of economic values is being applied to other societal questions, even the societal value of otters. The courts have ruled that polluters should "restore the environment to its original condition" or, if not possible, "to pay compensation for the total value of damages—including the loss of non-market benefits." Mandel, Michael J. (1989, August 21). How much is a sea otter worth? *Business Week*, 59–60. The National Academy of Science Board of Agriculture recognizes that current "federal farm policy encourages the heavy use of outside inputs" such as fertilizers and pesticides and grading rules, which "clashes with environmental policy." A new combination is required of organic and conventional farming that will "save money, lessen food safety concerns and be more 'environmentally friendly.' " Waterfield, Larry. (1989, October). Adapting alternative methods is not a simple task. *The Grower*. Washington, DC; Nowhere does the problem of balancing of societal resources and property rights become more difficult than in dealing with the protection of the environment. New approaches are suggested to evaluate and prioritize the nation's environmental problems that include ranking them on the basis of risks involved, and considering the appropriate application of economic models and incentives. Science Advisory Board. (1990, September). *Reducing risk: Setting priorities and strategies for environmental protection*. (Report to the United States Environmental Protection Agency). Washington, DC.

CHAPTER 4

Societal Model: The Propositions

This chapter develops the proposed framework in the form of three basic propositions, the necessary and sufficient conditions for the solution of many of the problems presented in the opening chapter. With the propositions as a higher order of abstraction, potential solutions are broadened to encompass this list of problems. Moreover, a new taxonomy is presented in conformity with the models developed relative to institutional requirements for the delivering of goods and services.

INTRODUCTION

The historical review in Chapter 3 provides support for the move toward the symbiotic balancing of the constrained viewpoint of laissez-faire with the un-constrained view of expanded government responsibility to groups within the society. We recognize the need for the continuing existence of both strains of thought, which are embodied in our history. While the constrained view has dominated the political, economic, and social policies of the century and a half following independence, both viewpoints existed side by side within our society. During the decades following the Great Depression, the liberal, unconstrained view dominated ideological values and government policies; the conservative, constrained view has dominated events of the past decade. We do not offer an amalgam of both views into a new centrist position, a kind of Hegelian synthesis. Rather the continued existence of both viewpoints is necessary in a symbiotic balance, where the advantages of both systems of thought, group consideration and individual concern (both true), can be exploited by society to its advantage.

In making explicit our assumptions about the role of government in our society and of man's attitudes about independence, elements of both the constrained and unconstrained visions are incorporated. We express constraint in that we propose no revolution relative to existing institutions; nor do we expect changes in basic human nature. Further, we assume as primary the continuing historical significance of the work ethic and the importance of the individual's desire to belong and to be within a social system. We also believe that client-consumers, staff, management, boards of directors, societal members, and government, as the key stakeholders connected to HSOs, will react to incentives induced by appropriate measuring systems—the constrained viewpoint. We accept as the function of government to ensure the right for the opportunities of pursuit and to take actions to lessen uncertainty for its citizenry. We are unconstrained in our viewpoint that the greatest number of persons in our society prefer independence and self-realization to support and dependency, and thus most people welcome the possibility of change even in the face of a limited potential.

To these ends, the propositions that form the conceptual framework have been developed. These propositions incorporate the truths of Smith, Marx, Keynes, and Buber in a Bohrian system of complementarity. These propositions are the basis of the societal model that focuses on the development of an accounting system to measure the performance of HSOs. In economic terms, with HSOs largely committed to promoting and/or maintaining economic self-sufficiency, a measuring system is needed that communicates more than a tracking of receipts and disbursements. Rather, what is required is a system that measures effectiveness and efficiency, that can produce a bottom line. The measurement system should induce optimizing the allocation of resources used, in the same sense that the profit metric presumably optimizes the use of its resources. Thus, measurement must be understood in the economic terms on which success/failure is to be determined and requires an extended discussion of basic economic tenets.

An interesting property of any measuring system, or for that matter any scoring system, is that in addition to being a means of reporting the results of a given action, it can induce the action that is ultimately to be measured and reported. Incentives to management based on profits, to sales personnel based on shipments to customers, and to students based on grades are also illustrations of measuring systems that induce behavior. Accordingly, any accounting system that is selected by society should consider this principle of inducing the kind of behavior that society prefers. Given that accounting systems are typically designed to measure and report on economic events, it is essential to understand what particular economic behavior our society seeks to elicit from its institutions and members.

The nature of economic goods must be defined since society assigns different types of organizations to supply different kinds of goods, which may require different kinds of measurement. How a society will perform in the optimization of its resources depends on the interfacing, interrelations, and interactions of these different types of organizations that supply economic goods.

Economic Goods

At the most basic economic level, our society is constructed so that there exists the potential for exchange of goods between producers and consumers. A good, by definition, must satisfy the needs and wants of one or more persons; goods are the means, satisfaction is the end. Accordingly, goods can range from the most tangible provisions of food, clothing and shelter to intangibles of play and the arts.[1]

In general, there are three kinds of satisfactions produced by goods: (1) those that satisfy a given person's need or want—consumer and payer are one; (2) those that satisfy another person's need or want—consumer is receiver of the good and payer is giver; and (3) those that satisfy the need or want of the group—the group is the payer and the consumer is a member of the group.[2]

Basically, the difference between the current accounting system in the PS and NPS is that exchanges of goods of the first kind have been accounted for in the PS and exchanges of goods of the third kind in the NPS. One possible explanation for the different ways of accounting of goods is that PS accounting systems are based on two principles. First, there must be an exchange that involves money value, and second, both sides of the exchange must have entered into the transaction by choice. Goods of the second kind fail the second principle so they cannot be accounted for. The probable reason that goods of the third kind have been accounted for only as exchanges of funds, and not as goods, is that the satisfaction of the recipient has not, in the words of Pigou, "been brought into relation with the measuring rod of money."[3] Accordingly, the accounting for this type of goods (nonprofits and governments) is based on the criterion of the sacrifice of funds. On the other hand, goods of the first kind are accounted for based on the benefit that the consumer enjoys, which is related to the measuring rod of money.

Moving toward a common accounting requires overcoming the difference between properties of the first and third kind of goods in their measurement. In which way should accounting procedures be made uniform: Should they be based on fund accounting or an consumer satisfaction? On what basis should the choice be made? Smith chose the satisfaction of the consumer: "Consumption is the sole end and purpose of all production; and the interest of the producer ought to be attended to, only so far as it may be necessary for promoting that of the consumer."[4] Hicks also incorporates in his measure of well-offness and income measurement the economic ability to consume.[5] The problem then becomes how to account for the consumption of goods of the third kind. If one recognizes that the recipient of the benefits/satisfaction is society as well as the individual, then the level of analysis changes. This leads to the question, on what basis should the collective produce goods of the third kind? The answer in theory is, to the extent that it improves the lot of its collective members in comparison to the costs incurred. Clearly, society already produces some types of goods of the third kind, for example, national defense, parks, and mosquito eradication programs. These goods are referred to as nonrival and nonexcludable goods, nonexcludable in that more than one consumer can simultaneously consume one unit of the good while no consumer can be prevented from partaking in the consumption of that good. They are nonrival because their production and consumption are not subject to economic exchanges having been decided upon in the political domain. As yet this type of collective goods has not raised accounting questions. There are also some goods produced by the PS for consumption by consumers that require government licensing, for example, cable television—these should be treated as nonrival and excludable goods.

Goods of the third kind that are rival and nonexcludable are typically of the type that are produced by HSOs, by private organizations based on funding by government. HSOs are hybrid entities performing social services to satisfy human needs. They compete in the market to acquire rival goods, yet like governments must generally offer their output services to all consumers. In most instances they are private in their decision making but public in their accountability. Are there criteria that determine how much of this type of goods should be produced? The answer is the same as above, that is, that society should produce this type of goods as long as it satisfies the need and wants of the members of the collective relative to costs. This is the organizational model proposed in chapter 2.

The following chart summarizes the combination of two types of economic goods that are discussed in this section, Type 1 where the consumer and payer are the same and Type 3 where the collective is the payer and the consumer is the member.

	Rival	*Nonrival*
Excludable	PS (Type 1)	PS & Govt.
Nonexcludable	NPS and Govt. (Type 3)	Govt. (Type 3)

Society has the goal of optimizing resources by using its institutions in an optimal manner for the production of various types of goods. Within this background of types of goods and consumers, the propositions for a societal framework are submitted.

THE PROPOSITIONS

The criteria offered as the underpinnings of the proposed societal model and related accounting system are:

1. Society as a whole is economically better off when there is a greater proportion of citizens participating in the social system—consuming and producing—than when there is a lesser proportion

2. Society as a whole is economically better off when it citizens are not risk averse, which can be defined as "one who starting from a position of certainty, is unwilling to take a bet which is actuarially fair"[6]

3. Society as a whole is economically better off when its citizens behave in a moral way—
   "humanity might indeed exist if no one contributed to the happiness of others, provided he did not intentionally detract from it; but this harmony with humanity as an end in itself is only negative rather than positive if everyone does not also endeavor, so far as he can, to further the ends of others."[7] (Immanuel Kant)

   "Nothing, in my view, more deserves attention than the intellectual and moral associations in America. . . . If men are to remain civilized or to become civilized, the art of association must develop and improve among them at the same speed as equality of condition spreads"[8] (Alexis deTocqueville)

We recognize that assertions such as these require logical proof, that the conclusions follow the premises contained therein in order that they be acceptable as a basis for further analysis. In addition, it will be shown that whichever proposition is taken as primary, whether one or two of the above, the other follows as a corollary.

However, before continuing with the proof, we address the question raised by Arrow's famous impossibility theorem as to whether criteria of collective well-offness can be posited. This proposition essentially says that, except for a dictatorial form of government, there cannot be a social choice function that satisfies minimally acceptable and reasonable conditions. In other terms, Arrow shows that in a democratic form of government individual tastes cannot be aggregated in order to arrive at a maximal social good. Thus, generally acceptable criteria must be promulgated that, on the one hand, satisfy the requirement discussed and, on the other hand, do not conflict with Arrow's position, In brief, it can be claimed that Arrow is looking at the problem from the bottom up; he asks whether it "Is formally possible to construct a procedure for passing from a set of known individual tastes to a pattern of social decision making."[9] We, in contrast, look at the question from the top down. Our approach is similar in nature to such other systemic choices as private property and freedom of speech. The protection of speech and private property in our society permit society as a whole, as measured by the average quality of life of its citizens, to be better off than if these rights were not guaranteed. There are certain systemwide choices that are made on the average, or some other such aggregate measure. Clearly, the protection of private property does not make everyone better off; there are some in our society such as the homeless who are worse off. If we were to abide strictly by Arrow's conclusions, all systemwide rules might have to be reexamined.

We start with an overarching statement: the United States of America is a society that in its economic dimension employs competitive, monetary, and capitalistic mechanisms to organize and operate those factors that contribute to its material well-being. We will not at this point examine the plethora of issues that the statement engenders, such as: Are markets truly competitive? Or, what type or proportion of society's capital should be owned by the PS? The statement is taken at its face value, as a given. However, the terms *competitive, monetary,* and *capitalistic* require analysis.

Webster's defines *competition* as the act of contending with another for a prize, profit, and so on. By definition, competition as a process produces winners and losers and may continue as long as there are competitors. In economics, the word competition has a technical meaning relating to market structure. One of the factors that is necessary for the existence of a purely competitive market is that there have to be many sellers and buyers where no one market participant can affect the actions of the market—where the market is impersonal.

As far back as the early nineteenth century, it was understood that a social system that operated on the principle of laissez-faire would, as part of its dynamics, produce a situation wherein some of its participants would be losers and forced out of the system. Before Keynes's *General Theory of Employment, Interest, and Money*, prevailing wisdom accepted *Say's Law* that full employment of resources results from automatic reactions built into the market. Keynes's analysis showed, however, that the return to full employment was not a necessary result of market forces. He argued that when private investment expenditures fall, the wages and profit in the industries that produce the capital goods fall, as well as those that supply the resources that go into the making of capital goods, such as steel and coal. This reduction in purchasing power propagates throughout the economy so that other sectors are impacted. The ultimate result is that the economy can be brought to its knees—a position from which it cannot rise; to Keynes, the lever for the economy is investment expenditures. Keynes concludes that government should, as part of its responsibility, maintain total effective demand at a level that sustains full employment. He suggests that government should vary its fiscal and monetary policies to achieve its goals.[10] There is hardly anyone today, on the left or the right of the political spectrum, that does not accept the proposition that government has a role to play in maintaining the viability of the economy— though there is considerable ongoing debate relative to proportion and degree. The human response to pervasive uncertainty is related to "a constructive role for government." It is argued that government, as envisioned by Rawls and Keynes, has a special purpose in society precisely because government can undertake actions to lessen uncertainty that individuals, acting alone, are unable to do.[11]

The U.S. economy is an advanced market economy. Another way of describing the U.S. economy is to say that it is made up of specialists, individuals, and firms that are thoroughly integrated into an economic system where market participants sell or buy goods in exchange for money. This economic game is played in terms of money, which places money at center stage; clearly, the degree of availability of money in the economy impacts the economy in at least two ways: in providing the participants in the economy with the ability to make transactions, and in its relation to the cost of money, that is, interest rate. There is an obvious relationship between the real and monetary sectors of the economy. (In recent years, as the analysis in chapter 5 suggests, the medium of money has often been substituted for the message of production.)

The term *capitalism* is taken to mean a pervasive private ownership of the means of production, and where labor and capital are connected in such a way that resources, including labor, acquired through market transactions are combined into products that are disposed of through market transactions. At the heart of capital theory is the notion of time; an investment in some means of production is made today in anticipation that the future product issuing from the investment will return a profit over time to the owner in addition to the original expenditure. Capital can take many forms, for example, machinery to produce cars, or a system for the education of the members of society. What they both have in common is the idea of profit over time—whether as fixed capital or as human capital.

The background has been laid for presenting evidence in support of the propositions. Additional support in the form of a more systematic analysis appears at the end of this chapter in Exhibit 4.2.

Support for Proposition One

Once again we invoke the words of Smith: "As it is the power of exchanging that gives occasion to the division of labor, so the extent of this division must always be limited by the extent of that power or, in other words, by the extent of the market."[12] There is implicit in Smith's concepts that economies of scale exist that are directly related to the size of the market for a good. Put in other terms, the greater the demand for a product, the greater the production. The greater the production, the greater the division of labor. The greater the division of labor, the greater the efficiency of production. If the Smithian analysis is coupled with the concept of declining marginal utility, that the satisfying power of each additional unit of a given good to a particular user is less than the prior one, we arrive at the essence of the first proposition, that society as a whole is economically better off when a greater proportion of its citizens are consuming and producing. It should be noted that a major component of this argument is the advantages derived from economies of scale. The proposition also applies to a world where there are constant returns to scale. Division of labor not only implies greater specialization of function relating to the production of a particular good, but also that potential specialization can lead to greater diversity of goods.

Support for Proposition Two

One of the ways that the division of labor is facilitated is through the use of capital goods such as machinery and equipment. Investors in capital goods try to anticipate the future returns that such goods will produce. Anticipation incorporates the assessment of the risks associated with the investment. Views of the future are made up of two components: On the one hand, the investor computes the benefits to be derived from the investment based on favorable factors, the upside; on the other hand, the investor is concerned with the impact of unforeseen variables, the downside. The combination of both sides results in the investor's subjective probability distribution. Thus, the assessment of risk is related to future events carried out by the investor who converts beliefs and opinions into a subjective probability distribution for investment returns relative to such future events. The investor with a more pessimistic view of the future will tend to arrive at a lower expected return, which could result in a decision not to invest.

This second proposition is also based on the same calculus as in the insurance industry: The group insures the individual against significant losses. The rationale of the insurance industry is the reduction of the downside that a particular insured party faces in a given circumstance. The insurance industry is capable of supplying this benefit, in a cost-effective way, because it spreads the individual risk among a large group of individuals and in some instances, society as a whole. The insured party, having the downside mitigated for a price, can take actions without being constrained by the concern for the downside. Whether life or medical, old age or unemployment, accident or mishaps insurance, the protection of insurance for the individual encourages risk taking. The more the risk taking by members of society, the more dynamic, innovative, and competitive is that society. Moreover, consumers with insurance will have a higher marginal propensity to consume.

Thus we see that the chain of reasoning distinguishing proposition two from proposition one is that society receives more output per unit of labor input, which is a consequence in part of the introduction of capital goods into the production process. But the investment in capital goods generally entails the assumption of a long-term risk that can have a negative outcome on the investor. This type of concern can be reduced in part by lessening the fears and concerns of citizens so as to encourage them to invest in the future both as consumers and as investors. It should also be noted that investment in capital goods is not limited to increasing the efficiency of a particular capital good, fixed or human; it also includes investing in new products and processes and encouraging research and development. Taking propositions one and two together produces an economic system that is both dynamic and utilizes fully its potential.

Support for Proposition Three

Proposition three is different from the other two in that the first two add to economic goods directly while the third addresses the negative aspects of a competitive economic system—a system in which the individual societal member "by pursuing his own interest . . . frequently promotes that of the society more effectually than when he really intends to promote it."[13]

If we view, as we should, society as a system, that is, as a set of interacting elements, it then follows that any reduction in the cost of maintaining the system is a benefit, assuming *ceteris paribus* relative to the other elements of the system. For example, lubrication is required in an automobile engine, which is a system to reduce friction. In a competitive economy system, moral behavior of its members can reduce the costs of law adjudication and enforcement, insurance, and other costs of societal maintenance. Is there some way to define ethics/morality so that it has the qualities to act as the friction reducer in our social system?

The positing of an ethical norm we label as *positive harmony*. The consequences of any action can only be assessed in light of what was wanted to happen; stated differently, we can only value the *is* by the *ought*—ultimately the ought resolves itself into an ethical proposition. We limit our assertion to the statement that society will be economically better off, not generally better off. This then requires that we show a connection between the asserted ethical norm of positive harmony and economics. Moreover, if research evidence connects the best available measures of economic welfare with the best available measure of human welfare, then we may cautiously broaden our third proposition to include human welfare in addition to economic welfare.

It is assumed that competition in the economic sphere produces greater output—however, with an increase in the associated costs of conflicts. Tensions manifest themselves in at least two ways, litigation and crime. The resources consumed in our economy by the conflict-resolving activity that is engaged in by some members of our society is wasteful. Accordingly any reduction in such costs benefits everyone. We concede that all of these costs cannot be eliminated; if they were, it would probably be at the cost of the elimination of competition. However, to the degree possible and desirable, an increase in positive harmony should result in a decrease in wasting of resources. Ethics as defined herein is an economic good; accordingly, society should devote resources to produce the economic good, ethics, to the point where the cost of resources allocated to ethics "production" is equal to the benefit derived from the reduction in conflict.

Economics is based on hierarchical choices in the satisfaction of needs and then wants. Once basic needs relating to survival are satisfied, then other choices regarding wants can expand. Such choices incorporate Maslow's hierarchy, which include the development of systems of ethics.[14]

Propositions one and two provide an appropriate structure for proposition three. Given a value system that incorporates proposition one's inclusion of members within the system and proposition two's provision for their support if they drop out of the system, an ethical environment is established. Likewise, given any ethical system (other than the polar extremes of social Darwinism or of a complete dropout from society), an awareness of self, other individuals, and of the group adds impetus for the implementation of proposition three.

An alternative articulation of the positive harmony principle is Feuerbach's statement: "The being of a man," he declared, "exists only in community, in the unity of man with man—a unity that rests solely on the distinction between I and Thou."[15] Buber, who recognized Feuerbach's contribution to his thinking, declared: "I myself in my youth was given a decisive impetus by Feuerbach . . . the essential human reality is neither one of individual or collective existence, but lies in the relation between man and man, and is a matter between me and you."[16] Feuerbach and Buber, stating the obvious with simplicity, exposed the superficiality of the debate between individualism and collectivism, the conservative versus liberal political poles. They anticipated the principle of complementarity propounded by the Nobel Prize-winning physicist Neils Bohr. In essence this principle states that an understanding of atomic physics cannot be achieved without resorting to expressions that are logically irreconcilable. Bohr observed that in some experiments light had a wave structure and in others it behaved as would a particle. Thus, he declared, if both are correct then reality possesses opposite properties that complete each other.[17] In the social world, the individual and group complete each other.

EMPIRICAL SUPPORT FOR THE PROPOSITIONS

Studies of investments in the development of human capital, such as the education, skills training, and health care of its societal members, provide empirical support for the propositions.[18] Schultz makes a fundamental contribution to economics in terms of his approach to the quality of populations. From an economic point of view, the payoff of public investment in these areas can exceed the returns from private investment as the result of individuals' increasing productivity and the potential for society to exploit directly and in more flexible combinations the changing educational levels, skills, health, and creativity of its labor force. The investment in health includes "child care, nutrition, clothing, housing, medical services, and care of oneself. The service that health care capital renders consists of 'healthy time' or 'sickness-free time' which contributes to work, consumption and leisure activities."[19]

Classical economics developed in Western Europe when subsistence was difficult and life spans were short. Approximately four-fifths of the national income in the United States is now derived from services and earnings and the remainder from property—which hardly could have been foreseen by Malthus and Ricardo. Schultz points out that Adam Smith and Alfred Marshall emphasized that knowledge and organization are both important components of capital—that the wealth of nations consists of the acquired abilities of its population. He emphasizes that concepts of capital formation must include investments in human resources. Like any other capital, it creates future income by improving economic productivity.

In an analysis of twentieth-century agriculture, he demonstrates that advances in knowledge and the inclusion of the value of human time have improved population quality. (Even in developing countries, after these investments, people can emphasize the quality of their children's upbringing compared to the quantity of children that they have.) Investment in improving knowledge (including entrepreneurial ability) and extending life span of societal members affects economic productivity and human well-being. The modernization of agriculture together with agricultural research has created a revolution in land productivity, for example, "the corn acreage harvested in the United States in 1979, 33 million acres less than in 1932, produced 7.76 billion bushels, three times the amount produced in 1932."[20]

Schultz states that it is a serious error when all outlays for education are accounted for as current consumption—the same accounting error is made relative to health. As a result of increased education and health, the real wages of production workers have increased over five times.[21] He cites the studies of other economists, Kuznets, Becker, and Knight, which empirically support that these investments result in economic growth with direct income effects to the labor force and to society, as part of the higher return from such investments to increase human outputs.[22]

Likewise, Heilbroner writes: "Thus the neglect of the national infrastructure has been an unmitigated disaster. No one has gained; all have lost."[23] He estimates that in order to bring the infrastructure back to its former levels would require an investment of about $500 billion, of which about $400 billion would be for the infrastructure of highways, bridges, and airports and $60 billion to $100 billion for elementary and secondary education (excluding higher education). He refers to the study of David Aschauer of the Chicago Federal Reserve Bank who has calculated that a dollar of public investment today is productive of more output than a dollar of private investment, and "that private profitability would rise by two percentage points—that is, from, say 10 to 12 percent—if infrastructure investment were merely brought back to its 1981 levels." He concludes that we as a nation must forgo short-run private gain. "In that case, we would see a change in the quality of life, as the numbers of school dropouts decline, the air gets cleaner, and the economy becomes more productive, the society more decent."[24]

Additional empirical support for investing in human capital is based on evidence from Taiwan. From a study of its industry Tallman and Wang derive "an open economy model that displays endogenous growth through the accumulation of human capital. . . . The evidence supports the theoretical suggestion that labor skill is a useful augmentation of the raw labor input measure commonly used in growth accounting studies."[25]

Recent studies suggest that good ethics may be good business. An Arizona State University study that attempted to relate ethics to the performance of excellent organizations concluded that "ethics does play a crucial role in the interactions between a firm and its external constituencies and in internal social contracts."[26]

Ethical considerations have moved in the PS from the boardroom to management and employees. In a recent article, specific methodology to improve the ethical climate within a firm is presented, starting with top management commitment, a written code of conduct, and follow-up seminars to assess and discuss the continuing results on decision making.[27]

Earlier we alluded to the connections between human welfare and economic welfare. There is also specific research evidence of this. Scitovsky, a leading welfare economist, has discussed

the many questionnaire surveys of self-rated happiness, which have been conducted both in the United States and abroad. In the United States, ten surveys were made at fairly regular intervals; the first in April 1946, the most recent in December 1970. People were asked to rate their satisfaction with their own lives on a three-point scale describing themselves as "very happy," "fairly happy," or "not very happy." In addition, they were also asked to give their demographic data including their income. Not surprisingly, people's self-rated happiness is positively correlated with their income in each of the ten surveys."[28]

TAXONOMY

The current classification system of profit and nonprofit (or nonbusiness) is based on considerations of the nature of organizational operations, ownership, and sources of funding. This blurs the appropriate economic functioning of societal institutions that provide goods and services of various kinds. The propositions, together with an understanding of economic goods, lead us to propose a new taxonomy (see Exhibit 4.1).[29] This taxonomy is based on the notion of the individual and the group and the source and use of resources, whether private or public. Under this changed taxonomy, institutions are classified as follows: (1) consumers who use their own resources for their own benefit—private profit sector (PPS), (2) consumers who use society resources for their own benefit, and society's benefit—societal profit sector (SPS), (3) groups that use individual resources for group benefit—group association sector (GAS), and (4) groups that use group resources for group benefits—group government sector (GGS).

Resources used to benefit the individual, whether private or public transfers, represent the profit sector and can be analyzed by microeconomic principles, that is, the neoclassical model and the societal model presented in this book. Resources used to benefit the groups, whether private or public transfers, represent the nonprofit sector and should be analyzed by macroeconomic concepts. As yet, satisfactions of a group have not been brought into an alignment with a money calculus for measurement. Accordingly, fund accounting remains as the most appropriate system for the present.

Illustrations of the PPS are the various privately owned companies producing goods and services in the existing profit sector. Health, education, and HSOs constitute the SPS. The GAS consists of private foundations and associations, usually private resources interested in the betterment of the group, such as disaster relief, cancer, and other civic and research entities. The focus of the GGS is the provision of services by the group for the maintenance and betterment of the group. Such services can be classified as external or protective, such as defense, police, and courts; and internal for societal betterment such as museums, parks, and religious organizations. It should be noted that membership organizations such as those formed around hobbies and lobbies, or trade groups and social clubs, which use private resources for their own personal benefits, should be classified in the PPS.

We refrained from presenting extensive statistical data as a basis for analysis of the economic significance of the NPS and of the HSOs. Some data such as the number of firms, their contribution to GNP, the assets employed, the number

Exhibit 4.1
Proposed Taxonomy of Economic Activity

The Beneficiaries

		INDIVIDUAL	GROUP
The Providers	INDIVIDUAL	(1) Private Profit Sector (PPS) e.g., Existing Profit Sector Social clubs, self-interest groups	(2) Group Association Sector (GAS) e.g., Associations Foundations
	GROUP	(3) Societal Profit Sector (SPS) e.g., Human Service Organizations Health Education	(4) Group Government Sectors (GGS) e.g., Maintenance of System Enhancement of System

	INDIVIDUAL	GROUP
Sectors	Profit	Nonprofit
Economics	Micro	Macro
Accounting Basis	Unified profit accounting: measurement of individual consumer satisfaction/benefits (proposed in this book)	Unified profit accounting: measurement of group satisfaction/benefits (area of future research)

of employees including volunteer labor, annual funding requirements, and so on, as reported in Weisbrod and O'Neill—were summarized in Exhibit 3.1. Our restraint is not based only on the admitted insufficiency of data. More important is the irrelevance of much of these data relative to policy questions because of the inconsistency and illogical arrangement of the current taxonomy. The object of a classification system is to include as many types as possible within a single membership group. However, an analyis of economic impact based principally upon the criterion of nontaxabilty prevents an appropriate analysis.

The submission of a proposed alternative taxonomy requires a collection of different as well as additional data to evaluate the impact on the economy and the society. The new system of classification is based upon the source and use of resources relative to the individual and the group. Based upon this taxonomy, we would conclude that the significance of Box 3 in Exhibit 4.1 has been grossly underestimated. The new system is applicable to a sizable proportion of our economy. In our opinion, the transfer of resources from the group for the direct beneft of individuals could amount to between one-quarter and one-third of the economic activity in our society.[30]

SUMMARY

The prior chapter described the welfare state with its current emphasis on work-related programs. This reflects a general consensus about the significance of social programs that are work-related, designed to promote self-sufficiency and independence. In order to respond to current demands for the measurement of the effectiveness and efficiency of societal resources used for these programs, three basic propositions are developed as a framework for a societal model. In specifying the economic benefits that can accrue to society, the propositions are also prescriptive for actions to increase the total and the average per capita income of the society. Logical proofs and empirical evidence support these fundamental assumptions. The accounting system developed in chapter 2 and discussed in chapter 6 is designed to measure the outcome for HSOs of their societal mission embodied in these propositions.

The proposed change in the societal economic taxonomy follows logically from the societal model developed in this chapter and the organizational model in chapter 2. All organizations that use resources for the direct benefit of the individual, whether resources are private or societal, can be measured by a profit calculus. Other organizations whose goal is to benefit the group should be classified in the not-for-profit sector.

The implementation of the three foundational propositions developed above can optimize for society the use of its resources. In order to account for an exchange of goods of the third kind (rival and nonexcludable), an accounting system is needed to induce the required kind of behavior based on these three propositions. It is a quantum accounting system, one that embodies the Bohrian principle of complementarity; it accounts for as well as induces individual competitive and cooperative behavior that directly benefit society. The accounting system that has been designed for HSOs from these propositions accomplishes this mission.

NOTES

1. Robert Mundell, the economist, stated the proposition as follows:

Hunger is a want . . . and food [in stock] a resource. Hunger creates the desire for food. Thus the availability of food for reducing hunger, combined with the ability to eat it, implies that food is a good. Available food, drink, and shelter are goods that can eliminate hunger, thirst, and cold; a symphony concert is a good that can satisfy a listener's love of music and a toy train is a good that can satisfy a child's taste for play. The concept of a good in economics is a very broad one. A loaf of bread is a good; and so is a car, a house, a painting, a Beatles record, a bed, and a dog. So might be air, a date with a girl, a swim in the sea, a conversation with a genius.

As quoted in Phelps, Edmund S. (1985). *Political economy: An introductory text* (p. 4). New York: W. W. Norton & Co.

2. In addition to goods that are purchased for direct satisfaction, goods are acquired for donative purposes such as gifts and charity. It could be argued that in both of these cases the action is based on the pursuit of self-interest. Nevertheless, there is an important distinction that should be drawn: Satisfaction can be achieved from someone else's satisfaction. To expand the latter notion, not only does this type of satisfaction arise for the donee, for example, a birthday gift; it can also result when the action is on behalf of the other person so that everyone is better off, such as from the performance of a volunteer fireman.

3. As quoted in Sen, Amartya. (1987). *The standard of living* (p. 26). Cambridge: Cambridge University Press.

4. Smith, Adam. (1976). *An inquiry into the nature and causes of the wealth of nations 2, 179*). Chicago, IL: University of Chicago Press (original work published 1776).

5. Hicks, J. R. (1969). *Income readings in the concept of measurement and income.* Cambridge: Parker, R. N. & Harcourt, Cambridge University Press.

6. Arrow, Kenneth J. (1974). *Essays in the theory of risk-bearing* (p. 90). New York: American Elsevier Publishing Company.

7. As quoted in Cornman, James W., & Lehrer, Keith. (1974). *Philosophical problems and arguments, an introduction* (2nd ed., p. 494). New York: Macmillan Publishing Co.

8. As quoted in O'Neill, Michael. (1989). *The third America: The emergence of the nonprofit sector in the United States* (p. 13). San Francisco, CA: Jossey-Bass.

9. "If we exclude the possibility of interpersonal comparisons of utility, then the only method of passing from individual tastes to social preferences which will be satisfactory and which will be defined for a wide range of sets of individual orderings are either imposed or dictatorial." Arrow, Kenneth J. (1963). *Social choice and individual values* (p. 59). New Haven, CT: Cowles Foundation for Research in Economics at Yale University.

10. Keynes, John Maynard. (1964). *The general theory of employment, interest, and money.* New York: Harcourt Brace and World (original work published 1935).

11. McKenna, Edward, Wade, Maurice, & Zannoni, Diane. (1988, October). Keynes, Rawls, uncertainty, and the liberal theory of the state. *Economics and Philosophy, 4*(2), Cambridge, MA: Cambridge University Press.

12. Smith, *An inquiry into the nature and causes of the wealth of nations, 1*, 21.

13.

As every individual, therefore, endeavors as much as he can both to employ his capital in the support of domestic industry, and so to direct that industry that its produce may be of the greatest value; every individual necessarily labours to render the annual revenue of the society as great as he can. He generally, indeed, neither intends to promote the public interest, nor knows how much he is promoting it. By preferring the support of domestic to that of foreign industry, he intends only his own security; and by directing that industry in such a manner as its products may be of the greatest value, he intends only his own gain, and he is in this, as in many other cases, led by an invisible hand to promote an end which was no part of his intention. Nor is it always the worse for the society that it was no part of it. By pursuing his own interest he frequently promotes that of the society more effectually than when he really intends to promote it.

Smith, *An inquiry into the nature and causes of the wealth of nations*, *1*, 477–478. As a moral philosopher, Adam Smith was concerned about society. The conventional interpretation of the above quoted statement, that is, that society is better off when the individual is better off, has been perpetuated in the theory and myth of economics. It should be observed that Smith claims that self-interest "frequently" achieves society's end, it does not always do so. An appropriate reading of Smith's work would place this writing within the context of his eighteenth-century antimercantilist position as well as his continual concern for individuals and their opportunities for development within his restricted society. The following statement is in our opinion a better reflection of his thinking: "He is not a citizen who is not disposed to respect the laws and to obey the civil magistrate; and he is certainly not a good citizen who does not wish to promote, by every means in his power, the welfare of the whole society of his fellow-citizens." Smith, Adam. (1982). *The theory of moral sentiments* (p. 231). Indianapolis, IN: Liberty Classics (original work published 1759).

14. Maslow, Abraham. (1943, July). A theory of human motivation. (Psychological Review). Cited in *New pathways in psychology: Maslow and the post-Freudian revolution*. (1972) (pp. 161–163). New York: Taplinger Publishing Company.

15. Rader, Melvin. (1969). *The enduring questions: Main problems of philosophy* (2nd ed., p. 510). New York: Holt, Rinehart and Winston.

16. Rader, *The enduring questions*, 510.

17. Bohr, Niels. (1951). Discussion with Einstein on epistemological problems in atomic physics. In Paul Schlipp (Ed.), *Albert Einstein: philosopher-scientist* (7, 199–241). New York: Library of Living Philosophers.

18. Schultz, Theodore W. (1981). *Investing in people—The economics of population quality*. Berkeley: University of California Press.

19. Schultz, *Investing in people*, n. 13, p. 13.

20. Schultz, *Investing in people*, 7.

21. Schultz, *Investing in people*, 144.

22. Schultz, *Investing in people*, 75–84.

23. Heilbroner, Robert. (1990, February 15). Seize the day. *The New York Review of Books*, p. 30.

24. Heilbroner, Seize the day, 31.

25. Tallman, Ellis W., & Wang, Ping. (1990, November). Human capital and endogenous growth: Evidence from Taiwan (Working Paper 90-9). Atlanta, GA: Federal Reserve Bank.

26. Axline, Larry L. (1990, December). The bottom line on ethics. *Journal of Accountancy*, *170*(6), 87.

27. Lane, Michael R. (1991, February). Improving American business ethics in three steps. *The CPA Journal, 61*(2), 30–44.

28. Scitovsky, Tibor. (1989). *Human desire and economic satisfaction: Essays on the frontiers of economics* (p. 23). New York: New York University Press.

29. Implicit in a binary logical system, which the matrix (Exhibit 4.1) presents, is the notion of an opposite. Once the notion of an individual is defined so is the notion of the group automatically defined. Moreover once the two mutually exclusive notions have been agreed upon, the ability then exists to define a four-cell classification matrix composed of combinations of the two elemental notions.

30. Box 3 in Exhibit 4.1 consists of group resources transferred for the direct benefit of individual members of society. Accordingly, it would include all social programs, whether services were performed directly by government or by firms under contract, health and education as well as program payments under social security, medicare, medicaid, unemployment insurances, and others.

APPENDIX: ADDITIONAL SUPPORT FOR THE PROPOSITIONS

Proposition One

A society's economic position can be represented by, X/N, where $X = (x_1, x_2, \ldots, x_n)$ representing a vector of goods and services consumed by society, and where N represents the number of individuals comprising society. X/N can also be thought of as society's average standard of living.

Economies of scale is a generally accepted concept in economic theory. In essence, this notion states that as the size of plant and the scale of operations become larger, the potential cost per unit of output becomes smaller. Today, technological factors contribute significantly to the realization of economies of scale, an example being the introduction of the computer into manufacturing processes. To realize the reduction in cost resulting from technology, specialization, and the division of labor, sufficient quantities of goods and services must be produced. In turn, for the optimal quantities to be produced, there must be a concomitant demand for what is produced. Moreover, the motivation for the producer to enlarge capacity to produce goods and services is unfilled demand. This phenomenon can be represented by $dC/dS<0$, where $C = (c_1, c_2, \ldots c_n)$ stands for the unit cost of X, and S stands for the size of plant and scale of operation. Usually, $d^2C/dX^2<0$, the reduction in cost, decreases at a decreasing rate. If that were not the case, $C(X)$, in a very large production facility, would approach zero. This does not occur since there are always some variable costs associated with production and, beyond a given size, the increase in the requirements for management outweighs the benefits of an increase in production.

In addition to the benefits of economies of scale, progress in economic conditions has been achieved through economies of scope, that is, the variety of goods and services that the economy produces. Variety is related to economies of scale in that new goods and services can only be produced if there are resources available. If not, then new goods and services can only be produced through a substitution of the new for the old goods and services. It can be argued that society is better off to the extent that it prefers the new to the old; however, in terms of quantity, it is still in the same position. Only through greater efficiency can lower costs through greater output be achieved. An increase in quantity and variety in goods and services can be enjoyed by economies of scale and innovation. Thus a society's economic state and desired change in state is a function of both low and lowering costs, and an increasing variety of the goods and services produced in the economy.*

As noted above, production is related to demand and demand is generally held to be related to production. This mutual relationship is usually referred to as the circularity of economic activity. Consumers spend income earned from their production on desired goods and services. The interrelationship between demand and production can be formalized through their equality with income: $D = I = P$, where D = Demand, I = Income, and P = Production.

At any point in time, the production/demand equality is presumed to hold.** In the short run, prices have the burden of equilibrating consumption with production. However, prices do not change either perfectly or instantaneously and therefore, a misallocation of resources occurs. In addition to income, demand is a function of prices which in turn are a function of costs. All of the relevant relationships and dependencies can be summarized as: $Pr(C)$, $D(I,Pr)$, $I(X,Pr)$, $P(C)$, where prices $= Pr (pr_1, pr_2, \ldots, pr_n)$. Through substitution, $D(I,Pr) = I(P) = P(X,Pr)$. Costs, C, is equivalent to the prices of productive resources, multiplied by the amount of resources used. However, all costs become income to the producer; therefore, $D(I,Pr) = I(P) = P(I,Pr)$. Thus it can be seen that, $D(I,Pr) = P(I,Pr)$. This result is a version of a general equilibrium in economics.

If we were to append to the general equilibrium framework the notions of economies of scale and scope, it would follow that society's standard of living increases to a larger degree than an increase in the joint number of consumer-producers.

It can be shown, without too many restrictive assumptions, that an increase in consumption without a related increase in production results in inflation which ultimately brings total consumption into line with production. Conversely, an increase in production results in a decrease in prices which also brings consumption into line with production. However, in both cases, the equilibrated level is below that which would obtain if everyone in society were both a consumer as well as a producer.

A summary of the above can be denoted as:

$$dX/dN > 0 \qquad\qquad d^2X/dN^2 < 0$$
$$dL/dN > 0 \qquad\qquad d^2L/dN^2 < 0$$

*For the purpose of simplifying the analysis, international trade has been excluded. However, the analysis could be broadened to include international trade without altering the conclusion.

** For our purposes, we have omitted the savings/investment aspects that a broadened economic analysis would include. Intertemporal consumption, that is savings and investment, does not affect the result if a long enough period is taken to apply to the analysis, since in the long run production will equal consumption.

Proposition Two

A more technical definition of risk-aversion is: an individual who is willing to accept a certain cash amount that is less than the expected monetary value (EMV) of a risky alternative. An example will clarify the meaning of risk-aversion. Assume that the probability (P) structure of a $5 per ticket lottery to win a prize of X is:

X =	no prize	P =	98.887%
	$100 prize		1.000
	$1,000 prize		0.1
	$10,000 prize		0.010
	$100,000 prize		0.003

Accordingly, the EMV of such a lottery ticket is:

$$E(X) = -5 + (.98887)(0) + (0.01)(100) + (0.001)(1,000)$$
$$+ (0.0001)(10,000) + (0.00003)(100,000)$$
$$= -5 + 0 + 1 + 1 + 1 + 3$$
$$= +1$$

A risk averse individual would not buy a ticket even though in the above illustration the expected return is positive. The reason is that the dissatisfaction of a certain $5 loss (the cost of the ticket) outweighs the satisfaction of possibly winning the prize. On the other hand, if this individual could combine with a large number of other individuals, each of whom will also buy a ticket, and all the members of the group agree to split evenly the total winnings among all the members, then it is very likely that the individual's decision will change. In essence, individuals insure themselves against absorbing the total cost of the ticket.

As implied by Proposition One, a society as a whole is better off in economic terms when its members undertake risky projects that reduce costs either through larger capacities or new methods of production. Similarly, society as a whole is better off when its members innovate new products and engage in research. Because such activities involve substantial risk, it is in society's interest that its members insure part of the risk. Among the risks to be insured, as contemplated in the present work, is that of destitution (in the extreme); in the usual situation, it is the inability to earn an acceptable wage. In either situation the individual is unable to earn an acceptable wage.

There are two forms of inability. One is a lack of saleable skills and the other is a physical, mental, or social disability. It is to society's long term advantage that its members do not so fear these prospects that they oversave and invest their savings in the least risky and most liquid investments. It is manifest that a consumer who is productive benefits society, whereas a non-productive one, does not. In addition, an individual who invests in productive projects benefits society, whereas an individual that invests in government securities (where the funds are used for current or past consumption), does not.

The justification of such government programs as social security and unemployment insurance is that these programs reduce, to some degree, the individual's concerns; however,

91

these programs do not address society's underlying problem, an increase in society's production and variety of goods. This can be achieved only if society has a mechanism in place that, to the greatest degree possible, reduces transfer payments devoted to consumption and increases investment for the production of existing goods and services and for research and development. The model presented in this book can convert transfer payments into productive investment.

Proposition Three

Morality is defined in terms of human conduct. In comparison, the word ethics usually refers to a system or code by which the morality of human behavior is assessed. The words right and good are part of the vocabulary found in discussions about ethics. The word right as in the phrase right behavior means behaving in accordance with some standard. The word 'good' as in the phrase "good book" means that something possesses desirable qualities, that is, has value for human beings, or that it satisfies a need/want. For our purposes, we define law as the standard which limits human behavior and ethics, as that which specifies how to achieve the good life. Another way of looking at the difference between law and ethics is that the former relates to what one should not do for others and the latter refers to what one should do for others; law is the lower limit of human conduct and ethics is the upper limit. Ethical behavior presupposes lawful conduct, but the reverse does not hold.

In a world where all of the economic participants behave ethically, consumption equals production (see prior discussion related to Proposition One). In contrast, an environment in which there is substantial unlawful behavior, there is a need for society to expend resources to preserve social order and prevent anarchy. A society that is in a state of anarchy will either develop an order that is based on power or it will eventually disappear. An ethical society which encourages economic cooperation, other things being equal, should outperform a society which is not ethical and encourages only unconstrained competition, with its concomitant costs.

An additional benefit to be enjoyed by a society whose

members behave in an ethical manner should be a decrease in the fears and concerns of its members. This conjecture is inferred from the <u>otherness</u> property of the concept of ethics. Competition in the economic sphere contributes to the efficiency and effectiveness of the economy. Competition also produces two negative effects. It is a winnowing process, so that at any given point in time there are individuals that are excepted from the economy. Therefore, it is reasonable for any individual to fear this prospect. This concern may manifest itself in egocentric behavior which may involve illegality or overprotection--either through hoarding or purchase of insurance. This state of affairs can be formalized as: $D(I,Pr) = I(P,U) = P(I,Pr) + U(H,N)$, where U = undesirable behavior, H = hoarding and N = insurance. It becomes obvious that a portion of society's productive possibilities is dedicated to the reduction of negatives. To the extent that resources are so consumed, society is sub-optimal. Ethical behavior mitigates the need for such expenditures.

The amount of resources society should devote to promoting ethical behavior should be less than $U(H,N)$. It is assumed that expenditures on the promotion of ethics, over time, will reduce undesirable behavior and its associated costs, such as, excess insurance, litigation, and criminal justice.

CHAPTER 5

The Methodology of Measuring Systems

We have discussed why we wish to measure—to evaluate the goal of achieving the optimal allocation of societal resources. In order to measure, however, it is necessary to understand the nature of measuring systems. The first part of this chapter deals with the nature of measuring, reporting, and control systems. The behavioral implications of such measuring systems are then discussed. Once the nature and roles of measuring systems are understood, the what to be measured can be determined. A brief review follows of how rules of measurement have been applied in the physical and social sciences, and to a subset, human services and economics, as to the *whats* to be measured. A reporting mechanism is needed. A reporting system that incorporates principles, techniques, and the rules of measurement as a feedback of actual to goals is called accounting. The approach to accounting is discussed in the final section of this chapter relative to the views of leading accountants concerning aspects of this question.

ESSENTIAL ELEMENTS OF MEASURING THEORY AND PRACTICE

According to the precepts of measurement and information theory, all measurement plans must contain the following elements: (1) a goal or theory around which the system will be built; (2) the set of properties or attributes (or surrogate, substitute, or equivalent attributes) by which the system will be evaluated; (3) the numerical scales (metrics) by which these properties will be represented (pounds, feet, dollars, etc.), that is, the unit of accounting; (4) the potential of periodic reporting to concerned parties (stakeholders); (5) the choice of metric and numeric scales for attributes, which can be converted and aggregated for feedback reporting using common data, that is, an integrated management information system; and (6) other factors, such as relevance and comprehensibility to users, cost of the system, and auditability of basic data.

Goals and Objectives

In broad terms, it may be said that a measuring system is enterprise-goal dependent. Ultimately, the intent is that all data are collected with respect to the goal and that such measures provide insights into the means of achieving and directing behavior toward that goal. The system's goal and the overall mission of an organization should be congruent. The organization must hone its mission so that the metrics selected for performance valuation are specific. As discussed below, the criteria used to determine product or services program effectiveness or efficiency can have profound effects on the organization's direction and motivation with respect to staff and management functioning and its policy and planning procedures.

Attributes

The set of properties or characteristics by which the system will be evaluated must, at the very least, be understandable to its users, allow for comparability in reporting both intra- and interorganizationally, and be relevant to the situations and contexts to which it will be applied. Direct measures of an attribute usually must have the potential of convertibility into a common metric so as to be denominated in monetary units. This is a common occurrence in accounting, going from attribute units to monetary units, for example, conversion of units of inventory into units of monetary value.

Metrics

The choice of metric may be less clear. However, the principles of mathematics provide some guidelines. Essentially, there would seem to be four basic options from which to choose: Measuring units may be nominal, ordinal, cardinal or ratio. Of these four, the nominal level is the "lowest" in the topology. Rather than providing quantitative data, its units are simply labels just as a name or address is a label. Clearly, these nominal values offer no basis for relative coding. Although job training programs can be compared according to size, client numbers, or funding levels, their addresses offer little as a comparative base.

Ordinal scales, on the other hand, do reflect some ordering patterns. For example, clerical, supervisory, and managerial classifications could be thought of as examples of an ordinal measure of job responsibility or skill. Each value has a position higher or lower than other values, and each of these relationships is transitive; however, with this system one cannot know how much higher one value is than another.

In addition to the properties of the ordinal system, the cardinal contains the property of scale. The latter imbues the cardinal system with the capacity to precisely represent distance. Therefore, rankings are always understandable. Two is always greater than one; four is always greater than three. With the inclusion of a ratio scale and of absolute zero, the cardinal system incorporates and establishes standard units of distance and proportional units of magnitude. The cardinal system permits the mathematical operations of addition, subtraction, division and multiplication. The ratio system provides a unit of relational magnitude between cardinal numbers: two is always twice as great as one; just as the ratio of fifteen to three is always five.

Periodic Reporting and System Circularity

It is essential that any organizational measuring system be capable of quantifying and making comparable the units of input and the units of output and outcomes at any given time in the organization's cycle of operations. Whenever such comparability is achieved, the system can be said to be circular. All organic systems, in contrast to mechanical systems, have cyclic features. Put in somewhat different terms, all organic systems have as part of their makeup major cycles of which they are a part. Examples of circular systems include the metabolic processes of humans and animals or the processes of rainfall as water vapor is turned to rain and back to water vapor once more. This universal property is also present in economic systems and in profit- and nonprofit-oriented organizations. Common characteristics of organic behavior abound. After determination of market in the PS or mission in the NPS, each organization must function to produce a product or render a service to a market in the most efficient manner possible. System requirements adapt from functional behavior.

The needs for measuring efficiency and effectiveness require the ability of the system to report on a periodic basis. The element of periodic reporting is a criterion that is most applicable to those organizations whose process cycles are longer than the accounting or reporting cycles. This is an obvious problem for organizations where the reporting cycle is shorter than the operating cycle, for example, wine growing and shipbuilding. As reporting periods grow shorter, this problem applies to any organization that reports during as opposed to at the close of its operating cycle. In that event, measures are required before cycle time has been completed; thus the measuring system must provide some mechanism for periodic estimates within the operating cycle. Therefore, a system should provide insight about its internal flows including the phases through which outputs become outcomes. Values must be attached to each of these transitional stages, expressing the interim state of affairs in terms comparable or convertible to those of the final output and/or outcome.

Management Information System

This last discussion of periodic reporting highlights the fact that the MIS must be more than the sum of techniques for reporting external measures of effectiveness. The MIS is also a tool for enhancing the insight and understanding of internal operations for decision making and control. An MIS must be developed using common data bases that have the characteristics of availability, convertibility to a money or other base, aggregatability (and disaggregatability), and reporting. Traditionally, the MIS of the profit sector has been said to play three roles, first as a scorekeeper; second, as an attention getter; and third, a problem solver. Within this context, the MIS should be capable of providing data for decision making, planning, and evaluation. Here the critical questions are, is this system fulfilling its function and can the system be improved? To allow this insight into the internal operations of any organization, the MIS must be capable of producing and manipulating disaggregated information. Perhaps the best example of a system that can deal effectively with both aggregated and disaggregated information is based on accounting for costs in the PS. Whenever feasible, current accounting requires both identifiable and standard product costs. The latter are based upon the premise that each function, product, or service can be divided into and examined on the basis of its component parts. To each of these functions and parts is attributed certain standards that incorporate quantity, quality, capacity, and cost variables. Each is also associated with three dimensions, output, projected or standard cost, and actual cost. When all of these features are incorporated, not only are the external reporting systems supported but also management is provided with a flexible and surprisingly strong tool for projecting costs and assessing the nature of the variances, or variations of actual from standard.

A final application of this aggregatable system would be to support and encourage communication among hierarchical layers of management. While all interested parties may ultimately be working toward the same goal, the evaluation process for program services measured and reported on at each cost center may differ from the criteria used by supervisory or executive management. In most organizations, the criteria and the orientation become broader as one works up the organizational ladder. To be effective, then, the system must ensure that senior management does not become so burdened with detail that it loses sight of the overall picture. Conversely, the supervisor must not be fed such generalities that he or she has no data to effect specific operations. However, while providing each level with its own situation-dependent information, the optimal MIS should also allow all layers of management to recognize their interdependence. Thus the needs for coherence in the totality must be recognized and each subsystem should be part and parcel of the pattern.

Relevance and Other Elements

The relevance of the metric is a function of the system's goals. The establishment of a relevant measuring system may require trade-offs that balance the factors of relevance, materiality, timeliness, and costs. Relative to financial accounting reports, information theory in fact shows that the more objective the accounting data, that is the more they are verifiable, the less their informative content; and the more subjective the data, the greater their informativeness.[1] The issue is to develop criteria and standards that balance the requirements for objectivity with the needs of the users for information. The system must also be verifiable with feedback loops that prove the units to the aggregates.

THE ROLES AND IMPLICATIONS OF MEASURING SYSTEMS

Measurement and evaluation systems have been used by societies for thousands of years. Developed initially to count and codify, these systems have evolved over time to assume an increasing role not only in business control but also more generally in the allocation of society's resources. Their existence has brought greater understanding of our resources, our wants, our potential, and our future. Their evolution has created new techniques for advanced planning, control, and decision making. The developments in measuring techniques are part and parcel of a general societal progression toward the optimal. Measuring systems are becoming more logical, more sophisticated, and better tools. From this perspective, measurement technique is necessarily embedded in the realm of the technical, and its practice is perceived as a neutral, calculative technique useful for the expression of an existing reality and for the apolitical distribution of resources according to needs/wants.

However, the vision of the measurement system as a neutral device is not one that is generally accepted today. For decades, in both the PS and NPS, measurement systems have been seen to have a profound effect on the behavioral patterns of stakeholders. To the extent that these systems are linked to reward or allocation systems, they can influence the behavior of staff and managers, who "choose" decisions that they believe will show maximum results according to the system of measurement that is in place.

In the discussion that follows, we assume that working individuals generally react to economic incentives. Further, we assume that profit is a key measure of management performance. We recognize the potential limitations of systems of reward from the experiences of the PS. Poorly constructed incentives can skew behavior toward inappropriate goals and can create imbalances among groups; moreover, profit as a single measure may be unrelated to direct efforts and contributions of specific staff members or groups. Since this is a book about HSOs, we confine the discussion to observations in this field.

The implication of this behavioral function is that the criteria used to allocate resources make an implicit statement about the goals of the program and the position the agency is to play in meeting societal needs.[2] To the extent that these implied goals are not in accord with the actual mission of the organization, service patterns can become skewed. In effect, performance criteria can become substitutes for the mission, directing staff, for example, to become less concerned with client outcomes than with closing the greatest number of cases. The optimal system must incorporate some goal. The reason is not only to provide the framework for assessment but also to provide the motivating force that directs the organizational participants toward the achievement of goals.

Human behavior is not aimless or purposeless but is motivated by and derived from the desire to meet some specific goal or to serve some need. In some cases, stakeholders may be directed by these criteria subconsciously, with no real awareness of the limitations they impose. However, in other cases, the noncongruence between formal performance criteria and the inherent motivations of staff are obvious. In these cases, staff may become frustrated as their inclinations toward service may be thwarted or discouraged. The tension that results may be a primary cause for what has been seen as an antimanagement bias among HSO staff. Middleton writes that "practitioners associate 'management' with corporate and bureaucratic forms, where, they believe, structural layers and procedures separate organization members from the values, clients, and sense of mission that are important elements of a nonprofit culture."[3] It appears that while organizations may need more quantitative methods and measures of performances to participate in society's allocative rounds, they must also be wary of selecting criteria that would reshape or redefine the reality of the organization's mission. To be effective, the selected measurement system must first support the organization's primary mission. And, when internalized by staff, the system must be conducive to the attitudes and motivation necessary for quality performance.[4]

While the behavioral implications have been generally accepted, a more controversial perspective of measuring systems has emerged that affects their functioning within the social and political domains as well. Realistically, measurement systems can be seen as social phenomena. They are communications systems whose development is less a progression in the technical sphere than an evolution in the social sphere. They are driven in part by developments in managerial techniques and in part by changes in social definitions of value. When defined in this way, accounting and measurement systems have implications beyond measurement and motivation. They can serve as proactive devices that, while interacting with the social, and by virtue of their association with the rational, can promote legitimacy, enhance communication, and advance the cause and position of those who manipulate them. A good example of the social conditioning of measuring systems is a recent study of the use of budgetary symbols by a state university. Management may significantly change the results of economic debate by modifying or adopting the language of the discourse. It appears that "as organization members articulate and promote their interests, they must express themselves in terms their external constituents can understand and value to present themselves advantageously."[5]

What is important to note from this last discussion is the common denominator of most measurement systems, their power to affect the development and direction of the organization. Measurements are not derived in isolation but are in part determined by who is asking the question and to whom accountability is owed.[6] Understandability, relevance, aggregatability, and periodic reportings are all essential criteria in the development of a measuring system, as is the ability to inform, motivate, and reward stakeholders who are the critical elements for the optimal functioning of any organization. Finally, the influence of goal direction on the behavior of stakeholders may be the principal function of measuring systems. Given the measuring system, the actions of stakeholders can be predicted.

MEASUREMENT METHODOLOGY IN THE PHYSICAL AND SOCIAL SCIENCES

The goal of some scientists to emulate and embody the same methodology as that of the physical sciences may not be possible. The physical sciences present functional relationships on a quantitative basis; the social sciences present correlative relationships on a quantitative basis. In effect, the quality variables can be kept constant for the physical sciences *in ceteris paribus* so that such functional relationships can be precisely measured. Only with macro phenomena can physical science deal with certainty. With micro phenomena in the physical sciences or for macro and micro in the social sciences, one can only deal in probability distributions. Thus, the social sciences can emulate the physical sciences in the specificity of their hypotheses, care in experimental design, objectivity (i.e., playing by the rules), and in recognizing the significance of controls, sampling, and statistical power. Both have in common the requirements of the imagination, patience, and persistence of the investigator.

There are needed methods of thinking based on specified rules to understand and to communicate the results of functioning of any system. Ideally, the system should have predictive powers and explanatory powers in terms of both axioms and hypotheses of the system's framework. Most systems are developed from observed phenomena. Preliminary associations of such observations can produce first principles, or hypotheses, the inductive element. These hypotheses are then tested and reconfirmed by the expected experimental outcomes, the deductive element. Continual successful outcomes strengthen the preliminary hypotheses, which can then result in theory formation. Despite wide latitude in application, the scientific method is one of spirit as well as practice. Such factors as hunch, luck, patience, and subjectivity can combine to produce a preliminary hypothesis and hoped-for results. However, rules to guess by, measure by, and report by must be disciplined.

The social sciences have attempted to emulate the scientific method as used by the physical sciences oftentimes without recognizing some essential differences in methodology. Physical sciences historically have indirectly confirmed their axioms by the logical consequences of experimental results or outcomes. Approaches to understanding the element *radium*, or the color *blue*, would be based upon theoretical constructs as to the nature of their elements and then, by "epistemic correlation," affirming or strengthening the basic concept from outcomes of controlled experiments.[7] On the other hand, the social sciences, including the evaluation of intervention in the field of human services, have to rely upon correlations in their experimentation, raising questions as to the effect of the observer on the observed and the difficulty of controlling for other variables in *ceteris paribus*.

During the past 150 years, within the generally accepted framework of economics, there have been attempts to incorporate basic conceptual units and explain the behavior of the firm and the individual consumer. In utility theory, unquantifiable utilities of wants have become part of the framework to explain the behavior of individuals in their use of resources. The human service field struggles with its efforts at measurement intervention for its justification in the absence of an integrated framework or specific societal goals. On the other hand, there appears to be a division in accounting ranks relative to the possibility and even the advisability of achieving a general framework under which applications can be deduced and where accounting concepts could be applied to various sectors of the society.

The differences in emphasis become manifest in the public image of these disciplines as to the performance of their practitioners—the impractical theoretician (economist), the well-meaning do-gooder (human service worker), the narrow-minded bookkeeper (accountant), and the opportunist (politician). The accountants track funds, trained for micro objectives and specific money metric measurement concepts; the economists emphasize theoretical designs with little apparent relevance to reality; the human service practitioners, often disinterested in the economics of their services, concentrate on the individual client within the subjective world of "help"; while the politicians resort to value systems of freedom, justice, brotherhood, and other "oughts," avoiding a definitive viewpoint.

Economics and Human Services

Economics. Historically, the field of economics has been devoted to the general problem of an optimal allocation of resources. Problems of efficiency and equity have directed economic thought in discussions of value of goods in use and exchange, and in the role of the pricing mechanism and markets for the distribution of resources. From Adam Smith onward, questions have been approached relative to the optimal method of performing society's work based upon individuals' decisions. The optimal efficiency and effectiveness in the allocation of societal resources have shifted largely to the micro questions of decision making by the individual firm and to individual utility.

In their approach to the question of economic behavior, economists have reached out to the fields of philosophy, political science, and particularly to psychology for underlying tenets to explain and quantify human behavior in economic decisions, such as utility theory. The science of economics, even 200 years after Adam Smith, still lacks a degree of completion. To its credit, the field of economics attempts to include, at least conceptually, the effect of externalities, social costs and benefits, as well as interest on capital as components of profit—which have largely been ignored in the field of accounting. There have also been historical shifts in emphasis between needs and wants. Historically, needs were attended to by the NPS and wants by the PS. (Needs are defined in terms of survival criteria and are closed-ended. Wants are defined in terms of satisfaction and are open-ended.) The fulfilling of basic economic needs for certain segments of society raised questions as to sources of support, such as societal or individual transfer payments. Wants were satisfied automatically by the effective workings of the market system.

Human Services. In chapter 7, we review the many attempts to find ways to measure and evaluate the economic benefit/effectiveness of social programs. It is clear that researchers and practitioners alike working in the field of human services as well as in welfare economics and accounting recognize the need for such a measure. However, for the most part, the problem has been approached from the perspective of the individual firm, program, and/or discipline. There is no conceptual framework that integrates the relationship of current social programs to the history and culture from which they emerged, to their primary mission, and to the concept of human capital as a vital resource to the economy of our society. The lack of a framework has caused difficulty in finding such a measure, one that could serve as an attribute and provide a common, readily understood indicator of effectiveness and efficiency for HSOs.

With the increased use of statistics and mathematics in the social sciences and with the influence of the paradigm from the methodology of the physical sciences, there have been continual attempts to measure the effects of intervention on social problems. Authors such as Rostker and Ramanathan have worked on methods for program evaluation by cost-benefit analysis within the development of a model framework.[8] As will be reviewed in chapter 7, their work has been useful in the development of macro approaches.

On the micro level, an in-depth review of program evaluation by Lipsey et al., characterizes the problems inherent in their design and results. From a "representative sample of studies," they conclude that "weak designs, low statistical power, ad hoc measurement, and neglect of treatment implementation and program theory characterize the state of the art in program evaluation." They point out that "program evaluation research today is based on the experimental paradigm, that is quantitative measurement of dependent variables with controlled designs to establish cause-and-effect relationships." Their representative sampling from the literature raises questions about the basic methods in use, the difficulties involved in their application, and the discipline required by the researcher. It is also apparent that measurement criteria must be selected in advance since it is manifestly improper procedurally and impossible quantitatively to collect data ex post to prove ex ante theory. Many of the studies that were reviewed did use "multiple dependent measures"; very few, however, "provide a multi-variate analysis." The authors conclude that "despite its current widespread use, the experimental paradigm is not an all-purpose program evaluation methodology." However, "this is not another polemic against use of the experimental paradigm in program evaluation nor a justification for some allegedly all-purpose alternate approach." Alternatives are mentioned to gain "insight and understanding of social programs" by "studying program process, case flow, service delivery, and so forth in a program monitoring or information system mode."[9]

The experiences of Lipsey have been confirmed by the GAO in its efforts at evaluation, which have been frustrated by numerous methodological problems: inappropriate initial design, deficiencies in experimental applications, inadequate data, questionable inferences and conclusions from the quantified results, and so on. Even with acceptable measurement outcomes for individual programs, there has been little or no basis of comparison and none for the aggregating of results because of the lack of common measurement denominators. These efforts of the GAO are further described in chapter 7.

While some researchers warn about the lack of understanding about science in the field of human services and the requirements of presenting verifiable data, there appears to be a movement toward the significant modification of the experimental paradigm and the development of some alternative approach to obtain pragmatic answers to programmatic questions. The search for an appropriate paradigm is exemplified by Zimmerman, who claims that there is a "misinterpretation of the contemporary scientific view of the nature of cause and effect" and wishes to "replace strict determinism in explaining causation, and discuss their implication for . . . research methodology and practice logic in social work." He recognizes probability distributions as part of prediction. He apparently differentiates between correlations and functional relations, pointing out that "there would be no presumption of causality, and generalization in its usual sense would not be required but temporary veracity [would] be accepted."[10] While he realizes that Heisenberg was referring to the molecular level, his critique about the "most recent formulation of science" misses the point that both random variation and conventional causality are needed.[11]

Measurement and Accounting

Accounting or measurement is an activity that is a necessary element in the functioning of any social system; it is in fact the counterpart to a feedback mechanism in a mechanical or electrical system—to measure the accomplishment of societal goals. Feedback and system behavior are mirror images of each other. A well-designed feedback system forces the system to behave in the desired manner. In the sphere of financial accounting, the ongoing debate has been between those who have claimed that accounting should be a positive (empirical) measurement system and those who have argued for a normative (conceptual) approach. A moment's reflection on this debate would disclose that the attributes chosen for measurement in the positive accounting system have to have been chosen normatively. Similarly, on the normative side of the argument, the attributes that are deemed preferable must also be susceptible to measurement.

Current accounting methodology contains elements of the positive and the normative. The basic normative principle underlying PS accounting is that of private property from which flows the fundamental accounting relationship of assets minus liabilities equals net worth. Concepts of private property are embodied in the Constitution of the United States and in the Declaration of Independence. The rights of the individual and the firm in the PS are based on the protection of the individual's liberty, which includes property right, the right to conserve, consume, invest, and protect one's assets. The ability to make choices is an unstated axiom to the models and underlies our societal institutions.

Economic decision making entails, in the words of Sorter, Ingberman, and Maximon, "predicting the amount, timing, and uncertainty of sacrifices and benefits resulting from a contemplated action and comparing them to the amount, timing, and uncertainty of sacrifices and benefits associated with alternating actions."[12] The difference between sacrifices and benefits that has taken place in a given period is defined as income. They define sacrifices and benefits in terms of cash flows, the emphasis of current accounting. Another approach is that of Kaldor's definition of social income as "the value of consumption plus the *values of the increase* in the stock of goods in existence." He goes on to say, "the change in the quantity of social capital, between any two dates, could in principle be measured by taking an inventory of goods at each of the two dates and valuing the different kinds of goods at end, at the same set of prices."[13] Setting aside the problems of measurement of goods and money, Sorter's approach should induce a set of actions from management that lead to the accumulation of money, whereas Kaldor's should cause the accumulation of goods.

Another factor that seems to follow for a societywide accounting is that it should have an aggregation property, that is, the sum of the parts should be equal to the whole. The current systems of accounting do not possess this characteristic; the sum of all of the individual income statements does not represent society's income for the period. For one thing, there is not a universal predicate underlying all of the individual financing statements; for example, the private sector accounts for its activity on the basis of sacrifices and benefits in terms of money, whereas the public sector accounts for it based on the receipt and disbursement of cash. The model developed in this book contributes to resolving the accounting and economic problems that have been raised as a result of Arrow's work.[14]

Accounting has been defined as a system that produces and communicates information that is useful in reaching economic decisions. Therefore, the problem is also one of meaningful reporting. The NPS with its cash report gives the appearance of objectivity but with less meaning; the PS reporting can be meaningful but subject to the vagaries of accounting interpretations that include judgment in the handling of similar transactions.[15]

The description of the measurement system that follows incorporates our societal institutions' goals and their implicit axioms.[16] The Lighthouse and General Motors should both base their accounting to reflect how their use of societal resources has helped societal members. Current economic methodology and its related accounting are based on axioms and propositions relative to the PS. The micro behavioral axioms of the firm and the consumer incorporate and reflect the implicit macro societal goals of the PS.

Discussion of Current State of Accounting. As stated above, the goal of current accounting is to measure economic events during and at the beginning and conclusion of a specified period in terms of money. Measurement principles and techniques for applications have been developed—from international and national macro accounts to the operations of a single organization or an individual household. Because of its widespread usage and apparent success, accounting in the PS has often been viewed as a potential model to be applied to the NPS. With direct or implicit relevance for the NPS, four distinguished members of the accounting profession have written articles that reveal current attitudes and underlying differences in applying basic questions to accounting practice.

Anthony emphasizes that accounting needs a focus that includes "definitions of key terms, the concepts of measurement and recognition, and the criteria for applying the concepts to standard and individual transactions. . . . The purpose of a concepts statement is to assess what financial reporting should be, not to describe what current practices are." He points to the historic change of focus from stewardship, and accordingly the balance sheet, to the performance of the enterprise in terms of its earnings, and accordingly the income statement. He emphasizes the need of a single attribute, since "accounting is a measurement system that uses the arithmetic operations of addition and subtraction," and therefore numbers must "have the same attribute." For usefulness to the decision maker, relevance, reliability, and their relationship to materiality are key factors in reporting. He also admits that the basic difference between his proposals and present practice is calculating the cost of capital supplied by shareholders. He concludes that "financial accounting desperately needs an authoritative conceptual framework. Without it, standard setters will continue to approach each issue on an ad hoc basis and argue from their own premises and concepts, which are not made explicit."[17]

On the opposite side, Gerboth assails the approach of a conceptual framework and emphasizes in its place the importance of professional values. He disagrees with the historical approaches of the Financial Accounting Standards Board (FASB) to conceptual issues such as the role of definitions, questions the nature and objectivity of science, and emphasizes the role of subjectivity in scientific understanding. He then discusses the essence of professionalism and concludes that "personal responsibility for the decisions forces a diligent search for the best obtainable approximation of 'accounting truth.' " Without the term, accounting truth, being specifically defined, he argues that "the key to accounting objectivity . . . [lies] in the integrity and personal responsibility of those who practice accounting." Accordingly, accounting "must take its directions not from its concepts, but from its values; it must find its security not in its intellectual structure, but in its professional conduct"; in effect in "the behavior of accountants."[18]

Another of the profession's distinguished members suggests that not-for-profits require different accounting standards from those of profits, stating, "We have tried to extend the accounting for one to the other without adequate analysis of similarities and dissimilarities.'' The bulk of the article questions the accounting treatment of buildings and other facilities owned by nonprofit organizations, which are classified as assets. In his opinion, such labeled assets contain significant elements of liabilities relative to their future use. Such service facilities do not produce income; rather they cause cash outflows. Anticipated costs of their operation and sources of funding should be projected in financial reports, since a nonprofit organization "provides services . . . [without] any expectations of recovering the full cost . . . [of the facilities and] of these services from the people that receive them.'' In this sense, they differ from facilities in the private sector, where such costs in theory are recovered in pricing to customers. His comments about the "confusing complexities of fund financial reporting" probably would be accepted by most practitioners. He also recommends a statement of receipts and expenditures to answer the question of mission realization "to show how the amounts spent furthered the purposes of the organization.''[19]

Briloff, a perennial gadfly and critic of the auditing establishment, recites the history of the "covenant," defined by him as the license given by society to certified public accountants (CPAs) for objective certification of financial statements that communicate the actions of management to creditors, stockholders, and the investing public. He points out that our complex society has evolved to the blending of the requirements of accountability by the private sector to the public sector relative to medical care and housing, and the reverse, "the private sector accountability blends inexorably into the public sector. For example, the banking, savings and loan, agricultural industries.'' The article concentrates on the failures of the auditing profession, also assigning various degrees of blame to the FASB, the Securities and Exchange Commission, and academe for the debacle of the savings and loan industry, HUD's corruption, and the merger and acquisition orgy. Directly and implicitly, his accusation of "accounting gimmickry" relates to the accounting framework. The creation of goodwill, "cost incurred on the acquisitions [are] buried in an amorphous, inchoate intangible quagmire''; the current emphasis on cash flow; accounting for research and development as period expenses; the substitution of tax-deductible debt for profit: these methods of accountability used by corporate enterprises "materially impact our society.'' After detailing two specific illustrations involving corporations that experienced a significant drop in market values, he comes to the heart of the problem: "In each instance the accounting could be fully rationalized by GAAP . . . form was given precedence over substance.'' In addition to the return to the "covenant" and to "professionalization,'' he states, "we already have a surfeit of accounting principles and concepts to accommodate our financial reporting, responsibilities it is now, for the accounting firms and academic institutions to determine which of the precepts should be implemented and under what circumstances.'' He also suggests that "the selection of the appropriate GAAP alternatives" should be the direct responsibility of the auditor and not of management.[20]

There can be no doubt that even with its limitations, there exist authoritative concepts of financial reporting even though the profession has not propounded one specifically authorized framework as called for by Anthony. From the pronouncements of the American Institute of Certified Public Accountants (AICPA) and the FASB, the Government Accounting Standards Board (GASB) and their predecessors (even with their qualified statements of application) from the SEC professional and academic journals and textbooks, generally accepted sets of rules currently cover the actions of accounting professionals. For a list of some of these pronouncements from the AICPA and the FASB as they relate to the NPS, see Exhibit 5.1. The International Accounting Standards Committee's proposed framework states that measuring of economic performance for a period is the primary objective of financial statements for its users. The framework includes definitions of assets, liabilities, and equity; principles of income recognition; balance sheet presentation; effects of relevance, reliability, and materiality; differentiating between substance versus form and between usual and nonrecurring events, and so on.[21] Tens of thousands of financial statements are prepared; it is doubtful if our modern society could function without authoritative accounting concepts and rules.

Anthony, however, is correct in his assertions. If GAAP cannot be applied equally to all types of organizations, profits and nonprofits, if all economic events that have occurred during the period as a result of the operations of an organization are not reflected on a consistent basis in the measurement reporting for that organization, if there are significant variations in the reporting of comparable events—then indeed the framework may require amendment, expansion, or replacement. Anthony is one of the few authors who discusses "nonprofit elements" and recognizes the advantages to be obtained in having a "conceptual framework for accounting that applies to both types of organizations"—as was proposed in FASB Concept Statement No. 3. By adopting the same accounting system for the PS and NPS, we should be able to develop a single measure of the effectiveness of the nonprofit entity defined in economic terms. This measure should also be able to summarize "the performance and status of an entity as a consequence of events that have occurred during an accounting period." It may be no more perfect than it is for the PS, but it should offer a readily understood measure that is appropriately relevant and reliable. It should offer stakeholders ranging from consumers to boards of directors and funding sources the basis for asking appropriate questions.[22]

Gerboth is also partially correct to the extent that professional training and professional judgment are required in the applications of principles and pronouncements to particular problems of presentation and reporting within the current framework. In practice, however, there may be too many choices from which the professional accountant can select unless there is an implicit or explicit framework. Moreover, the concept of income includes the probability of future economic benefits reliably measured. The professional must assess the degree of uncertainty based on available evidence, considering relevance to users and

Exhibit 5.1
Some AICPA and FASB Pronouncements Relative to the Nonprofit Sector

Issuer	Description	Date	Title
AICPA	Audit Guide	1973	Audits of Colleges and Universities
AICPA	Audit Guide	1974	Audits of State and Local Governmental Units
AICPA	Audit and Accounting Guide	1990	Audit and Accounting Guide: Audits of Providers of Health Care Services. (Replaced Hospital Audit Guide, 1972)
AICPA	SOP 78-10	1978	Accounting Principles and Reporting Practices for Certain Nonprofit Organizations
FASB	Statement No. 32	1979	Specialized Accounting and Reporting Principles and Practices in AICPA Statements of Position and Guides on Accounting and Auditing Matters[1]
FASB	Concept Statement No. 1	1978	Objectives of Reporting for Business Enterprises
FASB	Concept Statement No. 2	1980	Qualitative Characteristics of Accounting Information
FASB	Concept Statement No. 3	1980	Elements of Financial Statements of Business Enterprises
FASB	Concept Statement No. 4	1980	Objectives of Financial Reporting by Nonbusiness Organizations[2]
FASB	Concept Statement No. 5	1984	Recognition and Measurement in Financial Statements of Business Enterprises
FASB	Concept Statement No. 6	1985	Elements of Financial Statements[3]
FASB	FASB No. 93	1987	Recognition of Depreciation for Not-for-Profit Organizations[4]
AICPA	Task force	1988	Implications FASB #6 on Financial Statement Presentation
FASB	ED	1989	Financial Reporting by Not-for-Profit Organizations: Form and Content of Financial Statements
FASB	ED	1990	Accounting for Contributions Received and Contributions Made and Capitalization of Works of Art, Historical Treasures, and Similar Assets

[1] After comments by SEC, FASB undertook responsibility for all specialized accounting and reporting principles and practices in AICPA guides and statements of position.

[2] Expansion of No. 1 to incorporate objectives of not-for-profit organizations.

[3] Incorporates No. 2, extends elements of No. 3, and defines concepts relating to not-for-profit organizations.

[4] Depreciation optional for works of art and historical treasures.

reliability of information; there is also a threshold as to the effect of materiality relative to relevance and reliability. Every figure appearing on a financial statement includes a component of subjectivity—a reflection of the professionalism of the preparer. In fact, as already noted, the financial statements for the past are encoded with implications for the future, the greater their subjectivity, the more their usefulness. While recognizing the need for professionalism, Gerboth sees no use in further efforts to develop the framework.

There appears to be an element of circularity in Gerboth's argument of applying accounting "truth" and professionalism to an incomplete or implicit framework. The purpose of the framework is to provide concepts from which specific standards can be developed. The failure to develop such consistent standards allows different reporting of the same economic events and leaves a vacuum in the reporting of such events not covered by specific standards.

Briloff generally is correct in some of his assertions about failures within the auditing profession. However, he also does not come to grips with the fundamental question of a framework. Intellectually he is in agreement with Gerboth in terms of the requirements of professionalism and "truthful" accounting. He also misses basic problems inherent in the current auditing dilemma: (1) that financial statements under GAAP, with their emphasis on future cash flows, are projections of the future more than statements of the past; and (2) that statistical methodology used under GAAS is not primarily designed to uncover irregularities.

The four articles by Anthony, Gerboth, Mautz, and Briloff have in common their failure to recognize the impossibility of presenting a statement of income for the NPS without an appropriate concept of revenue generated. As representatives of a profession, they have failed to link the problem to a specific conceptual framework for all or part of the NPS. Anthony recognizes the need for consistent concepts and definitions applicable to both sectors, and presents an approach for the development of a framework on which standards would be built. He presents nary a hint, however, of how a statement of income could be created for the NPS. Mautz believes that a statement of receipts and disbursements can be presented for nonprofit organizations to reflect the degree of their realization of mission; he does not show how criteria for mission realization can be presented in a statement of cash receipts and disbursements—with or without accruals, and even after eliminating the confusing effects of fund transfers, restrictions, and so on. Gerboth never addresses the question of the NPS; he is avowedly against further methodological discussions of principles, concepts, and theoretical models.[23] Briloff would argue for the integrity of the auditor in his covenant relationship to society; he too fails to address the problem of a framework.

It should be recognized that in spite of these critiques, the existence of an authoritative framework for accounting is generally assumed by practitioners to exist. In addition to the usual references, comments, and discussions relative to concepts and standards, there has recently been promulgated a list of authoritative accounting literature, ranked by level of authority.[24]

SUMMARY

Measuring systems are the outcomes and embodiment of the methodological principles of classifying, summarizing, and reporting. They can function only within the context of stated theories and/or goals, when given a meaning. To be meaningful, the characteristics of measurement must be translated into units of attribute, which should be defined in terms of the goals and results to be achieved. An appropriate metric can allow measurements within and among systems and organizations. These together with other essential elements of a measuring system have been analyzed. Measuring systems inform stakeholders about organizations and can have significant implications for their behavior. The evaluation of management's functioning requires a means of measurement. For this purpose, an integrated system is required based on standard units with common data bases, with the potential of convertibility and aggregatability for internal and external reporting to hierarchical levels of stakeholders.

The methodology of measurement has been examined for an understanding of its application to the fields of human services, economics, and accounting. HSOs lack a framework within which to measure income based on a set of specified goals measured by a common attribute translatable into money, as in the PS. The field of professional accounting has failed to develop a conceptual framework that can be applied to HSOs. An analysis of accounting principles demonstrates that the key to creating the missing statement of income for this segment of the NPS is to define earned revenue consistent with GAAP; this is accomplished in the model and its accounting system as presented in chapter 2.

The cause of the previously described inadequacies in the present accounting framework is the absence of a unifying principle, one set of principles on which to base an accounting system that is general enough to account for all of society's economic activity as it relates to individual members. The resolution of this problem is proposed in the subsequent chapter.

NOTES

1. Cherny, Julius. (1983). *Liquidity and financial flexibility measures through a phase space approach to accounting* (Doctoral dissertation) New York University, pp. 81–93.

2. DeCaro, James J., Clarcq, Jack R., Walter, Gerard G., Welsh, William A., & Reilly, Dorothea. (1988, July–September). A methodology for utilizing federal data sources in program evaluation. *Journal of Rehabilitation, 54*(3), 46–50.

3. Middleton, Melissa. (1986, February). *Nonprofit management: A report on current research and areas of development* (Program on Nonprofit Organizations [PONPO], Working Paper No. 108, and Institution for Social and Policy Studies, Working Paper No. 2108). New Haven, CT: Yale University (p. 2).

4. Kanter, Rosabeth Moss. (1979). *The measurement of organizational effectiveness, productivity, performance and success.* (PONPO Working Paper No. 8), Institution for social and policy studies). New Haven, CT: Yale University (p. 3).

5. Covalski, Mark A., & Dirsmith, Mark W. (1988). The use of budgetary symbols in the political arena: An historically informed field study. *Accounting, Organizations and Society, 13*(1), 1–24. Great Britain: Pergamon Journals Ltd.

6. Kanter, *Measurement of organizational effectiveness*, 36.

7. Northrup, F.S.C. (1983). *The logic of the sciences and the humanities* (reprint). Woodbridge, CT: Oxbow Press (original work published 1947) (p. 119).

8. Rostker, Bernard. (1975). *An evaluation-management information system for vocational rehabilitation*. The Rand Corporation, Santa Monica, CA; and Ramanathan, Kavasseri V. (1985, Summer). A proposed framework for designing management control systems in not-for-profit organizations. (Publication No. 0267–4424). *Financial Accountability and Management, 1*(1), 75–92.

9. Lipsey, et al. detail the key aspects of program evaluation, which include design, that is, proper controls to determine causal links, statistical power required for work done in the field (citing its "close relationship to Type II error," the inability "of the researcher to detect an effect"), measurement sensitivity, which includes reliability and validity, and the failure of program theory and treatment implementation to be correlated, that is, treatment and expected changes based upon a conceptual hypothesis or program theory. Lipsey, Mark W., Cross, Scott, Dunkle, Jan, Pollard, John, & Stobart, Gordon. (1985, September). Evaluation: The state of the art and the sorry state of the science. In D. S. Cordray (ed.), *Utilizing prior research in evaluation planning. New directions for program evaluation* (No. 27) 7–28 San Francisco, CA: Jossey-Bass.

10. Zimmerman, Jerome H. (1989, March). Determinism, science and social work. *Social Service Review, 63*(1), 54.

11. Gould, as well as Heisenberg, in a discussion of randomness, was referring to the molecular level. However, "in the domain of organisms and their good designs, we have little reason to doubt the strong, probably dominant influence of deterministic forces like natural selection." Accordingly, Gould concludes that both are needed, random variation and conventional causality. Gould, Stephen Jay, (1989, September). Through a lens, darkly. *Natural History*, p. 16.

12. Sorter, George H., Ingberman, Monroe J., & Maximon, Hillel M. (1990). *Financial accounting: An events and cash flow approach* (p. 5). New York: McGraw-Hill.

13. Kaldor, N. (1986). The concept of income in economic theory. In R. N. Parker, G. C. Harcourt, & G. Whittington (eds.), *Readings in the concept and measurement of income* (p. 126). Oxford: Philip Allan Publishers Limited.

14. Arrow, Kenneth J. (1963). *Social choice and individual values* (p. 59). New Haven, CT: Cowles Foundation for Research in Economics at Yale University.

15. Briloff, Abraham J. (1990). Accountancy and society, a covenant desecrated. *Accountancy and Society, 1, 5–30. Critical Perspectives on Accounting*.

16. For example, assume that the goal of a given society was full employment of human resources regardless of output; a measuring system could then be developed so that the balance sheet would report upon manpower in place at a given time, and the period statement would reflect the amount of manpower used based upon some common attribute of work, such as hours, full-time-equivalent employees, or other.

17. Anthony, Robert N. (1987, May). We don't have the accounting concepts we need. *The CPA Journal, 57*(5), 36–45.

18. Gerboth, Dale L. (1987, September). The conceptual framework: Not definitions, but professional values. *Accounting Horizons, 1*(3), 1–8.

19. Mautz, R. K. (1989, August). Not-for-profit financial reporting: Another view. *Journal of Accountancy, 168*(2), 60–66.

20. Briloff, Accountancy and society, a covenant desecrated, 5–30.

21. Staff. (1988, May) Exposure Draft 32. *Framework for the preparation and presentation of financial statements*. International Accounting Standards Committee; London, England.

22. Anthony, We don't have the accounting concepts we need, 40. In the exchange of views discussed in the subsequent chapter, Anthony appears to take the position that the preparation of a statement of income for a nonprofit organization is not feasible.

23. It is a "mistaken notion that it is possible to avoid, minimize or control debate on basic issues by prior agreement on abstract principles." He argues that the search for definitions should be replaced by "substantive knowledge," investigations of the complex world in which accounting is involved. As "in law and in science, to the extent that objectivity is attained, it is primarily because professionals assure a personal responsibility in attaining it . . . the essence of professionalism—that makes the accountant's decision objective." Gerboth, The conceptual framework, 5–7. However, the circularity of his arguments becomes more apparent when "accounting truth" and professional integrity are applied to create an accounting system for reporting in the NPS. Concepts may be intuitive; proof is based on a framework of rules.

24. Miller, Jeffrey R., Smith, L. Murphy, & Strauser, Robert H. (1990, April). Sources of authoritative accounting literature. In Douglas R. Carmichael (Ed.), Accounting. *CPA Journal, 60*(4), 54–59.

CHAPTER 6

Profit and Nonprofit Accounting—
A Unified Approach

That the PS's and HSOs' accounting systems can be unified is demonstrated in this chapter. A brief analysis of the economic model of the PS, its accounting (measuring) system, and its significance and behavioral implications is first presented. Based on the centrality of the consumer, the economic model of the PS assumes that profit is a measure of individual, firm, and society's well-offness. Then an analysis of the measuring system used by the PS shows that the current accounting system fulfills the requirements of measuring systems as prescribed in chapter 5. Subject to continual criticism, the profit metric nonetheless is the accepted method of measuring, in the PS, its combined economic effectiveness and efficiency.

Two different approaches to accounting in the NPS are then presented. Their unsuccessful attempts should be compared to the proposed accounting system derived from the model. There then follows a discussion of the operating characteristics that are common to the two sectors and an examination of the degree to which their accounting systems can meet the criteria and measurement guidelines presented in chapter 5. Further analysis demonstrates that the accounting systems for the PS and HSOs contain the same goal of optimizing consumer benefits, applying the same measuring methodology, and functioning as organizations in the same manner. Differences between them are surface ones; organizationally, operationally, and financially output and outcome criteria are basically the same.

Now that the model for HSOs fills in the missing links to compute revenues and to complete their funding cycles, the accounting-measuring system for both HSOs and the PS can be unified. With the recognition of the equivalence of missions and outcomes to make profits, it is also apparent that the same system and its techniques can be used to measure efficiency.

THE PROFIT SECTOR

Economic and Accounting Model

Economic Model. In the PS, the satisfaction of consumer preferences, allocation of the firm's and society's resources, and survival of the individual firm (i.e.,
realization of profits) are all postulated based on the effectiveness of the market
pricing systems. According to textbook classical and neoclassical theories of
economics, an unregulated market will, by virtue of supply and demand interac-
tion, evince a natural tendency toward equilibrium in a Parieto-optimal allocative
state (i.e., a state in which no one individual can be made better off without
someone else becoming worse off). When competition exists and when no external influences limit the fluctuation or direction of prices, supply and demand forces
will tend to identify the value of each product and the direction in which returns
to investment will flow.

It is presumed further, in theory at least, that the profit measure automatically
subsumes all indicators for attentiveness to consumer wants, product quality, and
efficiency of production. To the extent that profits represent a quantity of value
created, an increase in the profits of a firm (without the corresponding decrease
in the profits of another firm) should also reflect an increase in the well-offness
not only of the firm but also of society as a whole; that is, by paying for outputs
an amount which is higher than the cost of related inputs, society (i.e., its consumers) has signaled its satisfaction with the goods and quantified the increase
in its overall satisfaction in an amount equal to the profits of the firm. From this
it follows that needs will be answered on a prioritized basis. Since resources are
limited and because firms are driven by the desire to optimize profits and cannot
answer all wants, they respond to wants of the highest economic value. In doing
so, the most responsive firms can earn the optimal profit, providing they utilize
resources in the most efficient manner.

Based on the assumptions contained in this analysis, the case for the profit metric
is made. Quantitative profit measures are assumed to reveal and ensure the optimal distribution of limited resources. The significance of the system is not only
that profits are a representation of the well-offness of the firm but also of the
corresponding well-offness of society. As discussed later in this chapter, the profit
metric also is consonant with the principal conditions and requirements for a
measuring system as set forth in chapter 5.

Financial Accounting in the PS. The financial reporting system measures the
performance of the firm under this economic model. Although the format varies
with the size or nationality of the organization, each set of statements will generally
contain the equivalent of a balance sheet and a statement of income and a statement of fund changes. By recording in quantitative money terms the resources,
activities, and results of operations of the organization, each of these statements
acts as a scorecard and a communications medium. They depict in monetary terms
such facts as the total and kind of resource under the control of the organization,

the total and kind of liabilities that offset these assets, the investments by the shareholders, and the net income for the period and its accumulation. The usefulness of these statements and the reasons why so much attention is devoted to their preparation and review are derived from their ability to report results on a periodic basis, matching within a time frame revenues and the use of resources, based on a set of generally accepted accounting principles (GAAP) and standards and methods of presentation, and audited by professional accountants in accordance with generally accepted auditing standards (GAAS). Moreover, the financial statements report information for the analysis of operations and about the risks undertaken. This is accomplished through classifications in the balance sheet according to the liquidity of its components and classifications in the other related financial statements of income and cash flows. The financial statements can be viewed as a method of reporting to interested parties such as management, investors, creditors, and the public, the efficiency and effectiveness of the organization in terms of its embedded goals. It may also be reasonable to argue that a profit organization, knowing that it will be judged in substantial part by the results reflected in the financial statements, will direct its efforts toward achieving optimal results as defined by such financial statements.

Criticisms of the PS Model. The economic model together with its accounting-measurement system is not without its critics. While this textbook economic theory is taught to generations of students, empirical evidence raises questions as to the applicability of theory. Moreover, realities of accounting practice have undermined not only the status of the system as a tool for measuring societal gain but also its ability to generate reporting that is comparable across different organizations.

A key criticism is that, aside from some agricultural markets, perfect competition rarely exists. Price floors and ceilings, limits on production or import and export quotas, institutional barriers, the actions of monopolies and oligopolies, and the creation of consumer preferences by advertising, the lack of data, and the rationality of the consumer and producer in decision-making are other examples of imperfections that disrupt the workings of free markets.

Theory has responded to these questions. It would take us too far afield to review current economic models of the firm under conditions referred to as monopolistic-competition, oligopolistic, and monopolistic behaviors. Suffice it to say, the underlying theory proffers a model that results in output control and curtailment depending on the firm's assessment of consumer demand for the product at differing prices, reactions of other firms, and other variables. The actions of the individual firms, nonetheless, are still primarily market/consumer driven, and accordingly resources are allocated in response to presumed demand schedules for products.[1]

Perhaps the most significant reason why profits do not adequately reflect societal benefit is that they do not include externalities, societal costs, or societal contributions. Some of these costs even when accounted for are displaced and borne by those who do not share in the benefits of the product. An example of these are the costs of medical care provided by society as a result of contamination from chemical products or cigarettes. Other costs such as smog, acid rain, or the extinction of certain animal species are generally difficult to accommodate within the pricing system. Likewise, government expenditures related to the PS are not reflected, such as direct or indirect subsidies to specific industries. However, these costs and subsidies should be considered in an evaluation organizational functioning and social welfare in the PS.

Some seventy years ago, Clark identified the importance of accounting for social costs.[2] Since then, economists and accountants have discussed their significance and their appropriate accounting for the economy. Ronen noted in 1974 that "Probably, the most appropriate and inexpensive source for such information [social costs] is the accounting system." He went on to say it is necessary to include such costs "to properly reflect the firm's contribution to the social product."[3] After the recent Exxon Valdez oil disaster in Alaska, in examining the issues that surfaced regarding the accounting for the costs of the incident, Rubenstein points up the inadequacies of present accounting and "speculates on accounting models the profession may be required to develop to accrue for such costs."[4]

In spite of obvious market failures and the social cost factor some economists maintain their support for the underlying theory. However, criticisms continually emerge to shake the basic concepts. Increasing industry concentrations, increasing product identification, internationalization of production and distribution with governments as major players, new modes of financing, and instantaneous communication have created changing structures within industry.[5] Likewise, the very roots of the theory have been questioned by rejecting the assumption that individual utility functions can be aggregated, that a measure of societal well-offness can be realized.[6]

Broadly speaking, there are three possible approaches to these criticisms. It may be that Milton Friedman has given a possible answer—that current neoclassical economic theory is perhaps more a question of usefulness than of theory.[7] The question involves not only the critique of the framework; one must also include the "cost" of the absence of a framework. The failure to provide a unifying conceptual scheme continually requires separate solutions to questions and the loss of a common language for communication, at least among professionals. A second alternative is to create another model with a different set of propositions, which can allocate societal resources in an efficient and effective way based on the assumed goals of the political body. A third alternative is to recognize its imperfections and to improve the actions of the market. This can be accomplished by introducing more players and better information; by encouraging investment, consumption, and education of societal members as to their choices in a more acceptable risk environment; and by encouraging the ethical behavior of all society's participants—the propositions developed in chapter 4. This latter course includes the recognition of trade-offs between macro and micro approaches.

It should be noted that accounting profit is not the same as profit defined by economists, nor can it be considered as the sole measure of organizational well-offness. As previously discussed, other variables such as market position, risks, liquidity, and so on, must be included. There are ways to convert accounting profit into economic returns, which generally are not used in practice. In the discussion of accounting framework in chapter 5, it was pointed out that one of the principal differences between economic and accounting concepts is the imputation of an interest factor on equity. Economists also prefer to abandon the accountants' historical cost approach in favor of current market and replacement cost, which may also incorporate interest/discounting features.

The Accounting Metric in the PS. The proponents of the existing system emphasize that the accounting measurement system for the PS offers a method of recording and communication that is understood worldwide. It presents a defined approach to the analysis of effectiveness and efficiency, with an inherent flexibility that allows for presentation of information for external reporting based on the aggregation of the same data, which can be used internally for all levels of management. Moreover, albeit imperfectly, it yields a method of comparisons of similar organizations that guides our economy and ultimately has a significant effect in determining the allocation of societal resources. As evident from the above discussions there are behavioral implications of accounting systems on management action. It has been suggested that an important aspect of any measuring system is its ability to induce and encourage goal-congruent behavior. To do so, it is essential that the performance criteria against which managers are judged correspond to the criteria against which the organization judges its own success. A review of management accounting reveals that the motivation issue can distort the congruence of management actions and societal benefits. While organizations theoretically should analyze their strategies and business opportunities from a long-term, discounted cash-flow perspective, most inventive criteria are based on short-term, profit-oriented measures. Changes in policies in accounting for research and development cost and emphasis on quarterly profits may be a factor in explaining the United States' industrial decline.[8] Further, on this issue, Briloff refers to the Lester C. Thurow study showing a time span for management planning of 2.8 years.[9]

There are problems surrounding the application of GAAP to PS accounting for the individual firm.[10] These problems are within the larger context of the questions of: (1) the primacy of the balance sheet or the income statement, that is, what is the primary goal of accounting measurement; and (2) the need for and/or the method of establishing an authoritative framework. While various accounting problems are known to practitioners and theoreticians, they have not arrested the flow of accounting reports; nor should they have. Rather they have spawned numerous attempts to resolve the concerns, most notable with the specification of standards, the amplification of GAAP, the exposure drafts and rules of practice of the FASB and the GASB, and with articles relating to the accounting system's conceptual framework.[11] The general inconsistencies of the PS's accounting system and its susceptibility to managerial manipulation have led some to criticize the system as resting on too "soft" a foundation. However, any evaluation of a system must recognize the inherent assumptions on which measuring systems are based, as well as the limitations of a single indicator.[12]

While GAAP provides some framework for the compilation of financial statements, this has not ensured complete consistency, either across time or organizations. There is not only a potential loss in comparability but also the possibility that accounting concepts may be manipulated to change corporate results. *The Wall Street Journal* commented on this situation: "The National Association of Accountants, a trade group of 95,000 management accountants has joined the ranks of those wondering whether the false values are being circulated by the [accounting] profession."[13] It further quotes a number of authorities who point up the weaknesses of the current accounting system in its use of historical cost for valuation purposes, its inability to incorporate the societal effect of business decisions, window dressing of financial statements, and the problems of measuring and reporting real growth. These accounting limitations may have helped to fuel the corporate takeover and merger movement.[14]

The application of accounting principles to practice often requires decisions with different results. This is inherent in the nature of the preparation of financial statements. Such applications of general principles vary because of the professional judgment about the particular application adopted and its effect on measurement.[15] Once the choice is made for the particular application, GAAP dictates consistency in the use of principles and their application.

It should be recognized that this reporting of profits by the individual firm is a best-estimate approximation based upon myriad assumptions and applications of these generally accepted accounting principles, rationalized in part by the normative economic model for the PS. The accounting measuring metric is a subset of statistical methodology, which is a subset of economic activities, which in turn is a subset of societal functions. The reporting of a firm's profits states nothing directly about the economics of its industry (competition, market position, patents and trademarks, labor supply, etc.), the social desirability of its product except in terms of consumer preference, its community relations, human resource management, or societal supports received or created, and so on. Even the efficiency of the firm's operations is subsumed in the profit metric, a combined measure of efficiency and effectiveness, which measures an organization's ability to monitor resources optimally within market forces. Some answers may be inferred from the financial statements together with the notes to financial statements and from comments that are contained in the corporate annual report. One could also expect that the accounting metric to be developed for HSOs would also have limitations—the very nature of measuring systems and the application of a set of accounting principles.

THE NONPROFIT SECTOR

Taxonomy

The current system of classification of the NPS has been briefly reviewed in chapter 4. Based primarily on donor and donee tax considerations, the need for a system's change was evident, and a revised taxonomy is proposed (see Exhibit 4.1) that is more in accord with current economic activity. The previous system of classification has abetted the continual confusion relative to an applicable accounting for this sector.

Accounting in the Nonprofit Sector

The exchange of views between Anthony and Folpe provides an analysis of the current differing approaches relative to accounting issues for this sector.[16] They share the belief that common accounting concepts should apply to business and not-for-profit (or nonprofit) business organizations. Nevertheless, they are in complete agreement on only one point: "The current situation in not-for-profit accounting is not a tolerable one . . . change . . . must come quickly . . . based on the fundamental needs of this important sector . . . for relevant, reliable and credible financial reporting."[17]

Their discussions point up the particular questions that an accounting system must resolve: (1) differences between the equity or capital sectors, (2) the treatment of contributions received and or pledged in terms of operating or capital support, and (3) the legal differences among contributions, whether unrestricted, partially restricted, or permanently restricted.

Their viewpoints involve the work of the FASB, criticized by Anthony and supported by Folpe, and that of the Government Accounting Standards Board (GASB), where they reverse their support position. The GASB was created in 1984 to deal with government accounting standards and measurement foci which include the importance of compliance with and comparisons to budget.[18] The underlying difference between them involves the primacy of financial statements, whether the balance sheet or the statement of income. For Folpe, it is the balance sheet; for Anthony, the statement of income. When measurement of net income is primary, matching of revenues and expenses can result in a balance sheet that may not strictly comply with definitions of assets and liabilities, as the financial valuation of economic resources and obligations relative to resource transfer in the future. When the balance sheet is primary, income is the difference in "real resources and obligations of an entity during that period."[19]

Whether funds are received for operations or for capital obviously affects the reporting process. Do the differences require a different accounting system or can they be resolved within an appropriate framework and treated with reference to *trade* practice? Can such questions as the recognition of timing of pledges, the nature of donations, additions to fixed assets and their subsequent depreciation, accruals, and other questions be resolved on the basis of current GAAP, or is a new framework needed?

When society makes direct economic transfers and/or indirect ones by donor tax exemptions to certain nonprofit organizations, how does society benefit? This should be the fundamental focus of a measuring system; this is the information required for an accounting feedback system. This is the same question that the

PS theoretically answers—the economic well-offness of societal members. By failing to focus on this overarching question, neither Anthony nor Folpe provides a reply. Interestingly enough, they both agree on one substantive issue—the nonfeasibility of measuring the value of services performed.

Folpe quotes Anthony: "The cost of providing services can be reported, but reporting the *value* of these services, or even the quantity or quality of the services rendered, is beyond the capability of financial accounting. Both the GASB and the FASB have commissioned studies on this topic. *None of the resulting reports has found that measuring the value of service in monetary amounts would be feasible*" [emphasis added]. Indirectly, Folpe adds support to Anthony's position of what accounting cannot do in stating:

This criticism seems particularly irrelevant inasmuch a neither FASB nor GASB has suggested in any of its pronouncements that placing a monetary value on such services and incorporating such monetary amounts in the basic financial statements is the appropriate way to satisfy this objective. Rather, disclosure of such information in non-financial terms as supplementary information to the basic financial statements has been put forth as the most feasible way to satisfy this objective.[20]

There is a certain irony in their agreement about the non-feasibility of achieving the objective of measuring the value of services, an original goal of the FASB. This book presents a conceptual framework which now makes possible the realization of the FASB goal.

COMMON CHARACTERISTICS OF THE PS AND HSOs

To date, the accounting profession has not been able to resolve two major differences between the PS and NPS: the ability to measure on a similar basis the value of goods and services and the nature of the consumer-payer in the NPS. Other differences also exist, such as the factors of equity ownership, taxable status, and sources of capital. There are, however, many functional similarities between the PS and the NPS. These similarities significantly outweigh differences, particularly once the two major issues which separate the sectors are resolved—as proposed in this book. These functional similarities are identified and reviewed under the headings of: Marketing; Management, Accounting, and Reporting; Organization of Product/Service Delivery; and Success and Survival.

Marketing

Until recent years' cutbacks in fundings from most sources, HSOs relied on serving those individuals for whom their programs were specifically developed. With the present fiscal constraints, although client satisfaction remains as the primary goal, HSOs can benefit from adapting proven marketing techniques. They can optimize their resource utilization by balancing the needs of potential consumer-clients (and their funding) with their organizational goals and current operating mix of clients, programs, staff, and funding.

"Client satisfaction is viewed as a primary and unifying goal, central to service and marketing objectives. . . . In marketing terms, social work is more user then seller oriented. Its ultimate accountability is to the consumer."[21] It should be emphasized that marketing concepts are conceptually the same for both sectors since the basic approach to the consumer is in the satisfaction of wants. As stated by Frances Hesselbein, the then national executive director of the Girl Scouts, "We kept asking ourselves very simple questions. What is our business? Who is the customer? And what does the customer consider value? If you're the Girl Scouts, IBM, or AT&T, you have to manage for a 'mission'."[22] Another recent article stresses the fracturing of existing markets and the identification of customers and "what they want." Instead of an extension of the usual model of advertising to create demand, the product is adapted to reflect consumer preferences. In this regard, some retail markets now make use of the checkout scanner. The coupon specialist can not only analyze purchases but can also assist in checking the effectiveness of specific types of advertising such as display, newspaper, magazine, and other media.[23] This is not dissimilar to HSOs' responding to the preferences of their constituencies and to their client-consumer demands for involvement in their service plan.

Management, Accounting, and Reporting

Hierarchical Reporting. The process of reporting of information to various layers of management is similar for the HSOs and the PS. The specifics of the type of information necessary for each management layer may differ more within the organization's hierarchical system than conceptually between an HSO and a PS organization at comparable levels of management.

As an illustration, a manufacturing plant in the PS provides reports to its hierarchical layers. The individual plant employee is evaluated from the point of view of his personal productivity by the foreman; the aggregate of the foremen by the plant superintendent or manager; the aggregate of plant managers by the vice-president in charge of manufacturing in terms of meeting schedules and standards (cost of production). This process is repeated for sales management and for other departments within the company. Finally, the company is evaluated by its success in its overall mission, that is, profits.

For HSOs, each group of stakeholders likewise requires information collected and aggregated for them. Typical stakeholders of an HSO are the following: clients, line staff, program supervisors, program directors, executives, boards of directors, funding sources, the general public, and volunteers. The reports to the various levels of management and to other stakeholders should reflect agency goals and the effective execution of these goals by management in an efficient manner based on the services of staff—oriented to the needs of and outcomes for the client. The evaluation process for program services measured and reported upon at each cost center differs from the criteria for supervisory or executive management and for the board of directors, even though much data from cost centers to supervisors to management layers are continual aggregates. As in the PS, the criteria become broader and the orientation differs at each level. For successful operations, all layers of management recognize their interdependence to maximize the effectiveness and efficiency of staff, management, the board, and the totality of the organization. The client as the "bouncing ball" may mean that more variables must be dealt with for the HSO than with standardized products as in the PS.

Staff Evaluation and Incentives. The basic requirement for staff and worker incentives in the PS and for HSOs must fulfill the twin determinants of equity and consistency. Piecework or incentive methods of pay within a firm and given labor market must equate each basic operation to a wage, where each operation rate is equitable among all the operations. The establishing of new hourly rates for changes in products must be consistent with past rates among the various operations and departments. In the PS these questions become largely quasi-automatic responses as good management practice; moreover, the market pricing mechanism, drives for profit, and management incentives provide visible evidence of efficient operations. For the HSOs, similar types of measurements can be used to evaluate staff—effectiveness based on client outcomes and efficiency based on service units (standard time).

Board of Directors. Surface differences tend to cloud basic similarities in board functioning. The establishment of organizational goals or mission and the feedback reporting of achievement are common denominators. From this foundation there flows the nature of the product/client service offered, its delivery and financing, survival, expansion/contraction, executive and personnel performance, quality standards, and so on. In the absence of a statement of income, the nonprofit board must assess success in other areas and by other piecemeal criteria indicators such as achieving mission, planning, financial stability, use of capital assets, and use and development of human resources.[24]

In the 1950s and 1960s, boards of directors were generally subordinate to the professionals within an HSO. The emphasis on the client, quality services and programs, the growing professionalism of social agencies—without, however formal outcome measurements—resulted in the professional staff's domination not only of the operations of the particular agency but also of the board of directors. In the last 20 years, the tendency has continued for HSOs to enlist successful and assertive executives from the PS; however, some board members confuse efficiency of operations with effectiveness of outcomes.[25]

Discussion of board development, philosophies, responsibilities, and remuneration of board members would take us far afield. Suffice it to say, recent developments in both sectors appear to bring them closer. The PS is examining its responsibility to its workers, their communities, and societal values, as well as the potentials for profit in the NPS; the NPS is searching for new funding sources, improved management techniques, professional development with cost and quality controls, as it attempts to balance between survival and clients' and community needs. Recent articles suggest that the PS can learn from the NPS in various areas of management, particularly in defining strategy and organizational mission, in having a CEO directly accountable to a functioning board, and in the motivation of key staff.[26]

Accounting. There are some differences between the sectors, notably the accounting for contributions in the form of money, property, or volunteer time. However, these are differences in kind and application and not in fundamental concepts. Differences in accounting within the PS may be wider than between the sectors, for example, compare the financial statements of a highly leveraged shipbuilder with a well-financed chain of fast foods. Basically, any financial information system records the transactions for an organization. A chart of accounts can be sufficiently flexible to accommodate multiproducts/services, departments, and cost centers as a function of an organization's size.

As has already been stated, the accounting goals of the two sectors currently appear different; however, other than the missing statement of income for the HSOs, the requirements for other financial statements are the same. Moreover, the same set of rules is applicable to their preparation, in accordance with pronouncements of the FASB. Funding restrictions and other significant events are disclosed in the notes to financial statements for both sectors. There is the same or similar terminology, and historical differences are being eliminated such as the accounting for depreciation on fixed assets and the accrual of liabilities. Certainly, internal control and other procedures applicable to accounts receivable, billings, inventories, and fixed assets apply equally to the two sectors. Standardized government contract terminology, contracting procedures, and reporting also diminish the demarcation lines.

While the external reporting system presents a combined measure of effectiveness and efficiency, internal systems have been designed to focus on and allow the reporting of degrees of efficiency. These systems serve as scorekeepers, attention getters, and problem solvers. Using the same data bases that compile external statements for periodic reporting, they offer routine information to staff and managers about the efficiency of operations, including their interrelationship with effectiveness. This data base represents the compilation of output quantities and material, labor and overhead determined at actual costs or in terms of projected or standard and actual costs. For purposes of efficient management, these dimensions of output, projected cost, and actual cost can be juxtaposed. The typical approach involves construction of budgets, and given anticipated output levels, the standards are converted into projections; corresponding actual expenditures are recorded, and the calculation of variances, or their differences, can be reported. Variances between actual and standard can be analyzed in a number of ways to reveal the effects on costs of changes in inputs and outputs, such as performance, volume, and price variables. This system can accommodate itself to the varying needs of analysis for different levels of management. Because of its ability to aggregate or disaggregate data within a structured format, the system can provide insight into operations for a specific work task, department, or division, and the level of the organization as a whole. It also can be utilized as a device for planning and research, aggregating and disaggregating prior standards and reassembling in terms of "what if" projections and analyses.

In brief, a standard costing system functions as a continual monitoring system providing feedback from ex ante planning and decision making to ex post reporting of efficiency and effectiveness. Standards can likewise be established for the marketing, sales, and administrate functions for market penetration, projection of units of product/service sales and proposed sales prices, distribution and marketing expenses, and general administrative costs. Variances can likewise be computed. Thus, costing and budgeting serve like a fourth-dimension camera, allowing visibility through both wide-angle and telescopic views in the past, the present, and the future.

The establishing of standards, their costing, and the computation of variances are conceptually and mechanically the same for HSOs as in the PS. For example, once the standard has been determined for the HSO in terms of service units (time measurement) as required for a given client service, then variances can be computed relative to amounts of time used and the effects of volume and price differences.

Organization of Product/Service Delivery

Customer or Service Order. For HSOs, the general concept of establishing a client's service plan at the time of initial assessment is not dissimilar to the taking of an order by a firm in the PS for the delivery of goods or services. Both the service plan and the customer's order can be translated into projected time and material costs, generally referred to as standards, as discussed above. The subsequent control of the order, whether persons or products, depends upon the procedures established, whether called a CIS or an inventory control system.

Unlike the PS, which generally deals with standardized unchanged specifications, HSOs deal with clients who may require continual changes in programs and goals while "in process." The consumer-clients' "production orders" for the HSO are more akin to customers' job orders in the PS. These changes may require special accountability, not unlike the construction field where "change orders" are separately accounted for.

The Firm. Among the common characteristics as discussed above is the essential role of the firm in marshaling the factors of production in response to consumer demand. This concept applies to both sectors: The success of the firm in the PS is measured by its bottom line or profit; for HSOs, the success of the firm will likewise be measured by its response to societal needs and the profit it engenders, based upon the calculations of the changes of net resources consumed by its clients in accordance with the discussions in chapter 2.

While the firm has two sources of payment from consumers, private and societal, there is only one type of producer and, accordingly, only one type of accounting required to account for the consumers' actions. The individual firm, private, public, profit, or nonprofit, brings together the factors of production and in effect measures its revenues based upon consumer benefits. The profit by the individual firm is its ability to respond to the market (consumers), and as a result, have its revenue exceed its costs. In some cases there will be the direct payers; in others, societal payers for the consumer. In any event, the profit calculation is based upon revenues less cost. Accordingly, the optimal allocation of resources is based upon the benefits to the consumer, indirectly calculated by the market in the PS or directly calculated for HSOs in terms of societal benefits.[27]

Success and Survival

In the PS, such factors as profitability, return on capital, market share, price earnings ratio, and maintenance of working capital are some of the variables that determine continuity of operations. For HSOs, most of these factors likewise have applicability. Like the PS, the survival of an HSO currently requires a budgeted and actual bottom line of receipts over expenses, cash flows to cover fixed asset replacement and/or expansion, and internal control of operations and assets. Even in the areas of fund-raising in the broadest sense, the HSOs are in competition among each other (and in effect with the PS) for individual and corporate donors, foundations, and the government funders. In the absence of outcome measurement, this competition has tended to require similar requisites of "success" for the HSOs, particularly in terms of satisfied clients, resolution of the particular social problem with which the agency deals, and (the appearance at least of) a well-managed entity.

With the introduction of the model, the characteristics of success and survival merge. It should be recognized that the gross income generated by the HSO must be incorporated into its funding cycle. In that event, the HSO will pay income taxes on its net profit based on the provisions similar to firms in the PS.

APPLICATION OF MEASUREMENT CONCEPTS

The accounting for the PS incorporates the basic measuring criteria presented in chapter 5, which measuring criteria likewise apply to the accounting system of HSOs as described in chapter 2. The application of common measuring criteria becomes a basic factor for a unified system of accounting for both sectors. In order to measure revenue and the use of resources over time, as presented in chapter 5, the criteria to be satisfied are: mission/goal, set of properties or attribute, metric, periodicity, unit of account, and other (i.e., relevance, cost, etc.).

Goal/Mission

In accordance with generally accepted economic theory, the goal of organizations in the PS is to maximize the return to the entrepreneur/investor. Variations of this goal include other models of organizational functioning that emphasize long-run stability, or liquidity, or maximizing cash returns rather than profits, or that stress risk factors, for example, minimizing the maximum loss possibility (minimax). Rather than profit maximization (maximax), in effect, these models attempt to incorporate the elements of risk, and/or liquidity, and/or long-run versus short-run considerations, such as some kind of optimality. Some critics have commented that in practice optimality becomes tautological—entrepreneurs behave as entrepreneurs behave. However, most economists and related professionals would argue that the general behavioral goal of firms in the PS is to optimize monetary profits, their attribute and metric.

In accordance with the measuring model developed in chapter 2, similarly the goal of HSOs is to optimize profit as measured by the return to society. The mission of the HSO is generally to improve the ability of its clients to function in society, the SS/I (HSO), or conversely to prevent the clients' increased dependence on society, the M/P (HSO). In each sector, the model of profit optimization is achieved by the firm by responding to its markets, that is, to consumer needs and wants. As heretofore described, the neoclassical model for the PS and the organizational model for HSOs are based on the satisfaction of consumers and consumer-clients.

Attribute

In the PS, profit is the accepted measure of success in attaining the goal. The optimization of revenues in relation to costs, measured in terms of the money/metric, results in profits, the goal achievement. The bottom line in the PS is a specific measure of performance that integrates the combination of effectiveness and efficiency of operations of a particular organization.

Effectiveness (together with efficiency) is relative. The degree to which an organization is effective varies with the ability of that organization to create value, geared to its markets and profitability, based on the efficiency in the use of resources when exploiting such market positions. Reporting of profits permits an initial comparison among PS organizations, which can be brought to a common denominator such as earnings per share, return on investment, and/or other indicators. Here the commonality of the profit metric becomes significant as a preliminary direct assessment of interorganizational functioning. However, for a more complete evaluation, other factors must be considered such as an organization's relative market position, patents, trade names, liquidity, risk, competition, cyclical exposure, trends, relations with labor, community, and government, and so on.

For HSOs, from the perspective of the SS/I, one of the most basic of human needs is work-related and economic. As discussed under Quality of Life in chapter

2, almost all individuals can be seen to require at least some livelihood that can generate means for their support. Needs are met only when the individual is a functioning and contributing participant in the economic mainstream, or not drawing upon societal resources. Thus, within the context of the SS/I, outcomes refer to changes in clients' abilities to move toward self-sufficiency and decreases in their dependence on societal support; while from the perspective of the M/P, outcomes refer to minimizing increasing dependence on such supports for their consumer-clients. The attribute selected must make possible the differentiation between outputs, or production, and outcomes, the economic results of the mission. For example, the output of an intensive training plan might be a certain number of client cases closed, or for a low-vision or blind person's program, a certain number of hours provided to increase the ability of the client to navigate the public transportation system. The outcome of the program would, however, reflect the more significant achievement of the clients in using their new-found skills to obtain and maintain an income-producing position. Thus outcomes are part of the final evaluation phase and deal with the aftermath of client adjustment to real-life situations such as independent living, employment, or school.

Obviously, a system of measurement for HSOs based on the number of kilowatt-hours used by clients would seem nonsensical; but so might the number of client cases closed per month without at least some method for assessing the effectiveness of their outcomes. The absence of an appropriate measuring system has resulted in other forms of evaluation to be offered, which in many instances may be as irrelevant as kilowatt-hours. Rating systems based upon the ratio of fund-raising expenses to total outlays may provide a necessary measurement in particular circumstances but not necessarily a sufficient one for assessing the agency's effectiveness.[27]

Metric

Each measuring system must revolve around some unifying goal converted into a specified attribute that can be expressed with a basic measuring unit. These conditions have been more obviously answered in the accounting systems of the PS. Here, to the extent that the purpose of business functioning has been accepted as a creation of monetary profit, goal achievement and the unit of measure have become almost synonymous.

The economic focus of this system requires the use of a monetary unit of measure. However, before assuming that use, recall that the choice of metric should be based on its ability to meet the general requirements of measuring systems as set forth in chapter 5 and the success of the money metric in the PS as described herein. It is suggested that each measuring unit should be understandable, relevant to the majority of the system's users, in accord with the precepts of a ratio system, and provide an ability to convert time and units of inputs, outputs, and outcomes to a common base. Given these, the choice of the dollar metric follows.

Periodic Reporting

Not only must there be consistent measurement within the organization's operating cycle, but also between periods. Periodicity has been described as an ability to generate intracycle estimates of performance. For financial accounting, if manufacturing and sales and/or service cycles were equivalent and actual inputs were comparable to corresponding actual outcomes, then no intracycle estimates would be required. The profit metric incorporates a flexibility that attempts to ensure that appropriate adjustment valuations can be made. In the United States, most of these allocative valuations are made in accordance with GAAP so that there is consistency in measuring both across time and across organizations. By comparing inputs and outcomes, together with appropriate adjustments for inventories, the organization can evaluate its effectiveness, its goal of profits.

Conceptually, organizational cycles are similar in both sectors. For example, a steel manufacturer's cycle starts at the point where it acquires iron ore, proceeds through the refining and manufacturing process, sale of its product, receipt of cash from sale, and moves back to the purchase of iron ore. For the HSO, there is a functional cycle of referral, application, assessment, treatment plan, program services, termination, and postterminal follow-up and outcomes. To complete the cycle, there must be payment for gross societal income as proposed in chapter 2.

Units of Accountability

Information systems should be founded on consumer-client data bases for purposes of internal control and internal and external reporting. Systems of recording of actual and standard costs based on time and in the selected metric can be applied and aggregated in both accounting systems. These units can be grouped in the PS by product, customer, and labor, and in the NPS by client, staff, and program as well as in both sectors by cost center/department and the entire organization.

Other Criteria

The interchangeability of the goal and attribute reported in the everyday metric of money enhances comprehensibility. While few may understand the foundations and applications of accounting principles, the ability of financial statements to present relevant information together with a single result in the form of a bottom line enhances general usage. The framework of GAAP permits the preparation of financial statements on a consistent basis with relevant information to users, whether management, staff boards, creditors, or other stakeholders. The use of common data bases for both internal decision making and controls and for external reporting also enhances the system's applicability.

Updated presentation of generally accepted auditing standards (GAAS) has been a concomitant of the growth of the field of professional accountancy. The development of concepts of relevance, together with materiality relative to financial reporting, permits timely reviews by the independent auditor within the bounds of reasonable cost constraints.

The costs of any accounting system involve trade-offs of desired information and its accuracy, timeliness, frequency of reporting, materiality, comprehensibility, and auditability. Given the requirements of a well-run organization for client and financial information on a regular basis, the incremental costs of implementing the organizational model for HSOs are negligible.

MEASURING THE PS AND HSOs BY THE SAME ACCOUNTING SYSTEM

It is apparent that the measuring and accounting systems of the two sectors converge once the key problem of quantifying the attribute of goal measurement is resolved. The overall goal and societal mission of the sectors become the same, that is, consumer benefits and satisfaction. Only the direct payers differ. Accordingly, the other measuring criteria—the metric, the matching cycle for income and expenses, a standard unit of accountability, and the other criteria (comprehensibility, auditability relevance, and cost)—all are the same.

The measuring criteria of both sectors now fulfill the requirements of a measuring system, which provides the ability to present a snapshot of the firm at any given time and its functioning for any given period. It allows the reporting data to be manipulated and reorganized for internal and external reporting to suit the needs of each different group of stakeholders, be it the hierarchical level of staff, management, board of directors, or community.

In recognizing that the relationship of market and profit in the PS is congruent to mission and outcome for HSOs, it then also follows that efficiency is subordinate to effectiveness and that the same system can be used for measuring and accounting for efficiency. As noted above, by the use of the standard measuring units and projections, the efficiency of the underlying system is integrated with market goals. Standard costing allows not only the reporting of results but also an examination of the causes and processes that may affect those results.

These common characteristics of the PS and the HSOs become the foundation for the unified system. The proposed model in optimizing consumer benefits from the services of both sectors can provide the basis of equating their measuring method. In fact, differences in accounting and reporting should no longer depend on the terminology of profit and nonprofit. All organizations by definition would be measured by profits based on optimizing societal/consumer satisfaction. The so-called profit enterprise, entering the domain of the so-called NPS and providing human services, should be measured by the same societal outcomes as a so-called nonprofit enterprise and not by its merchandising abilities. By the same token, the so-called nonprofit enterprise providing goods and/or services in the so-called profit areas should be measured by the bottom line of gross income less costs or net profits. With the same measuring system, all companies would become profit oriented in terms of their outcomes, their bottom lines. Payment of income and local taxes by HSOs would further dissolve differences. Some surface differences would continue to exist, such as the capital section of the balance sheet. These differences between sectors would be no greater than the accounting differences within each of the sectors, for example, the accounting questions involving firms in various industries such as a shipbuilder, a retail food store, or a firm of consulting engineers; or HSOs dealing with their ranges of services (training, counseling, recreation) for such diverse populations as the aged and the handicapped (physical, mental, and emotional).

Each firm would have two sources of income: the consumers, who use their own resources, and client-consumers, who use societal resources. Society becomes a customer and is billed by each HSO to the extent of its societal income generated. Funds are collected from the sale of such receivables. These procedures are described in chapter 2. The receivables must be appropriately valued in terms of expected realization—a common problem in accounting.

From propositions that optimize societal resources, concepts of revenue are derived for HSOs. The accounting system that has been developed to measure revenue uses as an attribute the change or maintenance in self-sufficiency of the consumer-clients for whom costs were incurred by means of societal transfers. Having developed this concept of revenue, the balance of GAAP can be applied to the HSOs. Since appropriate characteristics of measuring systems are already embodied in GAAP, existing concepts and standards can be used as has been mandated by the accounting profession. There is no need to redevelop definitions, conventions, and standards. Definitions (assets, liabilities), conventions (matching, depreciation), and standards (reporting, relevance, materiality) have been developed, are in use, and are familiar to firms and practitioners.

The result of a common accounting system logically induces a changed economic taxonomy for organizations within the society. As described in chapter 4, such classification scheme is based on the source and use of resources in terms of the individual and the group. All organizations that use resources for direct individual benefits make up the micro sectors, divided whether the resources used are private or group ones. Likewise, organizations using resources for the benefit of the group make up the macro sector, again divided whether private or group resources are used.

As described in chapter 9, several important areas of future research follow from this proposed classification system for both micro and macro sectors as redefined.

SUMMARY

In order to eliminate significant differences between the sectors in accounting and reporting of effectiveness in financial statements, for HSOs there were two missing elements: a definition of earned revenue for inclusion in the statement of income, and a method of ensuring that gross societal revenue reported in such statement of income can be part of the funding cycle for the individual HSO. These issues are resolved in chapter 2 by the development of the organizational model.

We have demonstrated the feasibility of a unified system to provide a bottom-line measurement of effectiveness and efficiency for all firms in their use of private and/or transfer resources for the direct benefit of the individual consumer. This unified accounting system, as discussed in this chapter, is based upon (1) common objective fulfilled of optimal satisfaction of consumer choices and benefits; (2) common measuring factors of goal, metric, periodicity, and other criteria; (3) common functioning characteristics of organizations; (4) common method to measure revenues produced and resources used; (5) common internal and external reporting to hierarchical levels of stakeholders; (6) common application of GAAP; and (7) common audit criteria of GAAS.

The payment to HSOs of their societal income generated together with the payment of income taxes suggest major changes for this segment of the NPS. Likewise, research in the PS could lead to significant modifications in its accounting. It should be noted that the model for HSOs did not develop from the shoe-horning of the PS's model. Rather, for the future developments, the reverse is true. As has been stated, the PS accounting model suffers from the problems of the economic model on which it is based: assumptions of market competition and knowledge and rationality of consumers' and producers' decisions, and a system that has an indirect measure of society well-offness. This is an area for further study as discussed under Future Research in chapter 9.

There are costs related to the lack of a conceptual framework and the related requirements for separate solutions and the absence of a common language. A unified accounting system permits a common level of understanding and realization that the mission/goal for HSOs is on the same level as profit is for the firm in the PS. The exchange of views between eminent practitioners in the field of accounting—and the articles referred to in the previous chapter—is of particular interest from this point of view and from a methodological perspective. The writers failed to raise their level of analysis to answer the basic question as to what information is required by stakeholders for relevant and reliable reporting. Information about what economic event for which decision maker and at what given time must relate to the goals of the enterprise within the mission of the sector of society. By raising the level of analysis, once it is recognized that both sectors are satisfying consumers—the individuals who are payers in the PS and society, which is the payer for HSOs—then one accounting system is applicable to both sectors. Accounting is a social system to measure the effectiveness and efficiency of the realization of societal goals, which should be based upon the economic optimization of its individual members. Such well-offness, while supplied from various sources, requires one system of measurement.

NOTES

1. The classical economic model assumes perfect competition. Accordingly, each firm reacts to a market that is outside of its control—a horizontal demand curve. Profits are a measure of efficiency. As markets become imperfect as the result of the development of and attachment to brands, the neoclassical model of the firm incorporates the concept of a sloping demand curve and, accordingly, profits become a function of the created markets, prices (a demand schedule), and supply costs. Profits are thus the outcome of a combination of marketing, of optimal pricing, and of efficiency in combining the factors of production (i.e., labor, material, and expenses), or outputs. Except in certain agricultural markets where no one producer can affect the price of a miscible product, the monopolistic-competitive model prevails. Accordingly, in this model, the producer-marketer profit reflects the effectiveness (outcomes) and efficiency (outputs) of the firm's operations.

The PS firms focus on demand assuming the supply (availability) of goods and resources; the HSOs focus on supply, the use of resources, and assume the demand. The function of the firm remains the same. The firms in the PS view the market of consumers and satisfy their individual demands; the aggregate of such demands is imputed to be a measure of societal well-offness. The HSO firm views its market and satisfies the demands from a societal viewpoint.

2. Clark, John Maurice. (1923). *Studies in the economics of overhead costs*. IL: University of Chicago Press.

3. Ronen, Joshua. (1974, May). Accounting for social costs and benefits. *Objectives of financial statements*. Vol. 2, p. 40. New York: American Institute of Certified Public Accountants.

4. Rubenstein, Daniel B. (1990, July). There's no accounting for the Exxon Valdez. *The CPA Journal, 60*(70), 40–45.

5. Galbraith, John Kenneth (1991, May). The sting of truth. *Scientific American, 264*(5), 136.

6. Arrow, Kenneth J. (1963). *Social choice and individual values*. New Haven, CT: Cowles Foundation for Research in Economics at Yale University.

7. The exchange of views between economic theorists Paul Samuelson and Milton Friedman is pertinent. Unlike Samuelson, Friedman is willing to settle for a system with correlative relationships and that has some predictive power. Friedman, Milton. (1980) The methodology of positive economics; Samuelson, Paul. (1980). The problems of methodology. In B. J. Caldwell (ed.) *Appraisal and criticism in economics: A book of readings* (pp. 138–174 and pp. 188–193). Winchester, MA: Allen & Unwin.

8. Haynes, Robert H. & Abernathy, William J. (1980, July–August). Managing our way to economic decline. *Harvard Business Review, 58*(4), 67–77.

9. Briloff, Abraham, J. (1990). Accountancy and society, a covenant desecrated. *1*, 5–30. *Accountancy and Society, Critical Perspectives on Accounting*.

10. The problems include: recognition of income and losses; timing of income for long-term contracts; allocation of costs to periods to be benefitted such as appropriate depreciation and amortization as current period charges; the determination and allocation of values of intangibles as current costs or future benefits; estimating future liabilities with uncertain maturity and amounts; fluctuations in the value of the dollar, the measuring rod over time and across currencies; the "cost" convention for the valuations of inventories and fixed assets; the valuation of investments at cost or market; the exchange of assets other than cash with uncertain market values; the accounting for predecessor's assets and

income in mergers and acquisitions; and numerous questions relating to distinguishing between legal form and economic reality.

11. Anthony, Robert N. (1987, May). We don't have the accounting concepts we need. *The CPA Journal, 57*(5), 36–45.

12. For example, see 1985 Annual Report, Union Pacific Corporation, Supplementary Information, pp. 45–46, which emphasizes the subjectivity and limitations of the standardized measure of discounted future net cash flows relating to proven oil and gas reserves in accordance with the Securities and Exchange Commission rule of present valuing such reserves at a 10% discount before income tax.

13. Berton, Lee. (1986, April 2). Away from takeovers to value accounting. *The Wall Street Journal*, 20.

14. Haynes & Abernathy; Managing our way to economic decline, 67; and Briloff, *Accountancy and society, a covenant desecrated*, 5–30.

15. Illustrations of judgments include: pooling versus purchase and the consequent valuation of assets (together with the computation of goodwill) arising from mergers and acquisitions; method of inventory valuations such as Lifo, Fifo, and Average; application of principle of lower of cost or market calculation for the individual item, groupings or total inventory; repair, retirement, replacement, and depreciation policies for equipment; matching wages and salaries with the related items of pension and medical costs for employees as future retirees; and the values of stock options and their timing as costs.

16. Folpe, Herbert K. (1989, April). Sorting out nonprofit accounting issues. *The Philanthropy Monthly, 22*(4), 5–14, and 1989, May 22(5), 7–14. Anthony, Robert N. (1989, July/August). Sorting out nonprofit accounting issues the author replies. *The Philanthropy Monthly, 22*(7), 11–16.

17. Folpe, Herbert K. (1989 May). Sorting out nonprofit accounting issues, *The Philanthropy Monthly, 22*(5), 14.

18. This raises the question as to the applicability of this standard to the PS, to reporting by HSOs as well as governments.

19. Folpe, Sorting out non profit issues, 1989, May, p. 14.

20. Folpe, Sorting out non profit issues, 1989, May, p. 11.

21. Genkins, Mary. (1985, Spring). Strategic planning for social work marketing. *Administration in Social Work, 9*(1), 35.

22. Byrne, John A. (1990, March 26). *Business Week*, p. 70.

23. Staff. (1989, August 28). Stalking the new consumer. *Business Week*, pp. 54–62.

24. Morrell, Lewis R. (1988, Winter). Yardsticks for performance of nonprofit management. *Directors & Boards, 10*(2), 37–39.

25. Mattar, Edward P., III. (1988, November/December). Directorship: The nonprofit board. *The Corporate Board* pp. 5–8.

26. Byrne, *Business Week*, p. 70.

27. The Council of Better Business Bureaus' Philanthropic Advisory Service, Arlington, Virginia, and the National Charities Information Bureau, New York; Moore, Jennifer, & Williams, Grant. (1991, April 9). Setting standards for non-profits. *The Chronicle of Philanthropy*, 26–31.

CHAPTER 7

A Review of the Literature

The literature review reveals that increased attention is being paid by both the accounting and human service professions to the questions of measuring effectiveness and efficiency to achieve optimal allocation of societal resources. The literature is reviewed from the perspective of the criteria for a measuring system and is examined as to its successes and limitations in meeting these criteria. These criteria focus on how the literature has been evolving and how it has contributed to the present model.

Derived from the fields of accounting and human services (and involving economic theory, political science, sociology, and welfare economics), a number of papers have generated insights into the state of our nonprofit reporting and management systems. Questions have been raised about HSOs as to the efficiency and effectiveness of their intervention efforts and the measurement and reporting of the results of their operations. There have been fragmented proposals, some partial insights, some suggested approaches. However, there have been no answers to the problem of an integrated system for an appropriate (regular and continual) system of measurement of both effectiveness and efficiency for reporting to the stakeholders of HSOs, with the potential comparability of results for similar (mission) organizations and the aggregatability of HSOs' results for the benefit of society.

The review, divided into the accounting and human service fields, includes in the latter a section on government efforts. Reference has already been made to the GAO and other governmental searches for systems of evaluation and validation. These governmental efforts and the questions that have been raised are valuable contributions to the human services arena. The contribution lies in their attempts to develop meaningful systems of outcome measurement within appropriate scientific methodological controls in order to effect legislation for desired societal goals as determined by political forces. As will be apparent in the discussion that follows, even with appropriate experimental methodology to evaluate programs, the GAO has been unable to aggregate research results in terms of common or convertible measurement bases.

In the discussion of the literature, where feasible, criteria are used to evaluate the literature in the language of measuring systems—what elements, what attributes, what metrics were used and what successes/limitations were noted in terms of these criteria. In this manner, the performance of the literature can be understood on the basis of the elements used and the missing factors.

ACCOUNTING LITERATURE

Performance evaluation and assessment have traditionally been the purview of accounting and profit-oriented reporting systems. At the center of these systems is a figure referred to as *profit*, a single measure that is assumed to represent an objective indicator of both effectiveness and efficiency. The essential differences between business and nonbusiness entities is that the latter have no transferable ownership interests, presumably lack a profit motive, and receive contributions, which differ from revenues from the sales of goods and services.[1] HSOs prepare no such profit-oriented accounting reports, nor to date has there been a serious methodology with which to develop one.

Some of these issues have been discussed in prior chapters. In chapter 5, the theoretical and empirical approaches to an accounting framework, concepts, standards, and applications were presented from a methodological viewpoint. The lack of such a straightforward metric within the nonprofit world and the absence of an agreed-upon, unified framework in accounting have complicated evaluation. In fact, accounting practitioners currently accept that fund accounting is the most appropriate form of accountability for the NPS in general and HSOs in particular. Standard reference books and articles dealing with the NPS are also concerned about efficiency, but for the most part, give lip service to the question of program effectiveness, the very raison d'étre of HSOs.

Accounting in the NPS

While actual systems may vary with the size and type of organization, each fund accounting system is organized to keep separate records of the various funds. These may be unrestricted (available for purposes management deems appropriate as for general operations), and accordingly expandable; temporarily restricted (receipt in one period for use in a later one); or permanently restricted (according to donor specifications such as endowment funds or by board decisions). When compiled, the data on fund activity is organized into the format of a balance sheet, a statement of costs, support, and revenue, and a statement of changes in fund balances—or some such similar titles. Both Anthony and Mautz point out that adding together free and restricted funds obfuscates a critical goal of a financial statement, that is to judge an organization's ability to meet operating needs.[2] It should be noted that no statement of income is required. In fact, it has not been "possible" or "feasible" to construct such a statement, unless income were generated by market-oriented services.[3] However, many financial statements also contain schedules of operating costs usually classified by functions. Footnotes are generally geared to the same legal restrictions and to the other requirements of generally accepted accounting principles (GAAP). The NPS could not come to grips with this question of reporting effectiveness and efficiency through the medium of a statement of income. Until recently, the conventional wisdom has held that many organizations provide service without expectations of repayment, often in a noncompetitive environment, and have been primarily concerned with accounting for their stewardship of funds.

The early attitude of the accounting profession toward the non-profits can be summarized in a 1988 article: "The AICPA issued, during 1987, ten proposed Statements on Auditing Standards. While reading those documents, one is struck by the fact that non-profit organizations do not have a low profile; they have no profile. . . . The past two years [1986–1988] has seen a flurry of activity affecting non-profit accounting and reporting, coming from the FASB, American Institute for Certified Public Accountants (AICPA) and industry, . . . Progress is slow due to the complexity of the issues. Further, achieving a consensus . . . from varying industries (health care, education, religious, human service) is proving difficult." Much of the historical effort of the profession has been geared to defining operating costs, such as the applicability of depreciation and the allocation of joint costs (of information and fund raising), as well as to clarifying auditing standards.[4] In the latter area, the AICPA has issued audit guides to assist the independent auditor in the examining and reporting on financial statements of voluntary health and welfare organizations, colleges and universities and other non-profit organizations.[5] Generally, both the FASB and the AICPA appear to consider that GAAP applies except where there is specific or imputed nonapplicability. A task force of the AICPA, however, has made the "tentative decision" that "a Profit and Loss Statement is required."[6]

The same lack of interest may also apply to the paucity of literature issued by the accounting profession relative to efficiency. The articles discussed relative to efficiency appear almost entirely in the human service literature, for example, the development of a set of management indicators which provide key information to improve decision making, financing, control and operating (efficiency and effectiveness) capabilities. These indicators (ratios, formulas, and other prescriptions) were generated by a team from a school of social work in cooperation with and financed by a firm of CPAs.[7]

Since the 1988 article, the "flurry" has increased to a small but steady flow reflecting the additional efforts of the AICPA, the FASB, the activities of the Government Accounting Standards Board (GASB), the release of the United States General Accounting Office, *Government Auditing Standards*, July 1988 (Yellow

Book), and related articles appearing in accounting journals relative to depreciation, accruals and the treatment of volunteers' time.

The Yellow Book makes reference to "Performance Audits" defined to include "economy and efficiency and program audits"; the latter refers to "effectiveness measurement. . . . However, the objectives in performance audits
are more comprehensive than those in value-for-money audits."[8] The outline
continues to refer to the accuracy of the system for measuring and reporting
on economy and efficiency as well as to give instructions to "determine the
extent to which a program achieves a desired level of program results"; to
"determine whether management has considered alternatives for carrying out
the program that might yield desired results more effectively or at a lower cost,
and to "assess the adequacy of management's system for measuring and reporting effectiveness."[9] It should be noted that "the auditor does not express an
opinion on the over-all level of performance," rather he reports on his "find-
ings and conclusions."[10] By precluding the auditor from giving an opinion, the
GAO implicitly acknowledges the absence of a common system of measurement. The GAO, however, has clearly presented the problem in its various
aspects of outcome measurement common to HSOs.

As this book is being completed, the steady flow has gathered momentum
with additional releases by the GASB and FASB. The GASB has issued thirteen
statements and a codification of governmental accounting standards.[11] GASB
No. 11 is issued to cover standards for management and reporting for certain
state and local governmental entities. In general, it attempts to incorporate considerations of the needs of users, the governmental environment and the goal
of accountability. Its focus is on the flow of financial resources, which requires
the continuing use of fund accounting—general or operating, capital and debt—as
well as on budgeting and the requisite compliance with legal restrictions. An
accrual basis for determining revenue and expenses is called for. An emphasis
of the system on interperiod equity—the reflecting of current year's revenues
in comparison to current year's services. There is also a GASB Financial Reporting Entity Project which defines a reporting entity and what related organization should be included and how they should be displayed in the financial
report.[12]

A committee of the AICPA has directed its attention to the applicability of
GAAP to not-for-profits. The committee lists existing standards, about two hun-
dred, for guidance and is reviewing GAAP and FASB pronouncements as to
specific exemption, non-applicability, and specific applicability (see audit guides
for colleges and universities and health care providers). It is making recommendations as to consolidations, combinations, and display for reporting entities. There are temporary comments awaiting FASB action.

The FASB's nonprofit project which dates back to 1977 commenced by "considering the specialized accounting principles and practices included in three
AICPA Industry Audit and Accounting Guides." This has resulted in the is-
suance of six concepts statements. Five concepts statements between the years

1978 and 1985 encompassed accounting for both sectors. In December 1985, concept statement number six promulgated specialized accounting principles for not-for-profit organizations. In March 1986, "initially to address accounting for contributions and the recognition of depreciation," the project added financial statement displays and in August 1989, FASB issued an ED on "Financial Reporting by Not-for-Profit Organizations: Form and Content of Financial Statements." In 1990, the board issued an "amended" statement of proposed standards for "Accounting for Contributions Received and Contributions Made and Capitalization of Works of Art, Historical Treasures, and Similar Assets."[13] Further action by the FASB is awaited by the profession (see accounting pronouncements relative to the nonprofit sector, Exhibit 5.1).

Are accountants being asked the same set of questions as are social researchers? A recent article deals with performance measures of a local transit system and the CPA's role in evaluation. The search for economic measures for examining performance criteria of government agencies has also been raised in the accounting literature. "Governmental financial support for numerous activities is often based upon performance criteria—the measurement of which has not been subjected to the intensive discipline that financial reporting has received. The author describes a typical scenario of this activity and the meaningful service that CPAs can play in promoting efficiency, understanding and cost savings."[14]

Discussion of Accounting Literature

For evaluating effectiveness and efficiency of operations of an HSO, an accounting system should incorporate: (1) information related to client outcome results; (2) standards relative to agency operations for purposes of controls and decision making; (3) mechanisms for regular internal reporting to hierarchical levels of staff and management; and (4) a mechanism for reporting to boards of directors, government agencies, and the public at large on a basis comparable with other agencies. Such a system should be integrated with data bases and reporting processes.

As the review of the accounting literature shows, the presentation of a balance sheet and statement of funds as the only public accountability by the HSO hardly responds to the above criteria. First, fund accounting contains no measurement of the effectiveness or efficiency of HSO programs or of the organization, other than in terms of its fund raising or survival capabilities. Consequently, providers of funds have no way of knowing which organizations are more worthy of support than others. Second, where other systems create and uphold surrogate goals for program performance, fund accounting systems may promote tensions between policy making and operational segments of the organization, between boards of trustees and senior executives responsible for funding and survival and those responsible for providing services to clients. Management indicators for the most part are efficiency oriented and thus have more meaning within the framework of effectiveness. In the PS, the plant that produced a single shirt of one size and one color could be amazingly efficient; however, it would run out of required warehouse space in which to store the unsold merchandise. Yet, as the literature indicates, in the absence of a profit metric, an illusion of measurement performance is created by the currently used, inadequate, fund financial statements and efficiency oriented internal reports.

The articles by individual practitioners discussed in chapters 5 and 6 and the various releases by government and private professional organizations attest to the more recent interest in the not-for-profit sector. The accounting profession, however, still appears to be looking at standards and not at framework, which will probably result in continued extensions in deadlines for exposure drafts, a divided profession, and a potential threat to the very existence of governing bodies.

HUMAN SERVICE LITERATURE

Juxtaposed within the debate of the position and future of human service programs are calls for economic justification and rationalization on the one hand, and assertions that the value of human services cannot be revealed by quantitative measures on the other. The literature covers such problems as the absence of a framework for evaluation, the use of economic tools such as cost benefit, the difficulty of applying analytical tools, the transfer of management and cost accounting techniques from the PS, organizational problems, and attempts at solutions to these questions. As might be expected, the review parallels the discussion of accounting with its emphasis on empirical studies in the absence of a conceptual framework. Some responses are reviewed in the following pages, together with a critique of their strengths and weaknesses, under the captions of Framework and Methodology, Efficiency, Cost/Benefit Analyses, Multiple Indicators, Other Organizational Elements, and General Accounting Office (GAO) and State Evaluations. The literature relating to Cost/Benefit Analyses is of special significance because it incorporates the basic approach used in the proposed organizational model.

Framework and Methodology

As previously stated, the HSO needs a conceptual framework for evaluating programs, staff, and the organization based on an integrated information system about all phases of operation for reporting to stakeholders and which can serve as a basis for planning and research. There is a need for a performance measure and its concomitant for service staff to recognize value in recording data, which must be related to client outcomes and intervention evaluation.[15] The lack of a concrete, generally accepted framework, as discussed under Methodology in chapter 5, has meant that even the basic definitions have been confused, such as effectiveness, efficiency, output, and outcome. Efficiency measures that are based on the summary of outputs have been used to portray effectiveness, which should more rightly be associated with outcomes. Accountability has also seemed to become synonymous with efficiency.[16] While there may be consensus as to what services should be provided, how they should be provided, and in what sequence they should be provided, there is little agreement on how to measure the effect of what services have been provided.[17]

Frieden and Nosek state that in spite of what seems to be a genuine interest in evaluation theory, there has been relatively little substantive work performed.[18] Despite all the attempts at program evaluation, numerous authors have commented on the lack of focus on outcomes and/or the development of a conceptual framework for a meaningful evaluation system.[19] There appears to be common agreement about the difficulty of applying analytic tools to assess diverse program effects and about the need for comprehensive evaluation of service delivery systems.[20] Nonetheless, enthusiasm for quantitative measures has emerged. Concern has also been expressed, however, to ensure that the application of present value concepts to human services does not skew the allocation of resources between the aged and the young, and a solution proposed to vary the discount rate for different populations.[21] Moreover, as discussed by Lipsey in Chapter 5, despite its widespread use, there are problems with the application of the methodology of the experimental paradigm for program evaluation.[22] While increasing attention has been devoted to the conceptualization of social work practice, little has been focused on issues of operating methodology. Without methodology, it is asserted that social work practice will continue to develop but in a manner that is "uncontrolled and irresponsible."[23]

Donors are asking for proof that their contributions are having an impact on the health and productivity of the HSOs' clients. Human service agencies are increasingly required to provide concrete and quantitative evidence of their performance.[24] The question no longer seems to be whether to measure but how to measure. Government agencies

invite proposals . . . to assist providers of health care services in assessing and monitoring a quality and level of care being furnished . . . to make available tools . . . to provide a means of monitoring and measuring services and outcomes . . . very efficiently delivered care that has a poor outcome is not effective and is thus "poor" quality care.[25]

In 1979, the Yale University program on nonprofit organizations identified a number of dilemmas encountered in attempting to evaluate HSOs. Some of the dilemmas pointed out were: lack of standard date collection and reporting regarding service provision and outcome, absence of clearly stated goals for clients and the organization (only qualitatively expressed), lack of criteria for short and long-term goals,[26] and problems inherent in comparing organizations using qualitative (subjective) effectiveness criteria.[27] Another dilemma that emerges is the relationship of the HSOs to their market. In the PS, the provision of goods and services is consumer-oriented, based on supply/demand feedback, which presumably emits signals on the appropriateness of price and quantity of services offered. However, for HSOs, clients who receive service may not be the payers for such services. The specific linking of supply and demand has been subverted to government or board policies.[28] Some of the literature describes the basics of the problem in terms of organizations with multiple goals and constituencies, which must deal with the complexities of diverse human beings who present a variety of needs, goals, and differing capacities to achieve them.[29]

The failure to develop analytical reporting may not only affect the amounts and kinds of funds received from external donors, but also lessen the possibilities of survival in competition against private industry. In the 1980s government expenditures increased, and as service eligibility standards widened, the traditional nonprofit arena has become more enticing to profit-oriented organizations.[30]

An analysis of the process of contracting for services (which focuses on both the effects on the government agency and the nonprofit service provider) predicts significant changes that include increased competition, an expansion of activities by profit-making organizations, and alternations in entrepreneurial management style, accounting, marketing, funding and so on. The article also points out that contracting of government services has the potential for growth of services without a concomitant growth of government.[31]

Questions raised in recent articles indicate a need for a system that will facilitate measuring effectiveness in the face of today's complex and fragmented human service delivery system. With widely divergent state/local structural arrangements, diversity of local resources, customs, target populations and the increased call for privatization and direct contracting of government services, it becomes even more critical to have in place a system that takes into account all variables, mandates adherence to centrally established standards and still permits local autonomy. The system needs to ensure equity. To accomplish this there is need for sophisticated automated information systems . . . "information is as critical as resources" . . . to enable clients to access and derive profits from services.[32]

From observations of the relationship of measurement systems to patterns of service and organization problem solving have come two major approaches to program evaluation: ad hoc studies and client outcome monitoring. Client outcome monitoring presents a systematic attempt to assess the impact of service on later client functioning. Its implementation requires the regular collection of outcome data for at least a sample of clients and agency programs. In contrast, ad hoc studies tend to be somewhat more selective. By focusing on specific programs and/or problems, these studies tend to generate a more detailed analysis of the relationship between services and outcome. While causal relationships may not be specifically measurable, contributions of the program to client performance may be reasonably determined.[33] Continual awareness is required, however, to detect unidentified variables or hidden assumptions when analyzing outcomes. Dean and Dolan conclude that to measure the earnings' impact of vocational rehabilitation intervention requires multi-variate analysis of service mix and such client demographics as health, age, sex, race, marital status, education, and prior training. These variables can then be functionally related to clients' changes in earnings and agency costs.[34]

Although there has been increased attention focused on attempts to evaluate outcomes in economic terms, difficulties have arisen due to lack of a priori statements on goals, definitions, data collection, and outcome measures and their timing. There are several examples of program evaluations that either failed to provide the information necessary to make a judgment as to continuation of funding or else required expansive, time-consuming studies in order to demonstrate the validity of the original program assumptions. Thus, even with program evaluations, results have not provided appropriate information to assist decision makers (funding sources or other stakeholders) as to whether the fault lay with the organization operating the program or with the program methodology itself. Additionally, the evaluations' results are not comparable among organizations with similar missions.[35] An economic answer to the question of effectiveness with the potential for comparability offers the base line to begin analyzing or looking for other causal factors.

Efficiency

The evolution of nonprofit management is seen as consisting of a cycle with shifts occurring periodically that first incorporate innovation, then problem-solving approaches, then management in the style of the PS.[36] Some writers have attempted to apply management techniques from the PS, which may cause effectiveness of outcomes to become confused with or subordinated to efficiency. The importation of profit style systems, which can confuse business managers who are accustomed to having profit as a guide, further adds to the tendency of equating efficiency and accountability of funds to effectiveness of outcomes.[37] The innovations of program planning and budgeting, management by objectives, and zero-based budgeting have been introduced but are often found lacking. On the other hand, the development of real performance systems has ''supplanted effectiveness and social impact as dominant values'' wherein management excellence becomes the agency goal.[38] The chief result of this management imposition has often been the growth of an antimanagement bias among practitioners who suspect that the system divorces them from their clients.

HSOs have increasingly focused on adopting current private sector business systems in a move to increase efficiency, cut costs, and improve services. To compound this approach, top managers have been recruited according to their track record in attracting funds. Top management is then either overtly or tacitly assigned the mission for the organizational fund raising. Program operation and design is left to middle management, who identify with the client/consumer, and tension is set up between practitioners and managers who perceive themselves as having different goals. Compounding this tension is the fact that usually neither group has an understanding of the value system and the knowledge base of the other group.

Other Organizational Elements

A number of other elements of the functioning of HSOs have been studied. These include the application of new technologies, the question of staff motivation and incentives, organizational conditions, potential conflicts between staff and management objectives, rational models impacting the public sector (i.e., decision making and the political process), dangers and benefits of new technologies, the unifying theme of the client, the use of feedback loops, and the needs and possible directions for future research and evaluation.[39]

Still another approach to evaluation of program outcomes is a national competition for excellence among agencies. Organizations with a similar mission are invited annually to submit program models, which are judged by a set of criteria in different categories. Each agency is rated on a common scoring system. "Each application was assessed using measures of client benefits and program productivity. Three to eight measures were used, depending on the program category."[40]

The literature has increasingly addressed the issues of evaluation from the management perspective. Not only has the introduction of management techniques had an impact on nonprofits but also the participation of top management personnel on boards and in consulting roles with these organizations. Such participation leads to the observation "that most non-profits fail to agree on a clear-cut set of objectives . . . and accept a broad and unquantifiable idea as a goal." They then go on to acknowledge that although this is a difficult process, it is essential that "key managers and board members of nonprofit organizations must define—and periodically redefine—exactly what it is they are in business to achieve. Further, they must define their goals with enough precision to be able to develop yardsticks that will tell them when they are making progress and when they aren't.[41] Another study proposes a "conceptual framework" for the selection of management indicators. It includes management reports on a feedback basis to respond to specified objectives to measure effectiveness and efficiency of the operations and financing of the agency as well as the effect on clients and the community.[42]

Ramanathan recognizes that "fund accounting . . . (fails) to link expenditures with results." To remedy this situation, a "conceptual scheme and control framework" for evaluating and improving management efficiency in nonprofit organizations is proposed, which also "integrates control and evaluation criteria within relevant aggregate benefit-cost perspective." He differentiates between outputs for efficiency measures and outcomes of effectiveness, which would be measured in terms of benefit cost-analysis within the particular agency. He emphasizes the integration of the common data components.[43]

Cost/Benefit Analyses

Researchers, practitioners, and governments have commonly grappled with questions of effectiveness.[44] At present, there is required reporting on government contracts of the economic outcomes of vocational services such as the measurement of substantial gainful activity.[45]

In an attempt to provide a needed framework, *macro* cost benefit analyses and *micro* program evaluation approaches such as those used by rehabilitation and manpower training projects focus on *before* and *after* clients' earnings as measurements of the clients' abilities to be self-sufficient and/or to improve their functioning. The logic behind cost/benefit studies goes back to the notable example used to support the passage of the Vocational Rehabilitation Act in 1920, as cited by Berkowitz: "The federal coordinating council for the vocational rehabilitation program stated the matter bluntly, 'The justification of vocational rehabilitation is based on its economic returns to society. It is primarily economic.' "[46]

In his seminal 1975 article, Rostker described a similar analytic process but one modified for what he recognized as prior failures of cost/benefit analysis. His proposed model incorporated measures for both efficiency and effectiveness and was based on the concept of a national labor market survey "to estimate the gain in client income attributable to the program." His survey would also provide program managers with data for detailed evaluation of the effect of treatment on clients with a given set of characteristics.[47]

A model using aggregated data from the experience of one state agency was developed by Berkley Planning Associates. Building on prior vocational rehabilitation models, Berkley "uses aggregate program data . . . for each of the state's vocational rehabilitation programs and information on all closures during that year." As noted above, the measure of benefits is based on a before and after approach—earnings at program closure versus earnings at program intake. Appropriate adjustments are made for retirement, mortality, continuity of employment, fringe benefits, changes in family labor force participation, repeaters, and for the present value of money. To adjust for this last element, Berkley discounts the future earnings stream at a rate of discount equal to the state's borrowing rate plus some modification factor for benefits not attributable to the program.[48]

The results of a series of workshops are summarized in an article on "the methodology and application of benefit-cost analysis as a means of evaluating the overall efficiency" of transitional employment programs. "The primary issue to be addressed and the benefit cost-analysis is the question of whether society is better off with the program than without the program," that is, do the primary and secondary benefits exceed the total cost?[49]

Multiple Indicators

The difficulties inherent in the calculation of a single outcome or benefit measure have led researchers to attempt to develop models to incorporate measures of effectiveness and efficiency based on multiple comparative key indicators. A team from the universities of Denver and North Carolina has developed measures relating primarily to the efficient management of community mental health organizations that use comparative key performance indicators such as "mixes of revenues, clients, staff, and services. . . . Performance comparisons can be both over time within an organization and in relation to comparable organizations.''[50]

Morrell recommends that multiple indicators be culled from five major operations areas: ''1. result achieved by the organization in meeting its mission, 2. effectiveness in strategic, space, and financial planning, 3. ability of the institution to achieve financial stability, 4. effective allocation and use of capital assets, and 5. use and development of human resources.'' It should be noted that the set of indicators used may be situationally specific.[51]

General Accounting Office (GAO) and State Evaluations

Another example of multiple indicators as a framework for program evaluation is their use by the GAO for the evaluation of certain government programs such as Women, Infants and Children, (WIC), Teenage Pregnancy, and other children's programs.[52] This use of multiple indicators is necessary and gives multidimensional information about the operation, outputs, and outcomes of various government-supported efforts. It should be noted, however, that varying multiple indicators or the use of a large number of indicators for evaluation lacks focus. A single focused outcome measurement, when used together with multiple indicators, could permit comparability for evaluation among programs geared to the same populations and administered by agencies with similar missions. The organizational model described in chapter 2 provides this focus.

The studies and reviews of the GAO, for the most part, are critical in spotlighting the defects of current program evaluation.[53] In general, in their program reviews, they found that the majority of the programs lacked appropriate evaluation techniques including the collection of relevant data, specificity of goal, control of variables, and evidence that the ascribed effects were actually caused by the programs, among others.[54]

The numerous reports prepared by the GAO for transmittal to the congressional leaders of the various responsible subcommittees cite the need for longitudinal studies, which require standard and continuous reporting and specificity of data and expected economic outcomes. For example, in a letter to Senator Chafee, the GAO states that ''even for those whose designs were credible, the ability to generalize from them to typical service settings is uncertain and the long term benefits are unknown because only one assessment of outcomes extended beyond 24 months.''[55]

The GAO also expressed concern about the lack of data collection in their transmittal letter to Congressman Coats: ''In the absence of national evaluations or comprehensive information systems, GAO could not determine whether the reforms have reduced the number of unnecessary and inappropriate placements.'' They go on to say, ''Neither the required state information systems nor the recommended national system includes the quality of care data needed to answer questions about the intended outcomes of the reforms for children and families."[56]

On the other hand, the GAO, in evaluating the outcomes in terms of cost effectiveness of eight major federal programs involving children, while observing the shortage of usable evaluations, nonetheless concluded that there was powerful research evidence about improvements in children's lives and the significant reduction of future costs for the populations served.[57]

As reported in *Gerontology News* in August 1987:

The General Accounting Office has stated in a recently released report that the Health Care Financing Administration [HCFA] does not know how effectively states' home and community-based services substitute for nursing home care and cannot evaluate whether these programs increase or decrease Medicaid cost. GAO recommended that HFCA develop methods to measure the ability of home and community-based services programs to prevent or postpone nursing home care and use these methods to determine their impact on the need for nursing home care.[58]

There are calls on the state level, as well, for evaluation of outcomes on an economic basis and for longitudinal studies that allow adequate time for measuring the effectiveness of these programs. New York, for example, has set up a statewide system for reporting the results of their supported employment program, through the design of a statewide MIS. This system (SEMIS) establishes standard data collection in order to measure cost/benefit of this approach.[59] Other state and local governmental units have also addressed these issues.[60]

Discussion of Human Service Literature

Some of the articles in the human service literature succeed in resolving pieces of the system's requirements, either from the micro or macro level of operations. None succeeds on both levels. Macro level studies homogenize averages post hoc, while the individual agency requires specific data ex ante for decisions. Rostker's combined macro/micro model has limitations: Macro statistical studies that incorporate measurement, membership, and averaging errors lose validity when applied to micro levels; for operational purposes, continual updating of program and population mixes and cost changes are required. Other micro or individual agency models that emphasize efficiency contain no proposals for "common denominator" outcome reporting. "Economic scarcity, political uncertainty, public scrutiny and policy pressures . . . [to be accountable] appear to be permanent features of our existence. Therefore, survival, efficiency and excellence in management have become [the] fundamental agency interests."[61] Moreover, it has been shown that both evaluation and research studies are often not used because they are neither integrated into operations nor timely.[62] While studies have yielded a richer understanding of the need for and difficulties in attaining quantitative benefit measurements, they have yet to meet the fundamental requirements of a reporting system.

To serve as a useful and dependable evaluation tool, reporting systems should be based on continually available data and must also provide their information in routine and periodic statements. The time required by most cost/benefit analyses and the cost involved in their preparation reduces their value not only to external stakeholders but also to management, which requires, for the short run, regular updates on activity for decision making and control, and for the long run, planning and research. The reporting of efficiency and effectiveness measures is valuable to the extent that it can be internalized by staff, enhancing insight and motivating behavior.

The competitive award process of the J. M. Foundation succeeds in alerting some stakeholders of rehabilitation agencies to relative outcome excellence by means of a scoring system. This is a carefully calculated and fair measuring system and a serious attempt at program evaluation. Its weaknesses lie in its failure to meet the necessary measuring concepts discussed—it does not produce an economic measure nor is it primarily client focused. Equally important, it is not internally generated, thereby lessening its impact on planning, decision making, and molding staff behavior. Thus, even the "best" does not provide a meaningful bottom line. Even after clarification of mission and specified outcome goals, the problem remains of measurement of success, a bottom line meaningful to staff, management, and other stakeholders, a measure other than cash availability. Like the excellence competition, the SEMIS evaluation effort produces externally generated data in evaluation; unlike it, the focus on benefits provides dollar amounts as well as a comparative site analysis.

The program models cited are top down and are not internally generated bottom-up evaluations.[63] For efficiency as well as effectiveness evaluation and for behavioral incentives for client, staff, and management, an internally integrated measuring approach is preferred. The literature revealed only one attempt at such a bottom-up/top-down conceptual control system, integrating pre- and post-client evaluation, using common data bases, differentiating between output and outcome criteria, and culminating in an organizational performance measurement based on cost benefit.[64]

The flexibility that seems to be the greatest benefit of the multiple indicator approach may simultaneously be its greatest drawback. While "top managers need management indicators to provide them with the information they need to perform effectively . . . there has been little systematic effort to meet this need." Their solution is to develop a conceptual framework for indicator analysis built around assessments of appropriateness of demand, appropriateness of process, long-term impact on clients and community, and definition and assessment of objectives.[65] Another problem arises because of the very specific nature and application of certain indicators, so that managers may be unsure of which are most appropriate to their cause. It is also unfortunate that most of the multiple indicators that have been developed either deal with the subordinate question of efficiency or with unintegrated or discrete measures of performance. Generally, they are situational, noncomparable, and do not have a bottom line.

SUMMARY

The literature reveals how each discipline (profession) carries out its own evaluation using its own system or methodology. Each discipline pursues solutions to the problem from its own knowledge base and its own inherent assumptions. Thus accountants, with their focus on fund accounting, look at the management of funds while the human service professionals struggle with program evaluation and ad hoc research studies. This separation has a profound effect on the behavior of all the stakeholders. It contributes to the difficulty of the various levels of staff (as well as to the various stakeholder groups) in understanding the gestalt of the organization and evaluating its effectiveness in achieving its mission. The board, for example, would read financial reports in a very different way if the bottom line informed it as to the results of the mission as well as the cash flow. Both information streams are required.

While some articles appear in the accounting literature about the NPS and government, there are none that deal with the missions of the HSOs as a contributing segment to the societal economy. Accordingly, there has not been a willingness to tackle the question of designing a measurement of income for this sector. This state of affairs is abetted by the human service sector, which, while looking for an economic measure, remains afraid that there will be a loss of concern for the individual if an economic criterion were developed. The concept of societal income provides the conceptual framework that unites both sectors. In fact, the human service evaluation models could more readily be applied based on the proposed organizational model. This model provides the information for specific program and client cost-benefit analyses, for integrating multiple indicators, and program evaluation, as well as for research on causal relationships and for planning.

The significance of the accumulation of client data changes when the focus is on outcome and when line staff/service providers see the direct relationship between their practice, client service, and recording of client data. In effect, too few members of top management attach importance or understand the significance of operations and mission; they are focused on survival rather than on outcomes.[66] Multiple indicators, while useful, generally are situational and noncomparable and do not have a unified approach or bottom line; likewise, quality assurance as a methodology focuses on process rules. The proposed organizational model focuses on outcomes.

In general, it is important to avoid the use of "frozen" client mix performance and goal data, homogenized in averages. Client information must accentuate the individual as well as totals for the client groups and the organization—it must be humanistic as well as mechanistic. The evaluation of the organization is, in one sense, the sum of the evaluation of the success of its individual clients. To function optimally, such a measurement system must first resolve the dilemmas that were noted above. This requires that each organization's objectives be defined in terms of its mission, that the units of input, output, and outcome be identified, and that comparability of reporting be achieved among like HSOs. Further, for the individual HSO, the system must establish integrated linkages between and among the services delivered, the processes by which they are provided, their cost, the clients to whom they are provided, the outcomes that are achieved, and the reporting mechanisms to the hierarchical stakeholders.

The next chapter details the components and the procedures that such an integrated system would comprise, with common language and data bases that are meaningful to staff at all levels and to other stakeholders, a system that not only gives control of and insight into the internal operations but also allows for an external statement of performance based on objective, verifiable data. It is a system that is not simply valuative but developmental, one that at the same time can look backward and forward, one that is able to contribute to the advancement of both client and staff.[67]

NOTES

1. FASB Concepts Statement, No. 4 (1980), December. *Objectives of financial reporting by nonbusiness organizations*, 3.

2. Anthony, Robert N. (1987, May). We don't have the accounting concepts we need. *The CPA Journal, 57*(5), 42; Mautz, R. K. (1989, August). Not-for-profit financial reporting: Another view. *Journal of Accountancy, 168*(2), 66.

3. "The value of services provided by most voluntary health and welfare organizations cannot be quantitatively measured by monetary data contained in financial statements." American Institute of Certified Public Accountants, Inc. (1974). *Audit of voluntary health and welfare organizations* (p. 1). New York: Committee on Voluntary Health and Welfare Organizations; Folpe, Herbert K. (1989, April/May). Sorting out nonprofit accounting issues. *The Philanthropy Monthly, 22*(4, 5), 5–14, 7–14. Anthony, Robert N. (1989, July/August). Sorting out nonprofit accounting issues. *The Philanthropy Monthly, 22*(7), 11–16.

4. Fetterman, Allen L. (1988, March). Update on not-for-profit accounting and reporting. *The CPA Journal, 58*(3), 22–29.

5. American Institute of Certified Public Accountants, Inc. (1981). *Audits of certain nonprofit organizations*. New York: Subcommittee on Nonprofit Organizations; American Institute of Certified Public Accountants, Inc. (1974). *Audits of state and local governmental units*. New York: Committee on Governmental Accounting and Auditing; American Institute of Certified Public Accountants, Inc. (1990, July 15 - effective date). *Audit and accounting guide: Audits of providers of health care services*. New York: Health Care Committee and the Health Care Audit Guide Task Force.

6. Fetterman, Update on not-for-profit accounting and reporting, 24.

7. Elkin, Robert, & Molitor, Mark. (1985, Winter). A conceptual framework for selecting management indicators in nonprofit organizations. *Administration in Social Work, 9*(4), 13–23.

8. GAO (U.S. General Accounting Office). (1988, July). *Government auditing standards (yellow book.)* chap. 2, p. 3.

9. GAO (U.S. General Accounting Office). (1988, July). *Government auditing standards yellow book*. chap. 2, p. 5.

10. GAO (U.S. General Accounting Office). (1988, July). *Government auditing standards yellow book.* chap. 2, p. 5.

11. Seville, Mary Alice. (1991, May). GASB moves ahead with MFBA: Credits to follow later; and Giroux, Gary (1991, May). Executive summary of GASB pronouncements. Douglas R. Carmichael, editor, *The CPA Journal, 61*(5), 54–55 and 55–57.

12. GASB, no. 11 (Government Accounting Standards Board). (1991). *Measurement focus and basis of accounting of governmental business-type enterprises*; and GASB (Government Accounting Standards Board). (1990, March). *The financial reporting entity* [Exposure Draft].

13. FASB (Financial Accounting Standards Board). (1990, October 31). *Accounting for contributions received and contributions made and capitalization of works of art, historical treasures and similar assets.* [Exposure Draft].

14. The author also comments that the lack of perfect information should not preclude reporting despite potential "distortions" and "obvious limitations of any service measure"; she observes that while the GASB has encouraged performance evaluation in accordance with the Yellow Book referred to above, a "number of years will pass before standards are set which require systematic reporting. In the interim, progress will largely depend on both researchers and practitioners addressing the problems and encouraging experimentation." Wallace, Wanda A. (1989, April). Performance evaluation of government agencies. *The CPA Journal,* 14–22.

15. Patti, Rino J. (1987, September/October). Managing for service effectiveness in social welfare organizations. *Social Work, 32*(5), 380.

16. Weissman, Harold H. (1983, June). Accountability and pseudo-accountability: A nonlinear approach. *Social Service Review, 57*(2), 323–336.

17. Gillman, Arthur E., Simon, Ellen Perlman, & Shinn, Eugene B. (1978, December). An outcome study of an intensive rehabilitation training program for young adults. *Journal of Visual Impairment and Blindness, 72*(10), 388–392.

18. Frieden, Lex, & Nosek, Margaret. (1985). The efficacy of the independent living program model based on descriptive and evaluative studies. *Rehabilitation Research Review.* The National Rehabilitation Center Information Center (NARIC), Catholic University of America, Washington, DC.

19. Patti, Managing for service effectiveness, 380.

20. Weissman. Accountability and pseudo-accountability, 323–336.

21. Avorn, Jerome L. (1984). Benefit and cost analysis in geriatric care, turning age discrimination into health policy. *The New England Journal of Medicine, 310,* 1294–1301; Welch, H. Gilbert. (1991, June). Comparing apples and oranges: Does cost-effectiveness analysis deal fairly with the old and the young? *The Gerontologist, 31*(3), 332–336.

22. Lipsey, Mark W., Cross, Scott, Dunkle, Jan, Pollard, John, & Stobart, Gordon. (1985, September). Evaluation: The state of the art and the sorry state of the science. In D. S. Cordray (ed.), *Utilizing prior research in evaluation planning. New directions for program evaluation* (No. 27), 7–28. San Francisco, CA: Jossey-Bass.

23. LeCroy, Craig Winston. (1985, September). Methodological issues in the evaluation of social work practice. *Social Service Review, 59*(3), 345–357.

24. DeCaro, James J., Clarcq, Jack R., Walter, Gerard G., Welsh, William A., & Reilly, Dorothea. (1988, July, August, & September). A methodology for utilizing federal data sources in program evaluation. *Journal of Rehabilitation, 54*(3), 46–50.

25. Solicitation by the Health Care Financing Administration, Department of Health and Human Services. (1988, May 4). *Federal Register, 53*(86), 16020.

26. Kanter, Rosabeth Moss. (1979). *The measurement of organizational effectiveness, productivity, performance and success* (PONPO Working Paper No. 8), Institution for Social and Policy Studies, 2–4. New Haven, CT: Yale University.

27. Kanter. (1979). *The measurement of organizational effectiveness*, 5–7.

28. Middleton, Melissa. (1986, February). *Nonprofit management: A report on current research and areas for development* (PONPO Working Paper No. 108, and Institution for Social and Policy Studies, PONPO Working Paper No. 2108), 21–22. New Haven, CT: Yale University.

29. Fishman, D. B. (1979). Development and test of a cost-effectiveness methodology for CMHCS (PS-246-767).

30. Stoez, David. (1989, March). A theory of social welfare. *Social Work, 34*(2), 101–107.

31. Kramer, Ralph M. and Grossman, Bart (1987, March). Contracting for social services: Process management and resource dependencies. *Social Service Review, 61*(1), 32–55.

32. Ezell, Mark, & Patti, Rino (1991, March). State human service agencies structure and organization. *Social service review, 64*(1), 30 and 22–45.

33. Hatry, Harry P. (1983). *Program evaluation and client outcome monitoring for state and local human services agencies, Urban Institute, Washington, DC.* Beverly Hills, CA: Sage Publishing.

34. Dean, David H. and Dolan, Robert C. (1987, January/February/March). Issues in the economic evaluation of the vocational rehabilitation program. *Journal of Rehabilitation, 53*(1), 13–19.

35. The following provide illustrations of issues discussed in the text: [re: elderly blind] Graves, William H., Giesen, J. Martin, & Maxson, John H. (1988, October). *Analysis of Title VII, Part C, independent living for the elderly blind grants, fiscal year 1986–1987*: Agency Rehabilitation Research and Training Center on Blindness and Low Vision, Mississippi State University; [re: community residential programs] *NARIC Quarterly, 1*(3) (1988, Fall) Silver Spring, MD: National Rehabilitation Information Center; [re: ambulatory patients] Friedman, Emily (1989, August 8). Outcomes analysis in rehabilitation, *Utilization Review*, pp. 5–6. On the other hand, for specificity of goal and innovative method of data collection, see DeCaro, Clarcq, Walter, Welsh, & Reilly. A methodology for utilizing federal data sources in program evaluation, 46–50.

36. Lewis, Harold. (1975, January 5). *Management in the nonprofit social service organization.* Paper presented at the Seminar on Education for Management of Social Services, University of Pennsylvania.

37. Weissman, Accountability and Pseudo-Accountability, 327.

38. Weirich, Thomas W., Deuschle, Linda, & Sklaver, Deborah. (1982). *The adoption of performance assessment in a CMHC.* John F. Kennedy Community Mental Health/Mental Retardation Center, Philadelphia, PA.

39. Geiss, Gunther R., & Wiswanathan, Narayn. (1986). *The human edge-information technology and helping people.* New York: The Hawthorne Press.

40. The J. M. Foundation—1987 National Awards for Excellence in Vocational Programs—A Profile of America's Finest Vocational Programs Serving People with Disabilities.

41. Harvey, Philip D., & Snyder, James D. (1987, January/February). Charities need a bottom line too. *Harvard Business Review, 65*(1), 14–22.

42. Elkin and Molitor. A conceptual framework for selecting management indicators in nonprofit organizations, 13–23.

43. Ramanathan, Kavasseri V. (1985, Summer). A proposed framework for designing management control systems in not-for-profit organizations. *Financial Accountability and Management, 1*(1), 75–95.

44. The "NSF will support high-quality research proposals . . . that could lead to significant public benefit if the research is successful," including "economic and social benefits to the nation." National Science Foundation Program Solicitation. (1987, June 22).

45. Supported Employment Briefing New York State (SEMIS), (1989, February 8).

46. Berkowitz, Monroe, & Berkowitz, Edward. (1983). Benefit cost analysis. *Rehabilitation Research Review, No. 5,* 1–35. The National Rehabilitation Information Center (NARIC), Catholic University of America, Washington, D.C.

47. Rostker, Bernard. (1975). *An evaluation-management information system for vocational rehabilitation.* The Rand Corporation, Santa Monica, CA.

48. Rostker, *An Evaluation-management information system.*

49. This paper outlines the techniques in terms of "the five steps necessary to conduct a successful benefit cost-analysis." Measuring benefits includes the concept of "discounting them to obtain a present value measure of the desirability of a project." However, after focusing on the commonality of such analyses using cost benefits, the author concludes that "each project will likely present a unique test of problems and difficulties . . . [and] adequate analysis may require a great deal of ingenuity . . . [and] the combined talents of many disciplines to . . . evaluate the benefits and costs of a particular project." Sav, G. Thomas. (1989, April, May, June). Benefit-cost analysis of transitional employment programs. *Journal of Rehabilitation, 55*(2), 44–52.

50. Sorenson, James E., Zelman, William, Hanbery, Glyn W., & Kucic, A. Ronald. (1985, January). Key performance indicators for community mental health organizations, managing with key indicators. *National Council on Community Mental Health Centers.* CO: University of Denver, School of Accounting.

51. Morrell, Lewis R. (1988, Winter). Yardsticks for performance of nonprofit management. *Directors & Boards, 10*(2), 37–39.

52. Shipman, Stephanie. (1989). *General criteria for evaluating social programs* (pp. 20–26). Washington, DC: U.S. General Accounting Office.

53. An apparatus with multiple indicators for improvement is now at hand. A report by the GAO describes six programs and proposes that "the valuative component of the framework is expressed as ten general criteria in a three-part structure that represents: (1) the need for the program, (2) its implementation, and (3) its effects" (sec. 2, p. 10). See their Table 2.1 for the ten general evaluation criteria related to the three parts of the structure. In particular, there is an extended discussion in the GAO report of "achievement of intended objectives" and "cost effectiveness." The GAO recognized the extent of the problems: "We encountered greater difficulty in generating indicators of the evaluation criteria for those program purposes and goals that were less concretely defined in their authorizing legislation than others." Chelimsky, Eleanor. (1988, Summer). Federal evaluation in a legislative environment: Producing on a faster trade. In C. G. Wye & H. P. Hatry (eds.), *Timely, low-cost evaluation in the public sector* (New Directions for Program Evaluation, No. 38, pp. 73–86. San Francisco, CA: Jossey-Bass.

54. GAO (United States General Accounting Office). (1988, August). Briefing Report to the Ranking Minority Member, Select Committee on Children, Youth, and Families,

House of Representatives. *A comparative evaluation framework and five illustrations* (GAO/PEMD–838–28BR). Washington, DC: Author.

55. GAO (United States General Accounting Office). (1986, July). Briefing Report to the Honorable John H. Chafee, United States Senate. *Teenage pregnancy: 500,000 births a year but few tested programs* (GAO/PEMD–86–16BR). Washington, DC: Author.

56. "In the absence of reliable information on the quality of care provided, the Congress may want to consider mandating evaluations of the effects that the reforms have had on improving program services and their outcomes for families." GAO (United States General Accounting Office). (1989, August). Report to Congressional Requesters. *Foster care—incomplete implementation of the reforms and unknown effectiveness* (GAO/PEMD–89–17). Washington, DC.

57. Searching for a system of measuring their cost effectiveness, a congressional committee requested the General Accounting Office (GAO) to develop a system of evaluation of "eight major federal programs that promote the health, education, nutrition and development of children." A research study was undertaken, a conceptual framework formulated, and three years later the Select Committee reported that there is "powerful research evidence that these key programs can make critical improvements in the lives of millions of children . . . reducing significantly the need for costly expenditures for years to come." The committee report also notes the "shortage of rigorous independent evaluations" and the use of these studies to direct the use of scarce resources for "sound investments in America's children and families." House Select Committee on Children, Youth and Families. (1985, 1988). *Opportunities for success: Cost-effective programs for children.* Washington, DC: Government Printing Office.

58. Staff. (1987, August). *Gerontology News*, p. 4. Washington, DC: The Gerontological Society of America.

59. Supported Employment Briefing New York State (SEMIS). (1989, February 8).

60. The New Jersey welfare evaluation program will include the "impact of welfare reform on employment, earnings and education attainment of public assistance recipients . . . benefit derived by public taxpayers and the federal, state and county governments," and thus should "provide policy makers and taxpayers with . . . analysis of . . . cost and benefits and its effects on welfare dependency." This new program aims to provide Aid to Families with Dependent Children "with opportunities for employment and self-sufficiency." Staff. (1989, April). Princeton firm will evaluate REACH. *Human Services Reporter, 11*(8), 2. NJ: Dept. of Human Services.

In New York, in response to questions of mission, management, and operations, there are significant changes being made in the organization of the Office of Vocational Rehabilitation (OVR) to define policy and coordinate operations so that rehabilitation services are performed in an effective and efficient fashion. (1989, July). *The New York State Advocate, 12*(7).

In Nevada, there was an economic evaluation of a rehabilitation program for older people with no vocational goals. The study concludes that "while there is room for improvement in this program, there can be no doubt of its efficiency, cost effectiveness and enormous value to disabled Nevadans." Nevada Bureau for Services to the Blind, Homemaker Rehabilitations, State Fiscal Year 1987. (1988, June). Conducted by Planning, Research and Program Development, State of Nevada Rehabilitation Division.

The Michigan Commission for the Blind, in designing an "objective" evaluation for their Independent Living Program for Elderly Blind, has taken the approach of a before and after assessment of the functional performance level of its clients, using a standard functional assessment scale. Research is in process as to the broader outcome. Nieuwen-huijsen, Els Reino. (1987, June 2). *The ICIDH as a framework for documenting small gains in rehabilitation*. Michigan Commission for the Blind. Saginaw, MI.

In Illinois, a government agency used the technique of a client satisfaction survey to "assess level of client satisfaction" regarding outcomes, timeliness, responsiveness of service providers, and so on. Staff. (1988). *Client satisfaction survey*. Springfield, IL: Illinois Department of Rehabilitation Services.

Suggested changes in the revision of the New York City Charter would include a statement of program goals by each of the city agencies by which each can, together with a program contract budget, "set(s) the stage for debating and defining policies" in order to "understand the city's priorities." A recent release by the New York City Charter Revision Commission Reform. (1989, September 27). Again in New York City, there is currently under way a census of nonprofit organizations "to help government officials, corporate leaders and the general public better understand the impact of nonprofits on the economic, social, and cultural life of the City." Nonprofit industry study—A joint project of the Fund for the City of New York. (1989, March 27).

61. Weirich, Deuschle, & Sklaver. *The adoption of performance assessment in a CMHC*.

62. Kimmel, W. A. (1981). *Putting program evaluation in perspective for state and local government* (Human Service Monogram, no. 18). Washington, DC: DHEW Publication # 0576–130.

63. Supported Employment Briefing New York State (SEMIS). (1989, February 8).

64. Ramanathan, A proposed framework for designing management control systems, 172.

65. Elkin & Molitor, A conceptual framework for selecting nonprofit organizations.

66. Gronbjerg, Kirsten A. (1990, June). Poverty and nonprofit organizational behavior. *Social Service Review, 64*(2), 228–229.

67. Brinkerhoff, Derick W., and Kanter, Rosabeth Moss. (1979, August). *Formal systems of appraisals of individual performance. Some considerations, critical issues, and application to non-profit organizations*. PONPO Working Paper No. 9, Institution for Social and Policy Studies, 1–7. New Haven, CT: Yale University.

CHAPTER 8

Empirical Applications
of the Model

Applications with illustrations provide specific approaches in practice to the concepts discussed in the prior chapters. These include the cornerstones of data accumulation and classification, the CIS and the FIS, and the reporting and evaluation of the information generated, the CES. Their design requires clarity of mission and definition of outcome to fulfill the mission. These determine the content and frequency of reports to hierarchical levels of staff and other stakeholders to fulfill the objectives of effectiveness (outcomes) and efficiency (outputs) in the use of resources. When the basic data are captured, they need only to be rearranged, resorted, and recomputed for client and program analysis.

The proposed statement of income is the key addition to the armory of management tools for evaluating outcome effectiveness. The only additional steps required are, for the SS/I application, the computation of the clients' NRC; and for the M/P application, clients' functional abilities in terms of activities of daily living, standards of morbidity and other indicators. The proposed financial statement for an SS/I agency as discussed in the case study appears in the exhibit at the end of this chapter.

This chapter offers a guide to an approach for an appropriate management system to enable HSOs to evaluate their current systems. Until now, this book has concentrated on the normative goals and philosophical underpinnings of the proposed models and on a proposed unified accounting system for the PS and HSOs. The view has been mainly from the "top down." The discussion that follows is from the "bottom up" and focuses on the methods and techniques for the accumulation of data and their subsequent integration into reports for the hierarchy of stakeholders.

Keeping in mind that each organization must define its own mission, and within the scope of that mission statement, define the specific goals of each service program and data requirements, the outline below serves as a directory for the details of the principal components of an accounting system.

The CIS

—CIS goals

—Client data

    Client profile

    Assessment and goal-setting

    Service plan and utilization

—Outcome data

—Evaluation

—Standard service units

The FIS

—Account classification

—Standards, budgets, and variances

—Illustration of budget, standards, and variances

The CES

—Staff performance and evaluation

—Reports and analyses

—Case study of societal income

Note: The combination of the CIS, FIS, and CES based on common data bases is referred to as the Management Information System (MIS)

CLIENT INFORMATION SYSTEM (CIS)

CIS Goals

The "shoulds" of any client information system are summarized as follows:

1. Should integrate the client's goal within the parameters of the organization's mission
2. Should portray the characteristics of each client
3. Should be consistently applied to clients with common needs, individualized for each client
4. Should be equitable as defined by the agency hierarchical allocation of resources to programs and types of clients within programs
5. Should permit feedback reporting of actual services rendered in comparison to services predetermined at time of intake

6. Should permit feedback reporting of actual costs in comparison to predetermined costs on a client (as well as on cost center and program basis) output analysis
7. Should allow assessment of predicted outcome, together with predicted cost, in comparison with actual outcomes and actual cost—outcome analysis

Client Data

For a meaningful management information system and for evaluation of effectiveness, some points must be stressed. It is essential that data be relevant to the care provider and also recognizable by the clients as pertinent to their presenting problems. An understanding of the relevance of the information being requested, recorded, and maintained can only be established where there is clarity of mission for the organization, the service being provided, and with a clear statement of realistic and measurable goals to be achieved.

Therefore, data to be collected by provider staff and to be maintained in client records is determined by the mission of the agency/organization and its goals (expected outcomes); agreed upon by all levels of staff. The data must be relevant to the provision of the service, pertinent to the presenting problem and to the anticipated outcomes. It must be aggregatable, comprehensive, and recognizable to all stakeholders, including the clients.

To determine the client data, there must be a mission statement for the organization and a description of the service. Where the organization provides multiple services, a mission statement for each service is required that includes expected outcomes, eligibility criteria, characteristics of individuals to be served, capacity of service units available (number of service units of full-time equivalent) staff, and service units needed (anticipated number of clients and average number of units per client). This service description should also contain information regarding costs of services, fee policy (if any), and third party sources of funding.

The term *client* is being used for the person served. Depending on the mission of the organization, the individual could be a patient, student, or trainee.

It is critical that the data be meaningful to the care provider and easily recorded. Where computerized information systems are not available, then written records should be so set up that basic data are recorded once and subsequent entries record change/status quo. If there are to be multiple users of the same data, then accessibility becomes an issue to be resolved. Resolution again depends on the nature of the organization, its size, and availability of records. The following categorization is suggested only as a guide; again, it cannot be emphasized enough, data to be collected are a factor of purpose and expected outcome of the service.

Data can be categorized in logical data groups (LDGs): client profile, assessment and goal setting, service plan and utilization, and output and outcome data.[1]

Client Profile. Client profile would include: (1) all identifying information, for example, name, address, telephone(s), date of birth, race, citizenship, language(s) spoken, referral source, and any other required data; and (2) presenting problem with pertinent data, such as client statement of problem, age at onset, use of formal support systems (other organizations used) past and present, data on informal support network (family and significant others), educational history, employment history, medical/psychological data, economic data (including current benefits/entitlements), client self-assessment, and other data pertinent to the assistance being sought.

Assessment and Goal-setting. This includes (1) functional assessment(s) by appropriate staff using standardized measures and (2) goals mutually agreed upon by client and staff with time frames and specific service objectives, translated into projected service units.

Service Plan and Utilization. The third LDG is the "service data," which identifies all elements of projected and actual service delivery. Examples of the data entered here include: client service history, that is, program referrals, requests for support service/assessment, dates of initiation of service, termination dates and reasons for changes in staff assignment, and scheduled evaluation periods/progress evaluations. The recording of all direct client service units as related to the service plan generates staff utilization data. Billing/payment/sponsorship files include data on third party sponsorship and payment of client fees, full or partial. Outputs are summarized for each program service as completed in terms of service units projected and used. Case notes are entered in the file in ordinary language and identified by type of note, originator of note, dates covered, and program/service to which the note refers.

Outcome Data. The fourth LDG consists of outcome data for analysis as part of the CES. All client data would be in the ongoing client service record. At a predetermined time, additional entries would be required as the basis for the calculation of societal income. For example, where job placement is the goal, the entry required is type of work, level of work, and earnings at time of follow-up. The follow-up time period depends on the nature of the services provided and the mission of the organization.

Evaluation

The act of evaluating clients from available data can be summarized:

1. Self-assessment by client
2. Validation by staff
3. Application to outside scale, or clinical criteria, as to where the client "is"
4. Projection to the outside scale, or clinical criteria, as to where the client "can be" within a specific time frame
5. Conversion of plan from "is" to "can be" in terms of standard service units by program services
6. Follow-up from plan "is" relative to the "can be" in terms of actual service units
7. Follow-up from outputs to outcomes

Service Units

Service units incorporate the specifics of client goals and service objectives with projected measurable amounts of defined treatments with quantified service units and operational predictions of outcome. However, quantification of these variables in and of themselves is insufficient. To ensure a commonality of information across service areas and to allow later aggregation of the information, service units must be defined along some uniform dimension, common to all programmatic and supportive service areas based on the agreed-upon standard hours in a workday and in a work year. For the purposes of this model, the key dimension is one of time, as in the PS. All services planned and actually rendered to the client population, whether in the form of a specific program, conference, or administrative function, should be defined in terms of predetermined standard time units.

There are various alternative possibilities for classifications of direct and indirect standard time units, for example, the separation of the time for direct program, therapy, and conferences from time required for such client-related administrative functions as telephone calls, letters, and so forth. This must be determined—whether only client contacts will be treated as direct and other time will be treated as overhead, including the delineation of the following: individual (face to face), family (face to face), telephone (individual/family), group contacts (more than one client), letter, support conference re client, conference on non-specific clients, no-shows, cancellation by agency, and cancellation by client. Other criteria that must be defined together with service units are for cost center and/or departmental transfers, for termination, and for any related accounting for transportation, meals, and direct financial support. These definitions have to be arrived at by service staff and agreed to by financial and evaluation staff and management.

FINANCIAL INFORMATION SYSTEM (FIS)

The need for budgeting and subsequent reporting builds on the projected service goals and objectives as developed by all levels of provider staff. Budgets include projections of anticipated client mix, program services to be rendered, service unit estimates equated with available staff time (capacity), and the expenses to support the services. Budget preparation then becomes an interdisciplinary process and the basis of a feedback system to actual results.

Account Classification

For control and reporting purposes, a three to four way account classification may be required to capture the multiple dimensions of data relating to expenses, departments or cost centers, programs, and clients. For example, depending on the size of the agency, its method of functioning, and cost control and reporting requirements, a six- to nine-digit code can be used: two to three for the usual accounting expense classification, one for departments or cost centers, two for programs, and two to three for client numbers. This would cover from 99 up to 999 regular accounting, payroll, and expenses accounts, up to 9 departments or cost centers, up to 99 programs, and from 99 up to 999 clients.

Standards, Budgets, and Variances

Based on the account classifications described above, for the purpose of control and analysis of the elements of efficiency, each program and cost center can accumulate the following:

1. Actual expenses, direct and allocable
2. Standard service unit earned in dollars (standard units of outputs × standard unit costs)
3. Actual services rendered in service units at projected costs (actual service units × standard unit costs)
4. Actual services rendered in service units at actual costs (actual service unit × actual unit costs)

Variances then arise as a result of:

1. Actual direct expenses differing from projected or budget; or actual direct expenses differing from budget adjusted for volume (depending upon the sophistication of the budget)
2. The analysis can be expanded to include the direct expenses, either before or after allocation to the cost center. (If after, the additional variables of method of allocation and volume affect the allocable cost per service unit)
3. Actual volume (quantity and type) of service units differing from budget. From this point of view, the type of service rendered, the volume of clients, and the client mix affect the volume of service units
4. Actual service units differing from the standard service units required for the particular service (efficiency)

Illustration of Budget, Standards, and Variances

A management control system should be established that encompasses: (1) the projection of the use of departmental facilities, (2) the projection of cost center and departmental expenses, and (3) the accounting on a timely basis for variances between projected and actual costs and an appropriate reporting system to direct staff and management.

Some budgetary problems include: (1) balancing of program capacities, client needs, intake, and counseling as well as their service requirements (telephone, office); (2) computing "production" in service-unit input or income generated by cost center when clients are still "in process"; (3) interim changes in client goals and program mix; (4) need to budget for fixed and variable expenses as a basis for proper volume variance accounting, for example, variances should segregate effects of client mix and actual service input and capacity; (5) ability of program staff to deliver services at standard input levels; and (5) absorption costing for each program that can create volume variances as a result of client variations in mix and/or absences.

The budgetary process permits management to project the mix of client types; their needs in kinds of service input units, that is, the service unit mix for these clients; and the estimate of service unit costs, which is a function of the level at which program costs (cost center) are absorbed (at what percentage of capacity). While it is assumed that all service units within a cost center have a common time base, and therefore cost equivalency—direct services, interviews, conferences, telephone calls, letters, and so on—the balancing of clients and their needs with staff and physical facilities is a major budget task.

In the illustration below, total costs for each cost center are first determined in terms of direct salaries based on client and program projections, by direct identifiable overhead, and then by indirect allocations of other salaries and overheads. The total number of service input units by each cost center is likewise projected so that the projected average cost per service unit can be computed for each cost center. From such averages, standards can be determined based on variations of service-unit costs for the specific services being rendered within each cost center and on client variations.

A necessary requirement for successful budgeting is the supervisor's involvement (together with provider staff) in the preparation of his/her budget in terms of costs, outputs, and outcomes. Such supervisor's budget would include a projection of the number of clients by type of client, a description of personnel within his/her section, projected service units required, other personnel and overhead expenses, projected client turnovers, and any special costs such as purchases of services, transportation, meals, and so forth. Special income should also be noted such as grants, tuition fees, and other third party sources. For the basic data to be entered in the CIS, for the information to be assembled by the FIS, and for accountability in subsequent reporting from the CES, the supervisor, together with provider staff, should be an integral part of the budget process.

The projections of total agency expenses should be part of a feedback procedure to incorporate the information presented below. General and administrative expenses of the hypothetical agency have not been included on the assumption that these expenses will be controlled by a separate budget. Such expenses could have been incorporated into the calculation of service-unit costs without affecting the illustration.

It is assumed that an HSO has four cost centers, A, B, C, and D, which deal with three client types, x, y, and z, and that it has a projected total agency expense aggregating $2,000,000.

Expense Classification	Amount
Salaries-Direct	$ 800,000
Salaries-Indirect	400,000
Overhead-Direct	500,000
Overhead-Indirect	300,000
Total	$2,000,000

Cost Center Distributions: Service Units

Cost Center	Client Capacity	Unit Capacity	Total Cost (000)	Average Cost/Unit
A	1,000	5,000	$ 325	$65.00
B	800	10,000	375	37.50
C	700	15,000	475	31.70
D	1,500	20,000	825	41.30
	4,000	50,000	$2,000	$40.00

It is assumed that the total cost consists of the following (all accounts in thousands):

Cost Center	Salaries Direct	Salaries Indirect	OH Direct	OH Indirect	Total
A	$100*	$ 50	$100	$ 75	$ 325
B	200	50	50	75	375
C	200	100	100	75	475
D	300	200	250	75	825
	$800	$400	$500	$300	$2,000

It should be noted that client capacity is not the same as projected number of clients since there are more "program clients" than clients. For example, assume that 1,000 clients take an average of four programs each (based on a subanalysis of client population by age, problem, goals, etc.); this affects in turn the standard number of service units required for a given cost center/program.

Service Units Calculations

Type of Clients	No. Clients	Service Units	Cost for Service Units (Avg. for Type)	Total Cost— Client Group
x	150	10,000	$30.00	$ 300,000
y	250	10,000	50.00	500,000
z	600	30,000	40.00	1,200,000
Total	1000	50,000	$40.00	$2,000,000

Budget and Actual Cost Comparison. The comparison on a line-by-line basis or by cost centers (programs or departments) of costs incurred in comparison to budget can be misleading. Even when actual and/or budget figures are adjusted by criteria of volume such as the number of clients, comparisons can obfuscate performance. Again, even if expenses are separated between fixed and variable, this artificiality becomes apparent since most expenses are relatively fixed in the short-run budget period. Aggravating the problem is the need to measure outputs in standard and actual service units. Such a comparison of actual and projected service units becomes crucial for evaluating performance efficiency.[2] An illustration will make clear the nature of the problem:

Assume that for a given cost center A the original budget projected 1,000 clients who would receive 5,000 service units of standard time at a total cost of $325,000 or $65 per service unit. Under the traditional method of comparing actual and budgeted amounts, if it is assumed that actual expenses incurred during the period were $315,000, then there would be a positive budget variance of $10,000. Further, such budget variance could be carefully analyzed as to differences between direct program labor, support labor, indirect allocated labor, direct identifiable overhead, and allocated overhead so that the components of the $10,000 positive budget variance could be presented. Further, assume that the summary of client time shows 4,500 hours or 90% of budgeted time. However, this kind of analysis might conceal the actual occurrences within this cost center. Thus assume that, instead of the original service units on which the budget was based, fewer clients received service and such clients received 4,500 service units, which are 800 service units above plan for this client mix. We can then compute for this illustration that there was a negative variance of $74,500: that it was the failure by that department to serve clients who required the higher number of service units per client that caused the apparent favorable results. The following is a summary of variances:

Earned by Department (in accordance with CIS) 3700 standard service units @ $65 each	$240,500	
Expenditures for the Period	315,000	
Gross Variance		($74,500)
Excess Units over Planned 4500 − 3700 = 800 @ $65 each		($52,000)
*Volume Variance		
$306,000 Standard @ 4500 Units $68 − $65 (normal capacity) = $3 × 4500 service units		($13,500)
Budgeted Expenses @ 4500 Standard units	$306,000	
Actual Expenses @ 4500 units	315,000	
Expense Variance		($ 9,000)

*Total expenses would be projected at various operating levels, for example:

Standard	Service Units	Center A Expenses	Cost/Center
100%	5,000	$325,000	$65 per SU
90%	4,500	306,000	68
80%	4,000	290,000	72.50
75%	3,500	280,000	80

The variance of $74,500 was caused primarily by the excess service units for the clients served to the extent of $52,000. The balance of the variance of $22,500 is a combination of volume, $13,500 (the cost of 5,000 service units planned for and 4,500 units used) and expense control of $9,000 (based on a variable expense budget of $306,000 at the 4,500 unit level).

Within the cost center, the mix can be further analyzed based on clients served. Assume that the client mix of 5,000 service units consisted of the following client types:

Type of Client	Number of Clients	Capacity Service Units	Actual Service Units	Standard Service Units
x	150	1,500	1,200	1,000
y	250	1,000	500	200
z	600	2,500	2,800	2,500
	1,000	5,000	4,500	3,700

An analysis of the above shows that the $52,000 variance of excess service units over plan was caused by the following client types:

x used 200 above standard @ $65/service unit	$13,000
y used 300 above standard @ $65/service unit	19,500
z used 300 above standard @ $65/service unit	19,500
Total	$52,000

While client type x used 20% above standard, client y used 150% above and client z 12% above, the mix variance pinpoints the problems in dollars. Client type x cost almost $90 more than planned, client y almost $80, and client z approximately $35 above what was planned. The cost of absences, cancellations, and program changes likewise can be computed in terms of applicable service units planned for scheduled meetings, classes, normal absences, and so on, by direct identification.

Variances have the additional advantage of not building substandard performance into averages, for example, in evaluating the average number of days from the referral to the first client contact. Average number of days may be at acceptable levels; however, the number of clients who are not so referred within the standard time period becomes more significant.

The above budget illustrates the measurement of elements of efficiency of an HSO. As discussed under the CES below, projections and actual results should also be reported on in terms of outcomes as well as outputs contained in the illustration. The results can be fed back and analyzed, classified by specific client, program, staff, and type of client, all relevant to the achievement of successful outcome. Projected outcome in the form of societal revenue generated should become the principal component of cash-flow projections, which would also incorporate such other significant expenditures as fixed asset acquisitions, debt repayment, costs of new programs, research, and any other cash requirements not included in the regular operating budget.

COMPREHENSIVE EVALUATION SYSTEM (CES)

The material included in this section is divided into three parts: staff performance, CES and other reports and analyses, and a case study in the preparation of a statement of income of an HSO. It should be apparent that the same underlying assumptions apply for evaluation of staff and clients and programs; and that common data bases are required for a full-functioning management information system for both internal and external reporting.

Staff Performance and Evaluation

Attitudes relating to clients, other staff members, and to the organization are quality factors of personnel evaluation common to all organizations. Factors such as elements of productivity, reliability, and effectiveness are quantifiable for HSOs. The system requires staff to focus on the consumer-client from initial application to closure; the evaluation of staff performance and client outcomes are interrelated. The reports of the front-line supervisor of outputs and outcomes on client results both move up to management and should be fed back to staff members to induce behavioral change. Such outcome goals for staff improve the efficiency of the supervisory function.

The system permits data accumulation about staff performance by staff member, planned and actual service units and costs, and in accordance with client outputs and outcomes. More specifically, the following can be calculated:

1. Productivity in service units versus projected within each time frame—for specific client outputs, the differences between rendered and projected service units, and actual and projected service unit costs
2. Reliability of initial assessments, that is, the ability to project clients' program needs, the frequency and type of client "change orders," the time frames for accomplishing the clients' programs relative to projections, and so on.
3. The type of service units rendered, that is, the actual mix by client, client groupings, and programs of direct client contact and indirect time.

4. The value of service units rendered in comparison to direct labor and indirect costs. The value in this instance is defined as the standard cost of the particular service unit.

5. Effectiveness measured by societal income of clients/client groups, programs—related to costs, standard and actual

6. The cost of time not allocated to clients, such as generalized conferences and meetings, cancellations caused by the agency, and planned and actual holiday, vacation, sick leave and other personal time

With a focus on outcomes and the inclusion of staff members in budget preparation, staff performance elements cited above can serve as a basis for an incentive compensation system. These performance criteria may reduce the significance of some of the current systems generally in use for HSOs that focus on process accomplishment. These include: number of clients served; percentage of case load seen (active case load divided by the number of clients seen); percentage of canceled appointments; percentage of late appointments; percentage of standard work hours accounted for in direct client contacts and indirect client time. The focus on outcomes responds to the criticism of quality assurance programs with their emphasis on process.

Reports and Analyses

The CES distributes the various reports generated—the outputs from the common data banks described herein under the headings of the CIS and the FIS. The information contained in these primary records—rearranged and analyzed—can be utilized for reports to hierarchical management levels and other stakeholders. Most of the primary reports are based on outputs such as client movements through programs and accordingly report efficiency. Only after the client completes the planned programs can outcomes be measured. Such efficiency analysis should be correlated with the outcomes achieved. The actual costs incurred can be compared to the projected or standard costs and variances calculated on a continuing basis by individual client, cost center, and program, as well as by cost center and/or department (and staff performance, as above). Likewise, agency costs such as absences, lateness, and cancellations may be better controlled. Statistical data such as client backlogs, client dropouts, and inquiries are also maintained. These can be reported upon in dollar amounts together with hours. There are also available quality-oriented reports containing descriptive data about clients, staff meetings, and programs as well as maintenance and other support services, and so forth.

The most important reports of the CES should be those relating to outcomes relative to the agency's mission. The statement of (societal) income should be the key indicator; other financial statements (the balance sheet, the statement of funds, and the statement of receipts and expenditures), overall comparisons to budgets, and standards and variance analysis are also significant. The concomitant of an integrated MIS and its relationship to the CES is the continual feedback and, in effect, the continuing research that can be performed by the individual HSO.

Operating results are functions of types of clients that differ with personal histories, types of personalities, and particular problems. Accordingly, descriptive quality statements are necessary to supplement statistical data about the individual client so that the individual is never obliterated by the numbers. The client as a participant in the development and changes in his/her plan must stay fully informed. Successful consumer-clients who are knowledgeable as to the relationship among mission, outcome, program, client mix, costs, and profits may be in a better position to serve as members of the overall decision team.

As already indicated, a well-managed agency requires current information on a continuing, updated basis about the client, the staff, programs, and the organization in terms of a total feedback loop. This would cover intake, client activities, and termination, and the efficiency and effectiveness of service delivery in terms of costs, projected or standard versus actual, and reasons for differences. The focus on such reporting should be on outcomes in terms of mission and variances in terms of original planning.

The number of reports that can be derived from the common data bases could overwhelm the potential recipients. Actual reports will depend on the nature of the HSOs' mission and activities, their clients, facilities, financial position, funding sources, staff and board sophistication, and community relations. There are also distinctive styles of management that affect the significance of information gathered and reported. Nonetheless, there are basic questions to which various stakeholders want answers on a continuing basis. At every hierarchical level, the required reports must eventually be defined together with costs within two broad categories, effectiveness of mission realization, outcomes and efficiency in use of resources, outputs and costs.

The general questions requiring information to arrive at answers include: (1) the degree of success achieved relative to mission—financial results, future funding sources, and cash availability; (2) what programs worked for what type of client—reasons for success/failure; (3) the results of marketing and competition for services together with client-consumer satisfaction; (4) feedback of projections—what was expected and what actually occurred regarding clients and program achievements and costs; (5) staff performance, personnel policies, and costs; and (6) other factors, such as overhead and administrative expense control; management relations with board, community, and funding sources; and facilities, research, and planning.

It is assumed that the HSO has clarified its mission, defined levels of reporting of outcomes to fulfill such mission, and installed an appropriate CIS and FIS to capture the essential data needed for evaluating and reporting of outcomes and the use and control of its resources to accomplish such outcomes. Where direct computer input is feasible, staff and management can be on-line with updated data about clients, program costs, service units, and so on. Even with such available information, hard-copy reports are necessarily aggregated according to staff level and information requirements. Based on these requirements, the reports would be distributed to designated service program staff, hierarchical levels of management, and board and other stakeholders.

There are four categories of reports that focus on the client as an individual or summarized as part of a group: client applications for services, the client in service, the client who completed services, and the client outcome. Other reports relative to staff and/or program service and/or cost center/department rearrange, re-sort, and summarize these basic client data.

As part of the functions of the executive director, there is a primary responsibility to review outcomes and report on the achievement of mission. These client reports must be integrated with the agency's statement of societal income. The system provides data for statistical analysis of variables of client type, program service, staff, and costs. The procedures contribute to the integration of research and practice enabling provider staff to analyze results for more autonomous practice, contributing to their professional growth. There are other reports that measure other aspects of the operation and do not directly involve client data.

The type of reports that follow relate to the individual client, client mix, client goals, program service, cost center/department, and organization, analyzed in terms of planned and actual costs, which can be regrouped by staff classifications and summarized for management and other stakeholders. The higher the level of reporting, the more the aggregating of data. The following list attempts to respond to these hierarchical needs for information; formats, recipients, and frequency of preparation depend on management style and needs. These reports achieve having client outcomes as the focus of management.

Applications for Service
—demographics of applicants, source of referral, nature of problem, services requested
Disposition of applications
—assigned to specific service, comparison to client request, denials—services not available, referrals to other agencies, other
—status of pending applications: how long pending, reasons for
Client case load: active, pending, inactive
—number of service units projected by client, client type, client goal, program service, cost center/department
—service units utilized, variance
Client completing service—outputs:
—planned/standard versus actual costs and variances
—by client, client type, client goal, program service, cost center/department
Client outcomes:
—planned/standard versus actual costs versus outcome income (societal)
—by client, client type, client goal, program service, cost center/department

Program Services—regrouping client output and outcome data

—analysis of costs, outputs, and outcomes

—inventory of clients in process, terminated, backlogs, capacity utilization, and so on

Service Staff—regrouping client output and outcome data

—analysis of costs, outputs, and outcome

—utilization and variances

Analysis of Variances—planned versus actual units and costs for agency, cost center/department, program service, staff and client levels

—efficiency

—other: changes in goals, dropouts, lateness, absences, staff fringe—holiday, vacation, sick, personal, and so on

Financial statements

—funding streams and cash availability

—balance sheet

—budget versus actual

—statements of societal income—effectiveness and efficiency evaluations by client and client types, program services, cost center/department, staff and agency

Other reports

—community relations, education

—maintenance and facility

—research

—long-term planning

Case Study of Societal Income

HSOs in general have as their mission the movement of their clients toward self-sufficiency and/or the maintenance of their clients at their present functional level. This case illustration of the computation of societal income represents an HSO whose primary mission has been vocational training and job placement.

The Center for Educational Advancement (CEA), formerly Hunterdon Occupational Training Center, located in Flemington, New Jersey, is a school that combines academic studies with vocational training and provides rehabilitation and vocational retraining facilities as well. The clients include the neurologically impaired and a significant number who are mentally retarded. The center receives some funding from the State of New Jersey, but its principal source of income is derived from a production, packaging/light assembly business that functions for training purposes as well. Used also both as a source of income and for training are the cafeteria, retail stores, maintenance shops, and other programs. CEA has a 45-member staff, a client capacity of approximately 150, and has been successful in placing approximately 30 clients in outside employment per year. In 1986, the same number were trained for continuing extended employment at the facility.

The statement of (societal) income presented below is based upon the actual operations of this agency. Calculating this agency's net societal profit was done by measuring the value of clients placed in permanent or extended employment. Other factors had to be considered: reflecting government support payments toward programs as on-account receipts against societal income generated; treatment of third-party reimbursements as revenue or cost reductions; reporting of special grants, donations, and other revenue; allocations of operating and/or administrative costs; value added for products and services created by the employees during the training process; accounting for clients who fail to complete their goals, including transfers and dropouts, costs incurred by other HSOs that contibuted to the results, and clients who remain as extended employees of the agency.

The questions inherent in the analysis of operations of an HSO may become more clear by an examination of the financial statements of the CEA for the year 1986, and their conversion to a statement of (societal) income for that year in accordance with the precepts of the model presented in chapter 2. Both the original financial statements and the restated statement of (societal) income are presented not only as an illustration for the mechanics of conversion, but also, more important, as a realistic illustration of opposing dynamic influences in the functioning of this organization.

As the statement of (societal) income demonstrates, 1986 was a banner year from the point of view of the accomplishment of the mission of the agency in terms of client as well as staff satisfaction:

1. 29 clients were placed in competitive employment during the year out of a total intake of 120 clients; moreover, 30 clients continued working as extended employees at the CEA

2. All seven programs contributed to this result

3. There was a noticeable improvement in the quality of the life-style of the clients placed in competitive employment. Longitudinal follow-up for most was positive in terms of continued employment. There was at least one case of a known increase in family productivity (the economics of which were not included in the statement of [societal] income)

4. A grant was received for the construction of an additional building to expand facilities

The model reflects these positive factors from the point of view of the welloffness of clients and of society. The currently accepted accounting model, on the other hand, shows diametrically opposite results:

1. The CEA operated at a loss after deducting production and administrative expenses, even after other sales revenues and government contributions toward training

2. CEA was financially weaker at the end of the year with an increased negative working capital as a result both of the loss and of funds expended for the new building above the amount of the grant

3. CEA became more vulnerable and more at risk with its expanded programs and staff

4. There was decreasing relative and absolute government support

The reaction of board members was generally negative in the absence of specific money criteria for the evaluation of outcomes, particularly in view of the increasing financial pressures. There was consequent pressure to increase efficiency without sufficient recognition of CEA's major outcome achievements in fulfilling its basic mission and goals. The paradoxes confronting management, the ambivalence of the board, and the failure to reward staff financially are not atypical:

1. There are differing objectives between staff responsible for programming and those responsible for funding, which can result in tensions among stakeholders, a kind of organizational conflict arising from varying agendas for different stakeholders

2. Financial survival influences choice of clients, programs, and staff remuneration

3. Funding ceases for innovation, experimentation, and evaluation

4. Grants for buildings result in: more or expanded programs, which significantly spread management efforts; a future increase in annual expenses needing additional working capital to carry the inventory of clients and spending for program fixed assets and/or supplies

5. The board of directors, coming largely from the PS, is efficiency oriented as it attempts to resolve an HSO's problems

We have defined this state of affairs as the "Janus Effect," named after the Roman god with two heads, placed back to back, looking simultaneously in two directions. There are opposing pulls of successful program outcomes in terms of mission and the requirements for financial survival. The situation is often aggravated by influences that do not appear in the PS such as:

1. Losing the more productive workers as employees, particularly in production-oriented workshops.

2. The counterproductive factors for placement such as government regulations that discourage employment by setting unrealistic minimum earning levels and failure to continue certain kinds of interim support, particularly medical coverage.[3]

3. Family resistance to client placement that fears failure, potential loss of income, change in stability of relationship with client or funding sources—the secondary gains from disability.

The financial statement that appears as Exhibit 8.1 at the end of this chapter presents the statement of income of CEA for the year ended December 31, 1986, in accordance with GAAP and the statement of (societal) income as adjusted to reflect the societal contribution of the agency. The following were considered and adjustments made as noted:

1. The elimination of public support, which consisted of contributions and other grants, since these items represented payments by society to CEA, including:

   a) building grant and other grants and contributions

b)   training fees from the State of New Jersey (in effect, societal income is the outcome of the State of New Jersey partial support of training expenses)

2. Subcontractor sales, gross profits on retail sales, and rental income were not adjusted since these amounts represented societal production

3. No adjustment was made to program expenses, management, general and administrative expenses, or interest

4. Gross societal income was computed from a listing of client placements

5. Transportation costs of CEA's clients incurred by another social agency, and paid for by government, were charged to program expenses as necessary to provide CEAs array of programs and services

The proposed model suggests other accounting adjustments for which data were not available. These include the adjustments for value of opening and closing inventories of clients in process and the reflection of differences between standard and actual program costs in order to compute the efficiency adjustment. While the individual output of production for each trainee was monitored, the CIS of the CEA did not contain actual or standard labor units of staff hours. Accordingly, the difference in value between the opening and closing inventories could not be computed; however, it was determined that such amount would have no significant effect on the resulting statement. While records of client completions of the individual programs were maintained both by individual client and by program, there was no system in place for the computation of standard and actual costs by client, which data are required for the computation of the efficiency variance. The computation of such variance is for management control purposes and does not affect the "bottom line" of the statement of (societal) income. Moreover, the CIS did not show societal support at the time of hiring. Therefore, for the purpose of this illustration, it was assumed that all the clients were on Medicaid but only half received supplemental security income (SSI)—a conservative assumption.

The above statement utilizes the "Compound Interest and Bond Tables of the Present Value of Annuity of $1.00 in Arrears." Twenty years of employment for each employee placed in competitive employment was projected. The interest rate of 10% was utilized based upon the then rate for a government bond for this period. The table indicates that the present value of $1.00 for 20 years at 10% is $8.5136. Accordingly, one multiplies the dollar change in net resources consumed for each client by 8.5136 to determine the societal income contributed for that client. The total societal income for the CEA is the sum of the individual societal incomes of each client.

When one looks at the age of the individual client and his or her anticipated period of employment considering morbidity and mortality tables, it is clear that a higher expected average could have been utilized. However, in dealing with this population and the uncertainties of future employment, an arbitrary measuring rule was established so that the value of future employment would not exceed 20 years for the purpose of this calculation. It should be pointed out that the difference between the present value of an annuity of $1.00 for 20 years and 30 years is approximately 91 cents, or 11%; and for 40 years, $1.26, or 15%.

One of the key differences between the organizational model as presented in this book and other cost-benefit studies is the assumption that the rehabilitation agency has created permanent human capital, which can be measured by the present value of its future income flow. Other models have used a certain number of years of income, which in our opinion do not fairly reflect the societal contribution of an HSO; moreover, some have not appeared to adjust for the societal income of the production of the clients during their training as an offset to their costs or made other adjustments described herein.

For the most part, accounting applications of GAAP are already in use by HSOs. Questions of measurement of inventory values, prepayments, allowances for losses on receivables, depreciation/amortization of capital expenditures and other items benefiting future periods, and accruals of income and/or expenses present the same issues of measurement as in the PS. Likewise, there are the same requirements of footnote disclosures of accounting principles, relevant information in the notes about mortgages, leases, and other significant contract data, status of pension funding, and disclosures about law suits, claims, other contingent liabilities, and special government rules and requirements as they affect the financial statements.

However, like the PS, as explained in chapter 6 (e.g., the arbitrary 10% discount factor in present-valuing oil reserves), rules will have to be promulgated that are indigenous to HSOs. The practical application of a computation of earned societal income is the key to the proposed statement of (societal) income, the measure of the creation of human capital. The interest rate to be used is readily available—as the function of the U.S. or other government agencies for the appropriate period of anticipated employment. The initial wages received are deemed to represent the client's societal contribution; subsequent increases are deemed to be a function of his or her employment.

The formula used to compute gross societal income in the accompanying statement of (societal) income was:

1. Compute the net societal resources consumed for each client at the time of employment and compare the age of the client at the time of employment to a standard working age of 55; this allows for morbidity and mortality for this population.

2. Determine the initial wage and benefits (for example, medical) when the client was placed in employment; this represents his societal contribution.

3. At the time of employment, determine the societal resources consumed for each client for the prior year.

4. Compare the age of the client at the time of employment to a standard working age of 55. (This allows for morbidity and mortality of this population.)

5. Compute the earnings of the extended employees and present value them for the period of their expected employment with the HSO.

Exhibit 8.1
Agency Statement of (Societal) Income

For the Year Ended December 31, 1986

	Statement of Revenue and Expenses*	Statement of (Societal) Income
Building grant	$ 99.4	
Other grants and contributions	159.9	
	259.3	
Revenues		
Training fees (State of NJ)	853.5	
Subcontract sales	687.6	$ 687.6
Gross profit, retail sales	58.4	58.4
Rental revenue	65.0	65.0
Other revenue	3.0	3.0
Total support and revenues	1,667.5	814.0
Gross societal income		2032.5
Total revenues	1,926.8	2846.5
Expenses		
Program		
Wages	456.4	
Staff salaries	659.2	
Payroll taxes	85.5	
Expenses	59.1	
Depreciation	68.1	
Other	211.4	216.0
	1,539.7	
Management and G & A		
Staff	164.8	
Payroll taxes & pension	33.5	
Depreciation	17.0	
Other	102.7	
	318.0	
Interest	117.4	
Total expense	1,975.1	1975.1
Adjusted total expenses	1,975.1	2191.1
(Loss) profit before taxes	(48.3)	655.4
Provision for Federal and state taxes measured by income (40%)		262.2
Net income - Net (societal) income	$ (48.3)	$ 393.2

* Audited financial statement

How is the reasonableness of this financial statement to be judged and critiqued? The answer must encompass the criteria for measurement enumerated in chapter 5, including ease of computation, availability of data, and comprehensibility of results. The financial statement took less than one workday to prepare. We utilized records and data collection systems that were not specifically designed to produce the information required for the statement of (societal) income. Even with the absence of data (an incomplete CIS) and some simplifying assumptions (such as sources of client support), the accompanying statement nonetheless is a reasonable approximation of the success of the agency's mission.

NOTES

1. Gordon, Arlene R., & Pollock, Risa. (1983, March). An information system in the private sector. *Journal of Visual Impairment and Blindness, 77*(3), 113–15.

2. Hayes, Robert D. & Millar, James A. (1990, July). Measuring production efficiency in a not-for-profit setting. *The Accounting Review, 65*(3), 505–519.

3. Roth, Wendy Carol. (1989, September 17). "Let Us See!" *Parade Magazine* p.16.

PART THREE

CHAPTER 9

Consequences and Implications

This chapter discusses in greater depth the consequences and implications of the models developed. The principal issues and their proposed solution are first summarized to provide a reference point for the discussion. Behavioral changes induced by the introduction of the model are viewed from the perspective of client, staff, other stakeholders, and the organization—the HSO. The model has direct consequences for the assessment of individual client changes from the intervention of program services, validation of program value, evaluation of staff, operational and internal controls, hierarchical reporting to stakeholders, and tax policy. The societal model also has long-run implications for the professions of accounting, human services, economics, and other social and political sciences, for the redefined profit and nonprofit sectors, and for approaches to the resolution of societal problems. These consequences and implications provide a basis for future research.

We have presented a general performance evaluation system for the measurement of the effectiveness and efficiency of HSOs embedded within a conceptual framework of a societal model. The societal model seeks to advance society's well-offness by taking actions that encourage its members to participate more fully in the social system, to make choices, to take risks, and to support an ethical and moral environment in which both the individual and the group are better off.

The organizational model responds to the current social scene, is congruent with the requirements for a measuring system, and provides the potential for a unified system of accounting that holds to the same standards when dealing with individual consumers, whether private or group resources are used. The information is derived from an integrated MIS that builds upon facts about client services and their outcomes accumulated in a CIS and FIS and reported upon in a CES to evaluate performance.

The proposed model recognizes the centrality of the consumer and the significance of optimizing consumer preferences whether the consumer is the individual purchasing the services and products of the PS or where society is the consumer-payer of the services and products of the HSOs. Equating society as the consumer-payer of HSO services permits the use of the concept of societal income as a measure of the effectiveness and efficiency of the HSO. The model, in bridging the gap between the PS and the HSOs, recognizes the common centrality of the consumer and, accordingly, that mission implies outcome just as market implies profit. This similarity also clarifies the role of efficiency in both sectors.

The measure of sales revenue, that is, gross (societal) income, is based on the overall mission of HSOs, the improvement of the quality of life for their clients as a result of the transfer of societal resources. The economic attribute selected to define quality of life is the consumer-client's movement toward self-sufficiency, also an economic goal of participants in the PS. These changes are measured by the change in the net societal resources consumed by the individual client. The revenue earned by the HSO is computed by present valuing the change over a prospective applicable period for each client. Therefore, gross (societal) income can be calculated for each HSO and its statement of net (societal) income can be prepared, which includes a bottom line measure.

The existing PS should be able to look at its own model to incorporate societal economic factors such as externalities, that is, social costs. It may even question the basis of choices and the role of consumer satisfaction in allocating resources in this sector. It is an area for future research. The proposed organizational and societal models have many immediate consequences and long-run implications, which are examined and which suggest other research areas to be addressed. It should be emphasized, however, that the accounting system derived from the organizational model can be implemented immediately. The principal ingredient required is the commitment of the board and management to an explicit statement of mission and a focus on outcomes. The rest will fall into place. The more complex societal issues that need to be addressed and incorporated into an action plan will take both time and a willingness to address these issues.

SHORT-TERM CONSEQUENCES

Measuring systems shape the behavior of management and staff and, as a result, the organization. Given the measuring or scoring system, the behavior of the players can be anticipated.

The adoption of the societal model and the organization model, with its accompanying accounting system, have important direct consequences for clients, staff, other stakeholders (board, funders, etc.), and the HSO. They are discussed in the sections that follow.

Client

A clear statement of mission for both the organization and the service, with specific objectives, time frames, and a goal in mind, focuses the client on outcome from the beginning. Engaged with staff under the same parameters, there is no secondary gain for either one to prolong or postpone completion. In essence, there is a real reward for or incentive for movement toward goal attainment, whether that goal is to achieve total economic self-sufficiency or to maintain an optimal level of functional ability. The potential partnership between or among client, staff, and management involves all parties in accumulating the evidence of the societal benefits (profits) from these investments in human capital. The results of the outcome analysis also provide the information as to causal factors contributing to failures or dropouts as well as to the underlying causes of the presenting problems.

The success of the agency and its net income are measured by aggregating the individual client's movements toward self-sufficiency and relative independence; these same factors likewise are some of the criteria for staff evaluation and compensation. It should be emphasized that the measurement of outcomes reflects changes in clients' self-sustaining behavior from the time of intake to program completion and follow-up. What has been developed is an accounting system that integrates client, service, staff, and managerial costs and financial data to provide a continuous and comprehensive understanding of the impact of services on consumer-clients. The client is not homogenized in statistical averages but retains an individualized reporting status. With the client as the crux and the raison d'être of the organization, the system should induce client, staff, management, and board behavior to achieve the common goal of the client's success.

The adoption of the organizational model with its goal of promoting economic self-sufficiency and its concomitant goal of supporting risk taking, immediately communicates to consumer-clients the commitment of the organization and its stakeholders to their belief in the ability of individuals to participate in the social system and/or to maintain their optimal level of functional independence. This, coupled with the clients' active participation and agreement on goals, contributes to the empowerment of the client. Risk taking, decision making, and goal achievement are all significant behaviors contributing to an individual's autonomy and sense of control. Recognition of the importance of government actions relative to graduated continuing adjustments of support systems during this period becomes essential. An understanding of the risks, process, costs, and benefits should enable consumer-clients who have achieved positive outcomes to make informed contributions to organization and community policy boards.

Staff

Like the profit metric, the system creates a focus useful for encouraging staff to operate with common goals in accordance with the mission of the agency and the requirements of individual clients as well as its own professional fulfillment. The development of a reporting system produces not only the necessary information for decision making, but also induces behavior on the part of decision makers based on the nature of the reporting system. Accordingly, staff and managers will find it in their best interests to optimize the use of resources consistent with the measuring rod. The model reduces the emphasis on process factors and replaces them with outcomes. For the practitioner, the model provides a framework and a methodology to systematically evaluate services and identify the key variables that contribute to success/failure. This is essentially equivalent to continual research and staff's continuing professional development.

Other Stakeholders

Net societal income is an indicator of mission outcome just as profit is an indicator of business achievement. Based on the needs and wants of their consumers, HSOs must analyze their missions to move toward profitability. The reporting of operating results in terms of net societal income permits comparability among HSOs in the same sense that earnings per share, or return in capital, permits comparability in the PS, providing an acceptable bottom line for board members. These financial reports can also provide significant information to government agencies such as the GAO and legislative bodies for evaluation of relative effectiveness on which to base political decisions.

The Organization—HSO

The model functions as a continual monitoring system of effectiveness and efficiency—a feedback loop that provides information for ex ante planning, decision making, and ex post analysis of client outcomes and program services. The components of the MIS relating to budgets, standard and actual costs, and program outputs and outcomes can integrate management decision making and controls and optimize outcomes and costs within the mission of the agency. As an information-generating device, the accounting system makes possible analyses of relationships among such variables as client demographics, kinds of programs, costs, staffing, outputs and outcomes, in terms of the criteria that measure success or failure in the creation of societal income. These relationships can be further focused by the use of sophisticated statistical techniques to segregate significant variables. The proposed system makes all data available for reports to government agencies when HSOs act as their agents; likewise for reporting to funders on special projects, grants, and so on. Computations for allowed HSO overhead can also be more accurately calculated, for example, to reflect the lower labor base, which requires deducting unallocated service time (staff meetings and training) and including such costs in overhead. Understanding what goes into the calculation together with the availability of data leads to a more accurate overhead rate.

In order to measure efficiency, based on standard units of time, the accounting and management techniques for both sectors also become interchangeable, conceptually and in application. As in the PS, standards of efficiency for HSOs become operable only within the framework of a particular set of market alternatives or market actions. An organization in a market economy allocates its resources in an efficient manner after it has optimized its market or outcome strategy. At best, efficiency factors may play a limiting or peripheral role in affecting the strategy of market or outcome efforts. Efficiency, based on outputs, should not be confused with outcomes, any more than production is confused with sales in the PS.

For HSOs, a standard unit of service as a management control measure can be related to standard costs. This permits the essential aggregatability of multiple services, however unique each service, which permits client, service, and financial information to be summarized and analyzed. Thus, once there is an understanding of the relationship of efficiency to effectiveness, or outputs to outcomes, then all the varied and advanced techniques that have been developed, such as job and process cost systems, standard costs, applications of overheads to direct costs, variance analysis, and so forth, can be used by HSOs. The HSOs should respond in their allocation of resources also based on their prospective profits, measured under the model of societal income.

The model ensures a continual longitudinal approach to care. This will result in different operating criteria for staff. The requirement to track clients even after services have been officially terminated can also contribute substantially to the development of program experience and to an understanding of the intervention process, a form of continual research. The need for special outcome research studies should be significantly reduced because of readily available data.

The significance of client data when the focus is on outcome means that service providers can see the direct relationship among the factors of practice, client service, and recording of such client data. The view from the top should require executive management to understand the up-down significance of mission and the relatedness of outcomes and data collection.

An organizational environment that highlights the evaluation of its achievement or ability to fulfill mission also has the information it needs for continuous strategic planning to ensure that it is always focused on mission and goals. Such strategic planning enables the organization to monitor its use of resources in relationship to outcomes, consumer needs, and satisfactory rendering of services. To ensure continuous evaluation and strategic planning, managers require information on (1) services requested, (2) demographics of consumers requesting such services and analysis of trends over time, (3) variances in over- or underutilization of staff, space, and other resources, and (4) funding streams and analysis over time of increase or decrease in sources of funding and relationship to costs. Strategic planning as a separate process can be a costly, time-consuming process; other disadvantages of strategic planning would not be a problem with the proposed model.[1]

The immediate consequence of the financial reporting by use of the model should shift the position of the HSO when seeking or negotiating funding. There are immediate benefits without the application of the societal model. The long-run implication, which requires a substantive change in tax policy, would replace, by market mechanisms, this short-run consequence. Historically, HSOs have been on the defensive in competing with other societal groups for a so-called fair share. HSOs can present objective evidence in support of their mission. The model presents a bottom line and uses a language with which certain donors and granters feel comfortable. Societal attitudes should significantly change with the realization of HSOs' contributions to the economy. A workable measuring system for the human service field that recognizes its goal to improve the quality of life in harmony with the culture of a work-ethic society is long overdue.

Measurement Methodology

In responding to societal problems prevalent in the current scene, the model incorporates the appropriate principal components of measuring methodology: specificity of goal, definition of attribute, metric convertibility into dollars, and periodicity of reporting, as well as relevance, comprehensibility, auditability, and cost factors relative to this system.

The dynamics of the operation of the system were analyzed at the end of chapter 2. An additional question must also be posed: Is the proposed system too "soft" to measure its desired goals? The answer has to be placed within the context of measuring systems in general. Most social and economic measures are "soft" in comparison to measures used in the physical sciences. Moreover, as has been discussed, there are limitations in the use of any single indicator, which ordinarily should be evaluated in context with other variables used. Examples could be found in such measures as the consumer price level index, calculations of the GNP, the poverty index, or the rate of unemployment. For example, to utilize the rate of unemployment as a measure (in addition to understanding the sources of data and the methodology of calculation) one must also examine changes and trends in unemployment by sectors or industry, area, sex, race, part-time and discouraged workers. As a single number, earnings-per-share figures suffer from the same limitations and the same softness. Profits may have a significant influence on investment decisions; however, they are only one of the components in decision making. Other information about the company and its industry must be incorporated such as trends, special occurrences that may have affected earnings within the period, evaluation of current and future competition, labor and market position, and risks, among others.

One can argue whether these measures reflect reality or induce reality, or some combination of both. A change in the method of measuring GNP could have converted the deficits run by the Carter administration into a surplus.[2] However, the question is not whether the measuring system is too soft, but rather whether it is useful or not. Accounting systems are useful when they can act as a feedback mechanism relative to the purposes for which they are designed.[3] They are not when they obfuscate policies and/or distort goal achievement—which they purportedly were designed to measure. It is generally accepted that society is better off with information, even when estimated. Such data may allow for comparability and encourage the continual improvement of data sources to confirm hypotheses, interventions, and evaluation of results.

LONG-RUN IMPLICATIONS

The adoption of the model has extensive implications for HSOs and other segments of the SPS. As well, there are significant long-run implications for the professions, for the PS and NPS sectors and society. The defining of revenue and the consequent potential for an HSO to prepare a statement of income should have a significant effect on the accounting profession and the field of management. The framework of economic policy will likewise be influenced because of the implications of the models. The functioning of HSOs will be affected by proposed changes in tax policy and, accordingly, its funding sources. The interrelation of the propositions and societal goals should likewise provide a basis for measurement to approach political solutions to other societal problems. The concept of "ought," generally considered as an ethical imperative, has been defined as an economic good, as a concomitant of the societal propositions.

The Organization—HSO

Because it provides common criteria to the consumer-client as well as to the provider, use of the model should cause an expanded awareness of HSO services. It also binds all constituencies and stakeholders to an explicit value system. When clients' problems do not interfere with their pursuit of opportunities, then the cost of the offered HSO services should be borne by the consumer-client. Moreover, based on the know-how developed, many HSOs should consider exploiting the market economy in the areas of their expertise; the model provides relevant cost and other management criteria.

The change in funding sources for the individual HSO should have a major repercussion on its operations. The elimination of the continual needs and pervasive influence of fund-raising for HSOs should not only eliminate tension between the fund raisers and the providers of services, but should also provide the appropriate shifts in emphasis within the HSO. The replacement of the "big hitters" of organizational life would permit a switch in focus so that programs would not follow funding but rather implement mission.

The individual HSO faces a double demand function in both satisfying the needs/wants of its client-consumer as well as the consumer purchaser of its marketable paper, representing the sale of its tax credits. The latter arises from our proposal that HSOs sell in a special market, the tax deductions based on their societal revenues generated. The demand would arise from consumer purchases of tax deductions and the supply from gross societal revenues generated by HSOs.

Professions

Accounting. Some of the questions raised by members of the accounting profession are resolved in the development of the organizational model and the resultant accounting system. Up to this point, HSOs have had no means to measure the value of their services rendered to clients, that is, their revenues generated, and therefore, a statement of income could not be prepared. The concept of societal income overcomes this gap. A statement of (societal) income can be integrated with the existing balance sheet and a statement of support, revenues, and disbursements. The mandated application of GAAP to the financial statements of HSOs is immediately feasible. The missing component of the framework has been built. The calls for evaluation by government agencies, the goals of the Yellow Book, and the needs of the GAO have been responded to by this bottom-line approach. There should be no differences in the standards of reporting by profit-oriented companies that operate in the area of human services when they use societal resources. The movement of clients toward self-sufficiency is a better measure than contract prices.[4]

Accounting systems should reflect the benefits of an enterprise's operation to the members of society. In recent years there appears to have been a shift in the accounting model's emphasis to the acquisition of cash instead of on the underlying economic realities of capital and consumer goods—which provide for the economic qualities of life, home, job, health, and other opportunities for making choices. The goal of society should be to make the individual better off—the rest is commentary.

Economics. Accounting in the PS is based upon the economic model of the PS. There is the assumption of an optimal allocation of resources based upon consumer satisfaction and the acts of self-interest from the interlocking market actions of consumers and producers. Individual preferences arising from the satisfaction of wants and needs are called their utility function by economists. In the simplified utility model, consumers presumably prioritize their demands based on their hierarchy of choices. Producers respond by bidding for resources and labor, the factors of production. According to this theory, the optimal allocation of societal resources is thus based on the choices of consumers in the markets and the reactions of producers. As part of this allocation process, entrepreneurial profit, the difference between revenues generated and costs incurred, represents the effectiveness and efficiency of their operations.

The current system of financial accounting in the PS reflects the ability of the individual firm to play the game of greed. The prescribed rules emphasize the acquisition of cash; we get what we measure. A change in the model can change the measurement system and behavior of its participants. For economic theory, the profit measurement developed in the model is superior to the profit reported in the PS. The latter is flawed since its measurement criteria preclude societal costs from the economic values created. Sales and service revenues do not reflect the broader societal and environmental effects of their products. Moreover, with the normative model the well-offness of consumers is a direct measure of societal benefits. The current PS model requires an indirect measurement based upon questionable concepts of the aggregation of individual consumers' preferences. When the individual is better off, it is assumed that private welfare is equal to or greater than social welfare—a derived computation for estimating societal well-offness. The compilations under the normative model measure social welfare directly, that is, where social welfare is equal to or greater than private welfare in order to determine society well-offness.

Future research in the PS should consider the problem of the inclusion of societal cost as part of the presentation of an individual organization's financial statements. Such inclusion will also focus the accounting on the depletion of natural resources, the costs of environmental concomitants of industrial production, as well as societal costs and individual, corporate, and social responsibilities in areas such as smoking, alcohol, and drugs.[5] Such research must incorporate the theoretical economic question relative to the relation of revenues generated and consumer well-offness, the indirect effects on other members of society, and the reporting systems that affect their behavior.

Political and Social Sciences. The societal model gives a framework for the making of political decisions to optimize the economic benefits to society's members. Within this framework, the organizational model not only permits the measurement of the individual firm's effectiveness and comparability among HSOs with similar missions, but also comparisons among groups. It can be one factor to assist in making the political decision for allocation of resources among competing groups. With a focus on outcomes, perhaps some of the factors for failures within the society can be more readily identified (e.g., in problems of racism, sexism, ageism, and drug abuse, among others), and solutions can be developed to deal with underlying causes instead of symptoms. The implications of the model would call for political actions requiring shifts in areas of government activities but also an increase in their responsibilities.

Education and Professional Training. Education and professional training should be modified to recognize an interdisciplinary approach. The relevancy of the fields of human services, accounting, marketing, economics, methodology of science, statistics, and other disciplines should be evaluated for integration at appropriate levels. The model provides a common framework for training and education for each discipline to develop its specialized knowledge and skills and to show how the application of measurement concepts in the various fields are interrelated.

While sometimes recognizing the nature of the problems, the literature has not responded to the heart of the question. The proposed model provides an economically based framework for the delivery of human services and for its accounting, which respond to the limitations of the conventional wisdom discussed in chapter 7. Its implementation will provide the data for ad hoc studies, for more complete cost-benefit analyses, for other systems of program evaluation, and for research that will contribute to new knowledge. The model provides a framework to serve as a basis for interdisciplinary communication and collaboration.

Sectors and Society

If an appropriate measuring system for what has been heretofore termed the nonprofit sector is to be implemented, there must be significant changes in tax policy. Societal contributions of HSOs can be appropriately measured, reported upon, and audited based upon the normative model presented in this book. However, the gross (societal) revenues generated as reported upon in an HSO's statement of income must become a component of its source of funding, in the same manner as sales revenues are funding sources in the PS. As proposed, a tax policy that would permit deductions by donors only to the extent of an HSO's gross societal income could accomplish this goal; contract sales from governments would have the same limitations. A market for such deductions would be a means to prioritize various HSO activities, thus giving to donors the ability to "vote" for the support of particular areas of human services and individual organizations within each area. The belaboring of "unfair" competition should disappear when organizations in both sectors pay taxes on their incomes, which have similar measurement criteria.

Society continually demonstrates its inability to resolve particular social problems. One of the causes of such failures and the consequent frustrations arising from the failures of "wars" against poverty, increasing health costs, and crime, is the absence of a general framework for reference. American empiricism and practicality (with its antitheoretical bias) are twin evils that contribute to the lack of an overall policy and consequent guidelines, together with the failure to establish hypotheses of intervention and criteria for measurement. This prevents a step-up in the level of abstraction, which would permit the recognition of interstitial relationships of problems and the reporting of both planned and specified outcomes.

This inability to provide societal solutions has been depicted in the current literature and has produced outcries for change. This is a direct consequence of the fact that social policy and programs are oftentimes in conflict with underlying (and nonarticulated) societal goals. The solution to some of society's current problems can be derived from the basic propositions, which point to criteria for their solution. The implementation of the goal of proposition one, to bring more individuals under the societal tent, impacts on societal decisions as to expenditures for education, training, and retraining: the improvement in the work force, in communication, in the market for goods, ideas, and people, and in the balancing of demographic changes with the inclusion of handicapped and aged persons. The encouraging of a dynamic and inventive population that is willing to assume risks follows from proposition two, societal expenditures for "insurance" in its broader sense. With a system of contracting of government services and the potential to measure program and organizational performance as proposed in this book, larger government expenditures do not necessarily mean larger government. The implication of the concepts of proposition three should significantly reduce societal cost of litigation, police, waste management, and the environment and ecology. The implementation of these societal goals should also result in a more ethical and moral society.

Taxonomy. The current system of classification, or taxonomy, clouds the economic functions of the varied institutions that provide goods and services for society. There have been recommendations for revision. The logic of the societal and organizational models leads to the proposal for a changed taxonomy. By using the criteria as to resources provided by or used for the individual and provided by or used for the group, the nature and composition of the profit, or micro sector, and the nonprofit, or macro sector, can be defined. It suggests major areas of future research of the models to the reclassified segments relative to their functioning, significance, accountability of, and reporting on transferred resources including the application of the models to: (1) other principal parts of the (redefined) SPS, that is, health and education; (2) the PPS to incorporate societal costs and provide a direct aggregatable measure of societal well-offness; and (3) the macro sectors. The proposed taxonomy suggests that the attributes and their corresponding money metric, which have been applied to the micro sectors, may not be appropriate to measure group-related outcomes. It suggests further that group well-offness may require attributes that can measure such factors as levels of health, education, leisure, art, conflict, and the environment.[6] A possible approach is the mapping of the vector of such attributes and their transformation into scales, which could then be converted into the common metric of money. National revenue accounts should reflect how the micro and macro systems perform, interact with each other and with international societies. Further research should concentrate on a national accounting system.[7] The goal of consolidated accounts for a society, after elimination of internal transfers, should be to present an appropriate measure of the well-offness of society's members.

THE FUTURE

The implementation of the organizational and societal models opens many areas for questioning and as such presents research opportunities in accounting, economics, human services, and related social and political spheres. Society should benefit from one accounting system for all sectors in its use of resources to achieve its goals. In essence, each assumed consequence and implication becomes a hypothesis for further research.

We look down upon the ladder by which we did ascend. It appears fashionable to take science to task, questioning the relationship of observations to theory, the difficulties of measurement as well as transferring misunderstood theoretical constructs from other disciplines. The questioning of human service methodology based on "science" requires an understanding of the scales of reference of the disciplines involved. In physics, Heisenberg's principle of uncertainty is valid

for the observation of sub-atomic particles; determinism in biology can be critiqued at the molecular level. These principles are not valid on the human scale.
We can deal at this level with a "deterministic" probability of 100%—for all
practical purposes a table is solid and stands regardless of the random movements
of its atoms.[8]

Gould wryly assails the scientist who gathers facts without a framework, without
a hypothesis.[9] The physical sciences can look directly at a question of causality,
the effects of an intervention, and precisely measure functional relationships by
holding other variables constant *in ceteris paribus*. On the other hand, it would
seem that the social sciences can only deal with measurement of intervention by
correlation because of the problem of holding constant other variables. Both the
social and physical sciences need the deductive-inductive method in their attempt
to place relationships of causality/association into a framework. Hypotheses are
based on and connected to observations, which can be tested as to consequences.
When predictions are verified, one goes back up to the hypothesis from having
gone down to the tests and observations.

A given set of problems needs a given paradigm for its solution. There are
no universal paradigms. One of the problems of utilizing an old or creating a
new paradigm is the persistence of questions left over from prior ones. Moving
an analysis to higher levels can eliminate nearsighted solutions with their ad hoc,
leftover residues. New paradigms are needed. New ways of problem solving for
the current conditions of the postmodernist arrogance of humanity—new ways
of thinking about problems that can be tested in an end-product analysis. One
approach is to break with the linear relationships embedded in our Western culture
from the Greeks, through the Renaissance and modern scientism. Can disparate
elements be brought together and can society and the lot of each individual be
improved at the same time? The physical sciences in their search for explanations of both macro and micro phenomena have recognized the need of complementarity principles in considering apparent contradictory concepts: for the macro,
electromagnetic forces and gravity; for the micro, in atomic physics, the hypothesis
of strong and weak forces. The application of the approaches used by the physical
sciences to social systems has been questioned. This parallelism from the physical
sciences can be thought of as metaphor or as an application of an underlying insight. Gould also comments about "how [an] interdisciplinary transfer can either
illuminate by expansion or restrict by inappropriate copying."[10]

Accordingly, a paradigm can be created using a Bohrian concept of complementarity rather than a Hegelian synthesis to deal with disparate elements. The concept of the symbiotic complementarity of deep truths, the opposite of which truth
is not false, is a system of Pareto mathematical optimality. It is a movement toward
an equilibrium wherein an individual can be better off without decreasing the
well-offness of another individual and without a cost to another individual or to
society—the goal of the model. In fact, the actions of individuals because of increased choices, which follow from the propositions of the societal model, can
induce changes in Pareto optimality toward a higher level.

The Chinese symbols of yin and yang are considered as the creative force denoting male and female, darkness and light, heights and hollows, land and water—the active and passive complementarity principle of nature in all its aspects. In physiology, there is complementarity within the person; an organism exists both free and dependent upon interrelated systems and subsystems. In biology, the complementarity forces needed to explain evolution are random variations and conventional causality. For the economic-political sphere, it now becomes clear that the either/or assumptions given by the proponents of the completely competitive economy or of the government intervention society should be restated. Society needs both the economic benefits of competition and the foundation of a strong ethical/moral system to encourage cooperation and to mitigate the negative elements and costs of competition.[11] The complementarity of both approaches is required. The use of either system by itself ultimately weakens the functioning of the society and the individual.

Within the paradigm of complementarity, the proposed societal model is based on the assumption that humankind has choices in the world of which it is a part. There is the scientific physical world of practically limitless space with relatively unchanging particles of energy, reacting to random variations over limitless time. And there are the social sciences, with space and time bounded by socially determined constraints. Within the forces of macro determinism and micro chance factors, humankind can deal with the essence of change and formalize its aspirations. To be meaningful, it must also measure its movements toward these goals.

NOTES

1. Hoffman, D. Lynn, Rowley, Daniel James, & House, Ronald B. (1989, November). An overview of strategic planning for human service organizations. *Journal of Rehabilitation Administration, 13*(4), 123–130.

2. Eisner, Robert. (1986). *How real is the federal deficit?* New York: Free Press, 43–46.

3. The question is posed as to how to account for any significant differences between originally planned costs and the subsequently instituted standard costs. "The comparison of the actual results with the original plan is of particular significance from the point of view of managerial decision making and pricing policy. On the other hand, the continual use of updated cost sheets has the advantage of current control and the pinpointing of responsibility." Herson, Richard J. L. (1964, August). The control of standard gross profit in the apparel industry. *The New York Certified Public Accountant*, 579–590.

4. As Peter Drucker points out, business can learn from the nonprofits. Some nonprofit organizations are becoming leaders in defining strategy and organizational mission, in having a CEO directly accountable to a functioning board, and (in their approaches) in "the motivation of knowledge workers." According to the same source, accountants and editors are observing an increasing interest in the NPS. "New information is now available on the important but neglected non-profit sector." Drucker, Peter F. (1989, July—August). What business can learn from non-profits. *Harvard Business Review, 88*(4), 88–93. Cited in *Future Survey, 12*(1), 1, 9 (1990, January).

5. Repetto, Robert & Magrath, William B. (1989, June). *Wasting assets: Natural resources in the national income accounts.* Washington, DC: World Resources Institute. Reviewed in *Future Survey, 11*(11), 11. (1989, November).

6. As previously discussed in Chapter 7, the GASB has been issuing pronouncements on accounting issues for reporting by governmental entities. (See note 6 and Exhibit 4.1, Proposed Taxonomy of Economic Activity.) While striving to accomplish its goals to develop standards for measuring outcome of public expenditures, it faces a similar dilemma as did the FASB, when the latter concluded that it was not feasible to value goods and services for the NPS. (See exchange of views of Anthony and Folpe in Chapter 6.)

7. Fogel, Robert W. (1987, December). *Some Notes on the Scientific Methods of Simon Kuznets* (Working Paper No. 2461) Cambridge, MA: National Bureau of Economic Research.

8. Gould writes that "if you wish to understand patterns of long historical sequences, pray for randomness. Ironically, nothing works so powerfully against resolution as conventional forms of determinism." Zimmerman understands that quantum theory refers to randomness on an atomic level. However, he missed Gould's explanation that this statement refers to "the smallest increments of evolutionary change at the molecular level" and that "in the domain of organisms and their good designs, we have little reason to doubt the strong, probably dominant influences of deterministic forces like natural selection." Gould, Stephen Jay. (1989, September). Through a lens, darkly. *Natural History*, 16.

9. Gould quotes Charles Darwin to the same effect: "How odd it is that anyone should not see that all observations must be for or against some view if it is to be of any service." Relative to science, he also comments as to "the same official persistence of a public myth about absolutely objective impartiality."

10. Gould adds that "conceptual locks are usually more important than factual lacks as impediments to scientific breakthrough." He doubts whether "Darwin would ever have been able to formulate the theme of natural selection without the available context of Adam Smith's nearly identical causal system for economics. Gould, Stephen Jay. (1990, January 18). Down on the farm. *New York Review of Books*, 26.

11. "I have understood it philosophically . . . the beauty of the idea of the pursuit of happiness. . . . This idea of the pursuit of happiness is at the heart of the attractiveness of the civilization to so many outside it or on its periphery. . . . The idea has come to a kind of fruition. It is an elastic idea; it fits all men. It implies a certain kind of society, a certain kind of awakened spirit. . . . So much is contained in it: the idea of the individual, responsibility, choice, the life of the intellect, the idea of vocation and perfectibility and achievement. It is an immense human idea." Naipaul, V. S. (1991, January 31). Our universal civilization. *The New York Review of Books, 38* (3), 25. Naipaul, like Smith, as a moral philosopher is also reacting to the restrictions of the societies about which he writes. Pursuit by itself, without other balancing factors, has the potential to become selfish, competitive, and destructive when carried to its reductio ad absurdum level. One could no more accuse Naipaul than Smith of advocating selfish competition for the benefit of society. The context of place and times must be considered.

Postscript and Guide to the Literature

As we go to press, the United States finds itself with growing economic and social problems—a stagnating economy, frictions among social groups, and lowered expectations for many in the immediate future. Solutions to the problems proposed by the two major political parties appear to be differences in degree, not in substance. It is paradoxical that the failure to develop workable policies coexists with the overwhelming data and knowledge generated by our society.

A partial explanation for this anomaly lies in the confusion that exists between measures of outcome and output, between cash accumulation and production of goods, and between cash savings and real investment. Current accounting practices reflect and reinforce these misunderstandings. In fact the absence of an accounting framework that takes into consideration the current state of the world distorts the decision-making processes in our society. For example, expenditures for equipment are accounted for as productive assets, whereas expenditures to improve the abilities of a labor force are considered expenses. In an economy which is becoming increasingly service oriented, this circumstance can have severe consequences.

The end of the twentieth century is a validation of Thomas S. Kuhn's notion of a paradigm shift. The paradigmatic elements of materialism and individualism have set the agenda and shaped the approaches to the solutions of the problems during this century. A major and pervasive portion of society, the business community, has been a significant instrument through which these beliefs have become the modus operandi of society. While we acknowledge the benefits that materialism and individualism have given to society, we must also recognize the problems that are associated with the benefits, the unintended perverse consequences. What is needed is a paradigm that recognizes and addresses the current problems. It would seem that the new paradigm should include humanism and community as elements.

The organizational model proposed in this book to measure the effectiveness of human service organizations in responding to social problems is located in the new paradigm. In addition the societal model proposed herein is also compatible with the new paradigm and can be used as a starting point for addressing current social problems.

For those readers who wish to pursue these ideas further, we have compiled a selected bibliography from the references at the end of each chapter. This list includes books that provide the basic economic and philosophical tenets that assisted us in developing the conceptual framework for the societal model. For those who wish to understand the principal issues and discussions underpinning the organizational model, we have included journal articles from the accounting and human service literature that highlight particular points of view and attempts at solutions. This also serves as a limited guide to publications that should be monitored in the future.

The *Federal Register* and releases from the General Accounting Office can offer directions of future government programs and assessments of past performance. Changes in accounting practice can be followed in the pronouncements of the FASB and the GASB. The various professional associations and their journals offer developments in practice and research. Addressing these issues, an increasing number of multidisciplinary groups are developing proposals with broader based solutions to societal questions, including graduate programs at various universities and think tanks, such as the Rand Corporation, Brookings Institute, the Urban Institute, and the Program on Nonprofit Organization, Yale University.

A *Handbook on Evaluation* is scheduled for publication in 1992 by the Council of Foundations. Lastly, we found that the *New York Review of Books* as well as the *Future Survey* are important sources for reports on the developments and trends in society's various intellectual pursuits.

Anthony, Robert N. (1987, May). We don't have the accounting concepts we need. *The CPA Journal, 57* (5), 36–45.

Arrow, Kenneth J. (1963) Social choice and individual values. New Haven, CT: Cowles Foundation for Research in Economics at Yale University.

Atherton, Charles R. (1989, June). The welfare state: Still on solid ground. *Social Service Review, 63* (2), 167–178.

Berkowitz, Monroe, & Berkowitz, Edward. (1983). Benefit cost analysis. *Rehabilitation Research Review, No. 5*, 1–35. The National Rehabilitation Information Center (NARIC).

Blau, Joel. (1989, March). Theories of the welfare state. *Social Service Review, 63*(1), 26–38.

Bohr, Niels. (1951). Discussion with Einstein on epistemological problems in atomic physics. In Paul Schlipp (Ed.). Albert Einstein: philosopher-scientist (7, 199–241). New York: Library of Living Philosophers.

Carmichael, Douglas R. (Ed.). Accounting. *The CPA Journal, 60* (4), 54–59.

Chelimsky, Eleanor. (1988, Summer). Federal evaluation in a legislative environment: Producing on a faster trade. In C. G. Wye & H. P. Hatry (Eds.), Timely, low-cost evaluation in the public sector (New Directions for Program Evaluation, No. 38, 73–86). San Francisco: Jossey-Bass.

Clark, John Maurice. (1923). Studies in the economics of overhead costs. IL: University of Chicago Press.

Dean, David H., & Dolan, Robert C. (1987, January/February/March). Issues in the economic evaluation of the vocational and rehabilitation program. *Journal of Rehabilitation, 53* (1), 13–19.

Ezell, Mark, & Patti, Rino (1991, March). State human service agencies structure and organization. *Social Service Review, 64* (1), 30 and 22–45.

Fetterman, Allen L. (1988, March). Update on not-for-profit accounting and reporting. *The CPA Journal, 58* (3), 22–29.

Folpe, Herbert K. (1989, April). Sorting out nonprofit accounting issues. *The Philanthropic Monthly*, 22 (4), 5–14; (1989, May) (5), 7–14; (1989, July/August) (7), 11–16.

Griss, Bob. (1988, December-1989, March). *Access to Health Care* I (3 & 4), Washington DC: World Institute on Disability.

Gronbjerg, Kirsten A. (1990, June). Poverty and nonprofit organizational behavior. *Social Service Review, 64*(2), 208–243.

Hatry, Harry P. (1983). Program evaluation and client outcome monitoring for state and local human services agencies, Urban Institute, Washington, DC Beverly Hills, CA: Sage.

Hayes, Robert D., & Millar, James A. (1990, July). Measuring production efficiency in a not-for-profit setting. *The Accounting Review, 65*(3), 505–519.

Keynes, John Maynard. (1964). The general theory of employment, interest, and money. New York: Harcourt, Brace and World (originally published in 1935).

Kramer, Ralph M., & Grossman, Bart (1987, March). Contracting for social services: Process management and resource dependencies. *Social Service Review, 61*(1). 32–55.

Kuhn, Thomas S. (1970). The structure of scientific revolutions. 2nd ed. Chicago: University of Chicago Press.

Linn, Lawrence E., Jr. (1986, December). The new economics of social welfare: An essay review. *Social Service Review, 60*(4), 590–602.

Lipsey, Mark W., et al. (1985, September). Evaluation: The state of the art and the sorry state of the science. In D. S. Cordray (Ed.). Utilizing prior research in evaluation planning: New directions for program evaluation (No. 27), 7–28. San Francisco: Jossey-Bass.

McKenna, Edward, Wade, Maurice, and Zannoni, Diane. (1988, October). Keynes, Rawls, uncertainty and the liberal theory of the state. *Economics and Philosophy, 4* (2).

Patti, Rino J. (1987, September-October). Managing for service effectiveness in social welfare organizations. *Social Work, 3* (5), 377–381.

Ramanathan, Kavasseri V. (1985, Summer). A proposed framework for designing management control systems in not-for-profit organizations. *Financial Accountability and Management, 1*(1), 75–95.

Ronen, Joshua. (1974, May). Accounting for social costs and benefits. Objectives of financial statements, 2, 317–340. New York: American Institute of CPAs.

Rostker, Bernard. (1975). An evaluation-management information system for vocational rehabilitation. Santa Monica: The Rand Corporation.

Schultz, Theodore W. (1981). Investing in people—The economics of population quality. Berkeley: University of California Press.

Scitovsky, Tibor. (1989). Human desire and economic satisfaction: Essays on the frontiers of economics. New York: New York University Press.

Sewell, Thomas. (1987). A conflict of visions. New York: William Morrow.

Smith, Adam. (1976). An inquiry into the nature and causes of the wealth of nations. Chicago: University of Chicago Press (originally published in 1776).

Weisbrod, Burton A. (1988). The nonprofit economy. Cambridge: Harvard University Press.

Weissman, Harold H. (1983, June). Accountability and pseudo-accountability: A nonlinear approach. *Social Service Review, 57*(2), 323–336.

Index

Accounting, as a social institution:
consequences of models developed
for, xvii, 185–186; as feedback of
results to goals in, xvi, 104, 190;
implications of models developed
for, xvii, 189–193; measurement
(*see* Measurement application);
social costs (*see* Externalities);
unified system for PS and HSOs,
as basis for, xvii, 45, 131–132, 133.
See also Organizational model;
Propositions

Accounting principles: accounting profit,
different from economic, 27, 105,
118–119; balance sheet or income
statement, primacy of, 39, 121;
current model, nonprofit sector, 3,
121–122; current model, profit
sector, 3, 116–117, 119–120; current
model, profit sector, criticisms of,
119–120, 190; current state of,
discussion of, 106; cycle of time and
reporting for, 27; economic
performance of an entity, goal of, 14;
as element in organizational model,
14, 26–29; framework for
accounting, discussion of, 26,
106–110; fund accounting

(unrestricted, temporarily restricted,
permanently restricted), 138; general
accepted accounting principles
(GAAP), problems in application in,
47n.5, 108, 119, 134n.10, 135n.15,
140; general accepted accounting
principles (GAAP), role of, 26, 27,
39, 40, 107, 119–120, 130, 132,
190; governing bodies, role in
promulgating, 108, 119, 139, 140,
141 (*see also* AICPA; FASB;
GASB); historical use of cost for,
119; income recognition and, 27;
industry audit guides and, use of,
139; inventory valuation, 27, 39;
literature review, in the NPS,
138–141; literature review, in the
NPS, discussion of, 141–142; model,
current, criticisms of, 120; model,
PS, as basis for current, 4; normative
(conceptual)—empirical (positive)
system, to measure effectiveness of
HSOs, xvi–xvii, 104; professional
and academic journals, in, role of,
108; professional concern about the
NPS, lack of, and, 139; receivables
valuation for HSOs, 39; revenue
defined for, 28. *See also* Accounting,